D0160337

The Principal Challenge

Marc S. Tucker

Judy B. Codding

Editors

The Principal Challenge

Leading and Managing Schools
in an Era of Accountability

JOSSEY-BASS
A Wiley Imprint
www.josseybass.com

Published by Jossey-Bass
A Wiley Imprint
989 Market Street, San Francisco, CA 94103-1741   www.josseybass.com

Jossey-Bass is a registered trademark of John Wiley & Sons, Inc.

Josey-Bass books and products are available through most bookstores. To contact Jossey-Bass directly
call our Customer Care Department within the U.S. at (800) 956-7739, outside the U.S. at (317) 572-3993
or fax (317) 572-4002.

Jossey-Bass also publishes its books in a variety of electronic formats. Some content that appears in print
may not be available in electronic books.

Library of Congress Cataloging-in-Publication Data

The principal challenge: leading and managing schools in an era of accountability / Marc S. Tucker,
Judy B. Codding, editors.—1st ed.
   p.   cm.—(Jossey-Bass education series)
Includes bibliographical references and index.
   ISBN 0-7879-6447-6 (alk. paper)
1. School principals—Training of.   2. Educational leadership.   3. Educational accountability.
I. Tucker, Marc S. II. Codding, Judy B., date. III. Series.
   LB2831.9 .P75 2002
   371.2'012—dc21   2002011039

Printed in the United States of America
FIRST EDITION
HB Printing 10 9 8 7 6 5 4 3 2

The Jossey-Bass Education Series

Contents

Preface

In the summer of 1999, the National Center on Education and the Economy (NCEE) was asked by Michael Levine and Vivien Stewart at Carnegie Corporation of New York if we would be interested in producing a plan for a "war college" for school principals, a new kind of institution that could model a very different approach to the training of these key educational leaders and managers. This request grew out of a meeting sponsored earlier that summer by Carnegie, the Ford Foundation, and the U.S. Department of Education addressed to the question as to where the United States was going to find the quality of people we will need to lead our schools.

Carnegie, like other philanthropic institutions, was growing concerned about the prospects for leadership in our educational institutions. Anecdotal data from many sources was revealing a very disturbing picture. The number of applicants for positions as principals and superintendents was declining. Experienced people seemed to be retiring at ever earlier ages. Even in the wealthy suburbs, applications were far below prior levels and continuing to trend downward. Recruiters were reporting ever greater difficulty in finding candidates with even minimal qualifications for positions in schools and districts serving low-income families. For the first time in our own work, there were schools in our network that had been without even minimally qualified principals for six months or longer because no one at all could be found to fill the job. More and more of the principals and superintendents we talked to were reporting that the pressures on them were continuing to grow and the rewards were diminishing.

Our friends at Carnegie asked us to focus our analysis and planning on the preparation of principals. Although they understood that lack of good training was not the only problem and that training alone was not going to provide a complete solution, they thought that other elements of the solution would prove less tractable and take longer to affect, so they hoped that we could find an approach to training that would prove to be much more powerful and effective than anything else available. Not long after Carnegie made the initial grant for this work, it was joined by the New Schools Venture Fund and the Broad Foundation.

All of us wanted to ground the design in the best research and widest possible search for best practices. The papers in this volume are the result of that commitment. They were commissioned not only as an aid to our work but also in the hope that they would provide information and analysis that would be useful to a much broader community of people who share our interest in the future of school leadership, in work on leadership in other fields that might bear on the way school leaders are trained, and in new developments in the education and training of adults that might be used to improve professional development in many areas of education. Whether or not you agree with the direction we have chosen to take, we hope that the ideas presented in these pages will prove valuable to you in your own work.

We are deeply indebted to Eli Broad, Dan Katzir, and Lynn Liao of the Broad Foundation; Kim Smith of the New Schools Venture Fund; and Michelle Cahill, Vartan Gregorian, Vivien Stewart, and Michael Levine of Carnegie Corporation of New York for the support that made the contributions to this book and all of the rest of the work on this program possible (although the statements made and the views expressed in this volume are solely those of the chapter authors).

Chapter One of this book, "Preparing Principals in the Age of Accountability," presents our own analysis of the issues surrounding the preparation of school principals and our proposals for dealing with those issues. We draw in our chapter on all the other chapters in this volume. But our chapter also relies heavily on research on the topic that we ourselves did over a period of two and a half years. In addition to commissioning the chapters in this volume, we conducted a program of "snowball research": interviewing leading experts in a variety of fields and then asking the person being interviewed to nominate others to whom we should talk. We continued this process for several months until most of the people being nominated were people we had already interviewed. Concurrently, we ran three large focus groups, talking with a group of principals from wealthy suburbs, another from inner-city schools, and a third from schools in communities of every description. When we were well into this process, we invited about twenty-five of the people we had interviewed—a very eclectic group—to Washington for a loosely structured two-day discussion of our initial impressions and hypotheses. Having used this meeting to further focus our research, we then continued with a set of visits to, among other places, several graduate schools of education and business, the National War College in Washington, the principals' professional associations, and a number of schools. When we had further refined our impressions and our analysis on the basis of these visits, Carnegie Corporation was kind enough to host a meeting of executives from a dozen or so foundations for a briefing and discussion in New York City. The names of all of these contributors are contained in Appendix B.

Following Chapter One are the reports commissioned for this study, presented in four parts. The first part deals with two important roles of the principal: the principal as instructional leader and the principal as moral leader.

In Chapter Two, Peter Hill, a leading Australian researcher with an international following, addresses the question of what principals need to know about teaching and learning. Now as never before in the United States, the heart of the job is organizing the school to promote gains in student achievement. But this is now mostly left out of the training of school principals, who are mainly trained now to manage the school organization, not its program. Hill draws widely on the international research literature as well as his own research and experience to present a considered, practical, and thoughtful view of the role of the principal as instructional leader.

In Chapter Three, Tom Sobol addresses the role of the principal as the moral leader of the school. Instruction, while central, hardly defines the whole job. In many ways, the moral and ethical dimensions of the job are paramount. Teachers and students always watch to see what the principal does when the hard choices have to be made between what adults want for themselves and what is best for the students. Principals who fall on the wrong side of this divide have little credibility with the best teachers and students. The issues are typically not black and white but are instead full of gray areas. Sobol's chapter captures these nuances and draws the reader effortlessly into the issues.

Part Two contains chapters that describe best practices in the training of leaders, managers, and other professionals in business, the military, and other fields.

In Chapter Four, Marie Eiter captures the main themes in the literature and relates some of the most important lessons from the business schools and the corporate universities in the area of leadership development. This is, of course, a vast field, so we asked Eiter to concentrate on providing us with a conceptual map of the territory on the issues that might have the greatest application to the world of elementary and secondary education.

In Chapter Five, Robert Hughes and Richard Haney describe the development of leaders and managers in the military, concentrating on the features of the military system that the authors believe might be applicable to the training of leaders and managers in the field of elementary and secondary education. The authors also describe the whole career development system for leaders and managers in the military and show how the design of the training system is intimately linked to the design of the other components of the career development system.

In Chapter Six, Gary Sykes, with Cheryl King and Jeanne Patrick, describes and analyzes models of preparation in a wide range of disciplines, from medicine and engineering to the ministry and business. The chapter covers a wide array of approaches to the education and training of professionals in this country from which individuals planning new ventures in education can usefully draw.

Part Three approaches the issues from an international perspective. In Chapter Seven, the only chapter in this part, Brian Caldwell, Gerard Calnin, and Wendy Cahill describe how school leaders and managers are prepared in many countries in the English-speaking world and draw parallels between the situation in the United States and elsewhere on the globe.

Part Four of this book is devoted to a situation report on the preparation of school principals in the United States.

In Chapter Eight, Carolyn Kelley and Kent Peterson describe the work of school principals in this country, their initial preparation, and the nature of the challenges facing the profession. In addition to describing the wide range of institutions providing certification and degree programs, this chapter also describes the policy framework and resulting incentives within which these institutions do their work. This thorough survey of the field was undertaken under the auspices of the Consortium for Policy Research in Education (CPRE), as was the following chapter by the same authors.

In Chapter Nine, Peterson and Kelley survey the field of continuing education programs for school principals. This kaleidoscopic review captures the often bewildering array of program and institutional types and documents the achievements and shortcomings of the offerings.

In Chapter Ten, Gerald Tirozzi takes a closer look at the role of the national associations in promoting the growth and development of school principals. These associations, like associations in most professional fields, take very seriously their role in keeping their members' skills and knowledge fresh and up-to-date. That role has been growing steadily in importance in recent years.

In the first of two appendixes, we provide a description of the program of the National Institute for School Leadership (NISL), the organization that emerged from the analysis contained in this volume. In the second appendix, we list the individuals and groups consulted in the course of preparing our work and designing what became the NISL.

We could not have done the work we were asked to do without the contributions made by the authors of the chapters in this book. We hope you will be as delighted with them as we were.

Washington, D.C.   Marc S. Tucker
July 2002   Judy B. Codding

Acknowledgments

We are greatly indebted to the other authors in this volume and the research and insights they bring to the fore. We are no less indebted to the many principals, superintendents, education and business school deans, military officers, researchers, and others with whom we talked as we did the research on which our work is based. We are also deeply appreciative of Guilbert Hentschke, Robert Hughes, Dan Katzir, Lynn Liao, Jerry Murphy, Kent Peterson, Tom Sobol, and Pat Wasley, all of whom took the time to read the manuscript and provide valuable feedback. From all these people we have learned so very much.

We cannot end without expressing our deep gratitude to Betsy Brown Ruzzi for serving as project director for this book, not only meticulously reviewing the manscript and providing guidance but also organizing virtually everything that had to be done to bring this work to fruition.

The Editors

Marc S. Tucker is president of the National Center on Education and the Economy (NCEE). He is the coauthor of the prize-winning *Thinking for a Living: Education and the Wealth of Nations* (written with Ray Marshall; Basic Books, 1992) and of *Standards for Our Schools: How to Set Them, Measure Them, and Reach Them* (written with Judy B. Codding; Jossey-Bass, 1998). He was the primary author of the 1986 Carnegie Report, *A Nation Prepared*, and a principal author of *America's Choice*, the report of the Commission on the Skills of the American Workforce. Designer of the National Board for Professional Teaching Standards, he is also cofounder and director of New Standards, an interstate consortium formed to produce state-of-the-art academic standards and performance examinations, and former head of the Committee on Standards and Assessment Policy of the National Skill Standards Board.

Judy B. Codding is vice president of programs for the National Center on Education and the Economy (NCEE) and director of the America's Choice School Design network, a program of NCEE. Before assuming her present position, she was principal of Pasadena High School in California, a large comprehensive high school serving predominantly low-income African American and Latino students. While in that position, she received the Rose Award from the University of Southern California for her work in greatly improving the academic performance of the students at Pasadena High. Previously, she was a teacher and principal of Bronxville High School and Scarsdale High School, both in New York, suburban high schools serving mainly high-income Anglo students. In addition, she has been an elementary and middle school teacher. She served as a charter principal of the Coalition of Essential Schools, a national high school reform effort. She is the coauthor (with Marc S. Tucker) of *Standards for Our Schools: How to Set Them, Measure Them, and Reach Them* (Jossey-Bass, 1998).

The Contributors

Wendy P. Cahill is a senior fellow at the Centre for Organizational Learning and Leadership at the University of Melbourne, Australia.

Brian J. Caldwell is professor and dean of the Graduate School of Education at the University of Melbourne, Australia, and consults in many nations on issues of education leadership and management.

Gerard T. Calnin is senior fellow and dean of studies in the Department of Education Policy and Management at the University of Melbourne, Australia.

Marie Eiter is responsible for the executive development programs and other related programs at the Massachusetts Institute of Technology's Sloan School of Management in Cambridge, Massachusetts. She was formerly in charge of the executive education programs at the Tuck School of Business at Dartmouth College and earlier headed Chase Bank's corporate university.

Richard J. Haney is an operations manager at Cubic Applications, Inc. He was a faculty member at the National War College and a senior analyst at the War Gaming Center at National Defense University. Haney is a retired colonel of the U.S. army.

Peter W. Hill is director of research and development for the National Center on Education and the Economy. He was formerly director of one of Australia's leading educational research institutes and chief executive of the education system of the state of Victoria.

Robert C. Hughes has had a distinguished career in the military, culminating in service as Provost of the National War College in Washington. He is currently acting director of the National Institute for School Leadership.

Carolyn Kelley is a member of the faculty at the University of Wisconsin-Madison.

Cheryl King is formerly a graduate student at Michigan State University.

Jeannie Patrick is an administrative assistant at Michigan State University.

Kent D. Peterson is a member of the faculty at the University of Wisconsin-Madison.

Thomas Sobol is Christian Johnson Professor of Outstanding Practice at Teachers College, Columbia University, and former commissioner of education for New York State.

Gary Sykes is a professor of education administration and teacher education at Michigan State University's School of Education and an authority on the professions.

Gerald N. Tirozzi is executive director of the National Association of Secondary School Principals.

The Principal Challenge

Chapter One

Preparing Principals in the Age of Accountability

Marc S. Tucker, Judy B. Codding

Why would anyone want the job of principal? Many school principals we know have the look these days of the proverbial deer caught in the headlights. Almost overnight, it seems, they have been caught in the high beams of the burgeoning account- ability movement. Now as never before, the public and all the organs of government are insisting that student academic per- formance improve — and fast. The federal government is put- ting ever-increasing pressure on the states to that end. The states, in their turn, are busy creating incentives for local boards and superintendents to raise school performance. And the local boards and superintendents are wasting no time in putting as much pressure as they can on the principals. And there it rests.

The principal experiences this set of pressures as a vise that is closing fast. The expectation that the principal will lead the school to levels of student achievement that are unprecedented for that school, for students from that social background, for children for whom English is not their native language, with budgets that mea- ger — all this seems to be the stuff of fantasy for the principal in the vise. If the principal and faculty had known how to produce unprecedented improvements in student performance before, they would have done it. What, they want to know, makes anyone think they can do it now, with little or no more money than they had before?

This enormous challenge is the icing on a cake that is, on the whole, not very appetizing to begin with.

The life of the principal is very different from the life of an average faculty member (see Chapter Eight). The typical principal supervises thirty professionals and fourteen support staff. There is no assistant principal in his school. This means that the average principal is responsible for a span of control six to ten times what is normal in private industry.

All day long, faculty, staff, and parents are making a beeline for the principal's office to resolve the problems they face. The result is a day — say, for a typical high school principal — that is a headlong dash that begins at 7:00 or 7:30 A.M. and does not end until 10:00 or 10:30 P.M. The principal's daily diary reflects a calendar set by everyone else. Typical entries would contains entries like these: "met with angry parent," "served with lawsuit," "met with grievance panel," "met with parent demanding that her son's grades be raised to level needed to get into college," "met with fire inspector on safety code violation," "attended expulsion hearing," "met with parent demanding that her daughter have a different English teacher," "visited classrooms (interrupted after fifteen minutes by emergency, unable to return)" . . . and the list goes on like that through dinner until the varsity basketball game is over in the evening.

Note that precious little of this day has to do with instruction. Principals refer to themselves as "one-minute decision makers" because they have a minute to decide one issue before they are confronted with the next one. Besides having to deal with the stress produced by this situation, the typical principal works an average sixty-hour workweek, compared to forty-five hours for the typical teacher.

So you would expect the principal to make comparably more, right? Wrong! Because principals have less political power and public support than teachers, teachers' salaries have been rising faster than principals' salaries. So although it looks as though principals earn more than teachers when you compare annual salaries, when you take into account the fact that principals are generally on a full-time schedule and the teachers generally work ten months a year, the hourly salary rate for principals is often actually lower than for teachers.

As the years have gone by and public trust in professional educators has turned to public disgust, the support that the principal used to get from parents and the community has evaporated, replaced by what seems like a constant battle, an endless series of demands that often easily escalate into abuse, from which there is no escape.

Over the past decade or so, many states have adopted some form of school site governance. The lofty goal was to relocate control of the school from the central office to the school itself and to share the enhanced power at the school level among a wider group of constituencies, to give them a greater sense of ownership and make the school work better. But the principal, a wry smile playing on her face, will tell you that it did not work out that way. The central office has as much control as ever over the budget, the curriculum, hiring, firing, and the assignment of key leadership positions in the school. The only difference from how it used to be is that the meager power the principal used to have must now be shared with a school site council composed mainly of teachers and parents who are happy to exercise whatever power they can get but who will take none of the responsibility for the outcome. So the principal has even less authority than before while being expected to accept much more responsibility.

The result is predictable. Principals are bailing out, and the pool of candidates willing to replace them is drying up at an alarming rate. Some schools with which we are familiar have recently gone six months or more without a principal because no one with even the bare minimum qualifications could be found for the post. This is not because no one has the formal qualifications. Getting the qualifications is one of the easiest ways to advance on the salary scale as a teacher or assistant principal. So there is a large pool of people who have the formal qualifications but who do not want the job. And who can blame them? Who would want a job that appears to be impossible, is thankless, and pays no more than other jobs in the same field that make more modest demands on one's time and psychic energy?

This situation would be regarded with alarm in the best of times. That is, it is always a problem when the supply of people seeking a key position falls below the demand. The only options available are to make the job more attractive, typically by raising salaries or lowering the qualifications. In education, time out of mind, we have usually done the latter, rarely the former. But consider where the country is right now. What we need are not just people who are willing to do the job and meet the minimum qualifications, even though these criteria would be hard enough to meet in many places at the moment. No, the job is no longer simply to "keep school," the job we have trained principals for over the decades. Today we need people who can do a job we have never advertised before, a job that currently serving principals were never expected to do. We need people who can lead and manage the school to much higher levels of student achievement at little or no increase in cost, in an environment in which they have much less control over the key factors that determine the outcome than similarly situated leaders and managers in most other fields. That is a very tall order.

Having said that, we are now in a position to break the challenge apart into its constituent components.

Making the Job Doable

First, the job itself must be made doable. This challenge has at least two dimensions: the structure of the job and the authority that it carries.

We have run focus groups of principals from many different kinds of schools and communities. The message is clear: the principals now in the job believe that they ought to be instructional leaders—that shaping the instructional program and providing effective guidance to the faculty in making the instructional program as effective as possible is the heart of the job. But the principals we talked to from the most advantaged communities told us that they could not possibly spend more than 40 percent of their time on instruction—too little, they think, to do what now needs to be done. And the principals of schools serving low-income inner-city schools just laughed. They spend all of their time dealing with emergencies. Attending to instruction, they say, is a luxury they cannot afford.

The fact is that one person can no longer do all that needs to be done. It is best then to talk about the "principalship," a function carried out by two or more people that involves providing the leadership the school now needs as well as the management needed to organize and administer the school at the top level. Among the possible configurations in a small school is providing the principal with a business manager who takes over many of the administrative duties. In a larger school, the job might be divided among a principal, a chief academic officer, and a chief of operations, or it might be given to a principal (or teacher) assisted by a business manager and a chief of staff. In a very large high school, it might involve multiple principals: one who is responsible for the physical plant and administrative services and a number of others, each in charge of an autonomous academic program, assisted in each case by a chief of staff or business manager.

There are many other possible configurations for the division of responsibilities among two or three individuals, but almost any conceivable arrangement is going to cost more money, which will have to be offset by savings made elsewhere in the system.

Note that the principal is the instructional leader in most of these configurations but not all of them. This is very important for everything that follows in this chapter. When we speak of the principal as instructional leader and when we describe a curriculum intended to develop the skills and knowledge needed by the principal acting in the role of instructional leader, we hope you will bear in mind this idea of the principalship and the possibility that the role of instructional leader may be played by someone other than the person who holds the title of principal. We have already noted that the environment in many urban schools is that the principal, no matter who is at his right and left hand, will have little time left for instruction after dealing with the inevitable daily ration of emergencies. A school district that ignores this reality and requires its principals to personally be the instructional leaders in every case may do so at its peril. Nevertheless, no matter which member of the leadership team performs this function, the principal should get the training for instructional leadership that we describe here, because it is essential that the principal understand this function and be able to support it knowledgeably, even if someone else is actually doing it.

Making Authority Commensurate with Responsibility and Accountability

There is another respect in which the job must be made more doable: the principal must have authority that is commensurate with her responsibility and accountability.

Imagine that you are the principal, this person who is being asked to produce great improvements in student achievement. You cannot select your staff. You cannot fire anyone who is already on your staff. You cannot award or withhold a bonus from anyone. Seniority rights for teachers means that overnight, you can lose people you have made an enormous investment in and have them replaced by people who couldn't care less about your agenda. You may have little control over the instructional materials that are used. Someone else controls the training agenda. Someone else controls how all but a small amount of your regular budget is spent. Someone else controls how the federal program money will be spent. Some people who work in your school report directly to people in the central office rather than to you. In some systems, you do not even have the right to assign teachers to classes because teachers' seniority rights govern assignment. Yet despite all this, if your students do not make progress on the state accountability measures, your school is likely to be put on a public list of low-performing schools. If performance does not improve, your school could be closed, the faculty disbanded, and you fired. You will be held responsible for the whole mess.

It is absolutely unreasonable to hold the principal accountable for student performance when that person has little or none of the authority needed to get the job done. No major corporation that expected to stay in business, no military unit of any size, no government agency that has earned the respect of the public would expect its executives to function successfully without the authority to get the job done.

State legislatures and school districts will have to deal with these issues, and it will not be easy, because others will have to cede authority to principals for this situation to be rectified. And it won't happen overnight.

So what can be done now to address the problems we have described? In answering this question, we should bear in mind that the low pay relative to teachers, the heavy supervisory load, the long hours, and much else that we have described as characteristics of the job have been with us for quite a while, though most of these problems have slowly been worsening in recent years. What has brought the situation to the crisis point has been the enormous anxiety and burdens brought on by the public's demand for greatly improved student performance.

A Historical Parallel

At first glance, the idea that schools and principals in particular should be held accountable for greatly raising student performance without the prospect of commensurately large increases in school budgets is simply unreasonable and should therefore be dismissed. But before we come to rest on that conclusion, it is important to remind ourselves of the situation that American business faced in the late 1970s and early 1980s.

American corporations virtually overnight found themselves facing unprecedented challenges from first Europe and then Asia. Their foreign competitors were bringing products to our shores that were of higher quality, were typically much more customized to individual customer needs and requirements, came to market much earlier in response to swiftly changing consumer tastes, and to the astonishment and dismay of American companies, often carried prices that were lower than the cost to the American firms of manufacturing the product, not counting the additional costs of marketing, sales, inventory, and transportation, to say nothing of profit.[1]

The short of it was that the American firms either found a way to greatly increase quality and bring their new products to market faster and do it all for a lower cost and price — or go out of business. Some went out of business, but many figured out how to produce higher quality at lower costs, and they did it very quickly.

So the experience of American business in the 1980s shows that it is in fact possible to greatly raise quality without significantly raising costs. But that same experience shows that this can be done only by rethinking the way the organization works, coming up with new strategies and processes, and then driving those strategies and processes through the whole organization using a new conception of executive development.

Firms found that they had to work hard to be very clear about their strategic goals. They had to translate those goals into standards of quality that they were going to meet. They had to come up with measures that would enable them to determine the degree to which they were meeting their standards and goals. Then they had to figure out how to empower the people who made the product or rendered the service to design whole new ways to get the job done. This process of redesign (they called it *reengineering*) of the basic processes pervaded these firms. To properly support the redesign process and the implementation of the new systems, the firms had to create new corporate cultures.

The Strategic Value of Executive
Development in Business

And they had to bring executive training from the shadows of the periphery of the firm right onto center stage.[2] Firms engaged in reengineering their basic processes quickly discovered not only that they had to have clear corporate goals and strategies but also that it was to no avail if the only people who knew about them and were dedicated to reaching them and using them were at corporate headquarters. If the goals and strategies didn't reach all the way down to the factory floor, they would fail. If the people on the front line did not know what to do and how to do it, the firm would inevitably go under. It was this realization that led firm after firm to establish corporate universities in this period. The top leaders of the corporation became the senior "professors" in the corporate university. They taught the next level down and so on in a "cascade" until the bottom of the pyramid was reached. In all the years that Jack Welch led General Electric, it is said that he never missed his biweekly teaching assignment at GE's corporate university at Crotonville, New York.

In this way, corporate strategy got out of the boardroom and into the bloodstream of the whole organization. One might ask why the corporations did not turn to the business schools instead of going to the trouble and expense of creating their own corporate universities. The answer is in part that the corporations had been quite critical of the university business schools for years and also that the corporations needed to be able to put their own corporate spin on the education and training that their executives received.

Whatever the reasons, the universities acknowledged both the threat and the opportunity, and they reached for the opportunity. All over the country, business schools began or greatly expanded their executive development programs. Whereas their M.B.A. programs enrolled individuals and usually applied the usual academic admissions criteria for determining who was admitted, the executive development programs typically reached out to firms, with which they made training contracts. The firms were asked to select teams of executives to participate in these programs. They defined projects that would be a focal point of the training program and that would be of real value to them. And the firms also contributed executives who would serve as part of the faculty for the program, ensuring that the firms' goals and values and "way of doing things" were reflected in the training. The business schools offered their best faculty for these programs and went out of their way to put together programs tailored to the needs of the firms.

The business schools made what in elementary and secondary education would be regarded as immense investments in curriculum and technology-based delivery systems (in some cases $1 million or more per course). In return, they reaped very large fees from the firms, which the firms were prepared to pay because their very survival was at stake.[3]

In a moment, we will compare the executive training in business to the training of school principals. But first, we need to discuss executive training in the context of the larger system of which it is usually a part — the system that most sectors of the economy create to develop their supply of capable executives. The case we have chosen is the case of the United States military.

The Iron Triangle

Virtually everyone we talked with in business and military education told us that they could not conceive of successfully doing their job unless certain systems were present in the place where the people being trained worked or would work.

We will illustrate the point using the military as an example.[4] Officers in the armed forces either move up at a predetermined pace or are expected to leave the service. Progress through the ranks is determined by promotion boards, which decide, on the basis of the written record, whether the officer goes on to the next stage of his career. That decision is made on the basis of the assignments the individual has had, how he has done in those jobs, the training he has had, and how he has done in that training. Promotion to the next step is both a promotion to a new rank and job and also the right to take the next appropriate training regime. In this system, jobs and the training for those jobs go hand in hand. Careers are laid out as a series of progressively demanding assignments. All officers are expected to counsel the officers reporting to them through this system and to participate in their education as coaches. Promotion depends in part on how well one has performed this function. The military does not simply send an individual to a particular school or training just because she wants to go any more than it would give that person an assignment simply because she volunteered for it. The qualifications for each job and career are known. One has to have the requisite training and previous assignments to qualify, along with the recommendations of one's superiors and, frequently, the right sort of results on the relevant diagnostic tests and so on. In short, the military sees job training and job assignments as two integral and highly related elements in a unified, coherent system of career advancement.

This "iron triangle" of carefully calibrated relationships among job training, job assignments, and career advancement is largely missing in American school systems. The pool of people from whom candidates for principals' positions come is made up of people who have selected themselves into that pool. Most people would agree that certain characteristics that are desirable in principals are inherent in the person's personality and that others are trainable. If that is so, then any sensible school district would do as the military does: identify the ones who have the right personality characteristics and make whatever investment in them is required to develop the trainable skills. It would create a carefully staged set of leadership positions in the school of increasing responsibility and step the potential executives through those positions, providing at each step the education and training appropriate for that stage in the progression, with strong mentoring along the way. They would make sure that this education and training was not just generic — addressed to what any principal in any American school district should know and be able to do—but also specific to the culture of that district and its own strategy for raising student achievement. This is what the military and many American business firms do, but few districts do it.

Good training has value in and of itself. But a good training system will produce much better results if it is mated to a sound executive development system. As you focus on the training of school leaders and managers in the rest of this chapter, we suggest that you keep this in mind.

We have told you something now about what the principal's job is like and how the challenges presented by the pressure to raise student performance are combining with other factors to cause a worsening shortage of people who can lead our schools to high performance. We have suggested that when facing a similar challenge to greatly improve organizational performance, American business created the modern form of executive development program as its chosen method for driving its survival strategies deep into the organization. And we have used the example of the military to show that such programs, though they may be essential, are not sufficient. We are ready now to examine the way principals are trained, with a view to understanding how and why that approach to training has to be changed to meet the challenges we have described.

The Training of School Principals Today

Most states require that people hired as principals have at least three years of prior service as a teacher.[5] Seventeen states require that the candidate pass an exam to get a state license to be a school administrator. But many of these tests are just basic skills tests and are generally quite easy (though not all candidates pass them).

Almost all states require that principals have a state-authorized credential or an advanced degree in educational administration (some states require both). The programs leading to these credentials and degrees are typically offered by departments of educational administration in schools of education in universities. Some non-degree programs leading to the credential are offered through professional associations, county offices, and school district training.

Recruiting for these programs typically does not involve selection criteria related to the candidate's potential as a school principal. Candidates are not generally interviewed. The schools offering the programs typically make no effort to identify potential school leaders. The result is that the pool of candidates from whom the districts select principals is generally composed of people who may or may not have any aptitude or desire for the job or be regarded by their employers as suited for it. Indeed, some have a well-developed distaste for it.

The doctoral programs offered by the universities, on the one hand, often have little or no coherence.[6] In too many cases, very little is expected of the students in these programs by way of performance that would shed some light on their suitability as school administrators. The state-approved credential programs, on the other hand, are often "hyperrational." Categories of skill or knowledge are specified, means for achieving them must be documented, procedures for supervised fieldwork must be specified and are audited, and periodic program reviews are undertaken. Notwithstanding all this, however, the substance of these programs is typically very thin indeed. And there is typically very little connection between the curriculum as taught and the actual demands, conditions, and problems of everyday practice.

The educational administration departments of many schools of education at the state universities and state colleges where credential and nondoctoral work are the norm are generally regarded as "cash cows" by the university.[7] That is, they are expected to produce a substantial surplus that can be used to fund programs that the school cares more about. One consequence is that almost anyone who meets the most minimal academic qualifications will be admitted, and an absolute minimum of effort on the part of the student will be accepted by the faculty to earn a grade that will enable the candidate to obtain the necessary certificate or degree.

In their effort to keep costs down, these schools rely heavily on adjunct faculty. The adjunct faculty, often practicing or retired school administrators, frequently offer anecdotes from the world of practice that students find a refreshing antidote to the theory expounded in their other courses, which often seem quite irrelevant to the problems they actually face. But anecdotes from the past are not going to prepare these students for a future shaped by the new and much higher expectations of the accountability movement. And they are no substitute for a carefully thought out curriculum combining the disciplined acquisition of craft knowledge with the conceptual underpinning that these students need.

So all in all, it is no surprise that when principals who are succeeding in leading their school to substantial gains in student achievement are asked to identify some connection between their capacity and the way they were initially prepared for the job,[8] they are unable to do so, pointing instead to personal characteristics and what they learned on the job and from colleagues.

The programs made available to practicing principals by the graduate school administration programs are, on the whole, no better than those for aspiring principals. Scattershot and lacking in coherence, they are only rarely connected in any significant way to the specific goals and strategies of the districts in which the principals work. We found nothing comparable to the kinds of executive development programs common in business and the military.

In fact, the connections between the academy and the employers in the field of public education can in most cases be described as tenuous, standing in strong contrast to the relationships between some graduate schools of business and the modern industrial corporation or the very close links between training units and operational units in the military. By and large, it is still the case in education that the customers of the graduate schools are individuals, not school districts. The faculty of the graduate school of education determines what the curriculum will be, with little or no input from the employers of the executives being trained. If this had continued to be the case in business, as it has in education, few executive development programs would have survived in the business schools; the corporate universities would have done the job themselves, hiring individual university professors as consultants as needed.

There are programs that do not answer to this description.[9] We know of some that have been using the case method for years and others that work hard to make strong connections for their students between their courses and the actual challenges of practice. We found some graduate programs that do not rely overmuch on adjunct faculty and some certificate programs that are paying attention to the new demands on school leaders posed by the standards movement. There were some that were clearly valued by their students for the knowledge and skills they provided and some that worked hard to screen out individuals who they thought would not profit from them.

But these are the exceptions that prove the rule. As one would expect, some of the most effective programs can be found at a handful of elite institutions. Stanford pioneered the use of the case method in education administration. The Harvard Graduate School of Education, among many examples at that institution that might be cited, makes wide use of cases it has developed as well as cases developed by the Harvard Business School, the Kennedy School, and other institutions. The University of Wisconsin uses cases, simulations, and role-play to base its program in situations that mirror the kinds of problems that practicing school administrators face every day. And programs like those at Wichita State and the University of California at Fresno also expect their students to get deeply involved in problems of practice and use many of the techniques of the best executive development programs (like action research and problem-focused curricula). Some of the most promising programs we found were in the form of collaborations between universities and particular jurisdictions, like the collaboration between Teachers College and Westchester County, between the Chicago School Administrators Association and Northwestern University, or between the San Diego Schools and San Diego State

University. These programs involve both aspiring and practicing principals, are generally very intensive, focus on leadership and problem solving, and are deeply embedded in the work of particular school districts and the strategies they are using to raise student performance. Here as elsewhere, we see the result of the insight, drive, and charisma of a handful of leaders.

But when we looked at the most promising programs closely, we found more often than not that they were built on too small a scale, many had too little institutional support, and they were typically poorly funded. Virtually all suffered from lack of investment in the development of powerful curriculum materials. None had all the elements one would look for in a program that is likely to meet the full scope of the challenges we have described here. And there are far too few of them.

Why Have the Universities Failed?

Without question, there are a growing number of people in our universities and in the other organizations responsible for training the next generation of school leaders and managers who are very much aware of the shortcomings of the programs we have described and eager to do something about them. We have met many of these people and have come to admire their determination. We shall describe some of the challenges they face and some of the policy changes that must be made to improve their chances of success.

The question as to why the universities have, on the whole, failed is crucial. Our universities have at least their share of people of good will who are committed to public education and who want to do the right thing. There are no villains here. So if that is the case, it is likely that the problem lies in the situation in which the schools of education find themselves, the policy environment they face, and other incentives to which they must respond. If that is so, the answer lies in changing that environment and those incentives. One could argue that the current system has evolved in response to the incentives governing the relationships among the universities, school districts, and state departments of education, as follows.

First, the universities are accountable to the states for approval of their degree programs and certificate programs. To the extent that these programs are not equipping school leaders for the world we have described, the state shares some of the accountability.

Second, the people who sign up for these programs are full-time teachers who are taking the courses to entitle them to an automatic pay raise given for courses taken. It is likely that a large fraction have no intention of becoming school principals. One could say that they only want their ticket punched. More charitably, for many young people who have taught for several years, this appears to be the only viable way to stay in the profession and earn more money. They are simply responding to the incentives they face. But the result is that they are typically angry when the people who teach these courses make any serious demands on them.

Third, some adjunct faculty members lower their expectations of their graduate students in education administration programs when those students threaten to drop the course, because the faculty members are compensated on the basis of student enrollment.

Fourth, because there are no clear quality distinctions among programs and because these students already have full-time jobs (and often family obligations), they tend to select the programs that are least demanding of their time and energy. This puts pressure on programs to lower their standards to maintain enrollment.

Fifth, given the low expectations of the students in these courses, it turns out to be relatively easy for many universities to hire adjunct faculty to teach the courses at very low cost.

Sixth, at the major public research universities, reduced state support in recent years has combined with the formal incentives and informal academic norms in these institutions to push faculty to seek research grants and publish in journals rather than make useful connections to school practice and practitioners that could strengthen their teaching. This does not necessarily signal a lack of interest in making these connections, but it has the same result.

Thus we have a situation that meets the needs of all of the actors involved *except* the students who will be taught in the schools where the graduates of these programs serve as principals.

The tired teachers taking the courses get their automatic pay raises for very little investment of real effort. The university makes a profit on each person occupying a seat in the program and is not disturbed by anyone from the state inquiring as to the quality of the professional education offered. The people running the program do not have to go to the considerable effort and expense that would be required to develop and teach an appropriate curriculum, to say nothing of the expense and effort that would be required to really connect the program with the actual practice settings that would give it life and meaning.

There are policy measures that could be taken to address at least some of these issues. The states could impose tough licensure standards that reflect the changed nature of the job and administer equally tough performance assessments to the candidates. Under current conditions, that would absolutely guarantee that the trickle of people into the principalship would dry up completely unless the state at the same time substantially increased principals' salaries, abolished school site councils, sharply curtailed the scope of teachers' bargaining rights (thus giving principals more scope to choose their staff, reward individual faculty members, and get rid of poor performers), and much more. You may or may not think that these are good ideas, but they are, we think, responsive to the analysis we just presented, and anyone who wants seriously to address the problems we have described must either entertain these ideas or come up with others that have an equal chance of meeting the challenges. Our point here is that much of the general failure of the universities to address these challenges is attributable to the policy environment in which they work and is not likely to change much until that policy environment changes.

The states are slowly adopting a set of administrator licensure standards recommended by the Council of Chief State School Officers (those of the Interstate School Leaders Licensure Consortium, or ISLLC) as well as an examination administered by the Educational Testing Service (ETS). These are not performance standards. They are necessarily very general, because their designers intended them apply to everyone from school principal to big-city superintendent. It is as if the same standards applied from second lieutenant to four-star general. No less important, they were constructed by analyzing the job as it has long been done by experienced educational administrators, which means that they do not reflect a determined focus on the greatly altered current environment and therefore the job description with which this chapter began. It is therefore not surprising that although the ISLLC standards include instructional leadership, they do not feature it. Nor are they a good guide to the kind of training that would equip the principal to be an effective redesigner of his school to get much higher student performance at little or no increase in cost, the heart and soul of the new job description. Nor is the ETS exam designed in a way that is likely to encourage the development of principals of the sort we described in the introduction to this chapter.

There is one policy development that we do think may have promise. The National Policy Board on Educational Administration has stimulated an effort to create for school principals an institution with a mission parallel to that of the National Board for Professional Teaching Standards. Its role would be to create performance standards for board certification of principals who are accomplished practitioners of their profession. The existence of such a certification program could be an incentive for many principals to participate in a demanding program designed along the lines of the business schools' executive development programs, if the brief history of the National Board for Professional Teaching Standards is any guide. But that will be true only if school districts and states provide an incentive to principals to make the investment of time and money necessary to prepare themselves to meet the certificate standard and take the examination.

There are two other points to be made in connection with the question as to why the universities have not done better in this field. One has to do with money. Good business schools, like good medical schools and good law schools, have very ample budgets. Their budgets are ample because they can charge handsome fees.

They can charge handsome fees because their graduates have the potential to make very high salaries that are connected in part to which graduate school they attended. These graduate schools honor their applicants by admitting them to their programs, and their graduates honor their alma maters by giving them generous gifts. There is no such virtuous circle in educational administration. Which graduate school you went to makes little difference as one goes up the ladder. And there is no pot of gold there anyway. Few school administrators of any rank make enough to have a university building named after them. That is not likely to change.

There is an irony here. The virtuous circle for business schools results in those schools' having the funds to make significant investments, as we have pointed out, in the development of powerful curricula for their students, which in turn enables them to provide successful programs that get their students ever more powerful curricula. One of the more interesting trends is the development in business schools of opportunities for candidates for the M.B.A. to focus on the education industry. Presumably, this reflects the development of education as a major business opportunity in the American economy, but it could presage major capital investments by business schools in the development of education leaders and managers of a kind that the education schools have never been able to make. Here again, state policy and private philanthropy could put the education schools on a more equal footing with respect to capital investment if they choose to do so.

The last reason the universities have not done what needs to be done has to do with a choice that graduate schools of education made many years ago. That was the choice to model themselves on the schools of arts and sciences, not the professional schools. Graduate schools of education below the top rank are often populated with professors of education sociology who yearn to be members of the sociology department in the school of arts and sciences and professors of mathematics education who are not really accepted as equals by the professors in the mathematics department of the faculty of arts and science and have nowhere else to turn to find out where they stand in the status hierarchy.

We are pointing to some of the deepest cultural differences within the university. The incentives in the modern graduate school of education to reach out to the world of practice are weaker than they should be and weaker than they need to be, though many individuals in these institutions are working hard to make those connections despite the lack of formal incentives to do so. The people who lead our universities will have to work to change those incentives if they want to see their institutions play the role they should be playing in educating and training our school leaders in the years ahead.

The District-Level Lack of Management Development Systems

Summing up, then, we can say that while the modern school district faces much the same kind of challenge that American business and the military faced beginning in the late 1970s, it lacks some of the basic structures that are needed to do the job, structures that have long been taken for granted in business and the military.

Both sectors decided that they had to make enormous changes in strategy and culture. Both knew that the only way to drive those changes through their organizations was by using training strategies. But in both cases, there were certain well-developed basic infrastructures in place that they could count on.

Among these structures is the modern system for identifying, training, and selecting leaders and managers to make sure that there is at all times a strong pool of candidates available, as noted earlier. Another is the carefully defined sequence of positions that aspiring senior managers have to go through that enable them to systematically develop the skills and knowledge that senior managers need, as described earlier, and at the same time, the sequence of formal courses that provide the "just in time" education, training, and

professional development they need both to do the job they have
and to prepare them for the next step in the sequence. Military
officers typically also have access to a well-constructed mentoring
system. Such systems can also be found in the private sector—for
example, in law firms, where each partner is usually responsible for
mentoring a group of associates. Rare is the district that has any of
this in place. We know of very few school districts that come close
to having all the components of a well-designed management
development system.

It is also true that the infrastructure for the initial preparation
of leaders and managers and for their continuing education and
training was in better shape in the business sector and in the military than in public education. The fact that the corporate university evolved in partnership with the university graduate schools of
business is a testament to the responsiveness of the business schools.
The corporate university, a recent innovation, might otherwise
have evolved to largely replace the university as a source of continuing education and training for experienced corporate leaders and
managers. In the case of the military, the war college system is the
corporate university, and it has been both healthy and around for a
long time.

In the case of the military, the employer and the trainer are the
same organization. Just as in the business case, the employer decides
what the employee needs and either provides it in-house or buys it
from another source, often the university. In any case, the management development system provides the standards to which the education and training will be done. As we have noted, it is because
the standards are universal within the system that officers in charge
can reliably make plans even for people they have never met,
knowing only what their formal qualifications are, because those
qualifications incorporate universal standards. Only the ISLLC
standards are available to perform this function in education, and
we have described the shortcomings of those standards.

One's instinct is to assume that these ills are unique to the
American education system and to look for someone or some class

of institutions on whom to blame the problem. But the assumption is dead wrong. The broad institutional weaknesses reported here are endemic to elementary and secondary education systems throughout the English-speaking world and probably beyond (see Chapter Seven).

Starting with the People on the Job

The question is where to begin to address those weaknesses. The normal instinct is to attend first to the initial preparation of school leaders. There are good reasons for this. Here, as elsewhere, it makes more sense to do the job right at the beginning than to have to pick up the pieces later. But our judgment is that if resources are limited, the first priority should go to addressing the problems faced by the school leaders who are already on the job.

The case for giving initial priority to the school leaders already on the job is much the same as the case for businesses' giving priority to the development of their executives in the late 1980s and early 1990s. Recall that the business world, when its competitive position was attacked as never before from abroad, attended first and foremost to the executives already on staff. These were the people they had to rely on to turn the firm around. These were also the people who, because they were already on board, were most subject to the influence of the corporation's agenda, as opposed to the agenda of university professors who may or may not understand and be sympathetic to the goals and strategies of the firm.

The analogy holds. The agenda of standards-based reform that is now driving government's agenda for greatly raising student performance is far more deeply embraced by school districts, especially large school districts, and even more particularly big-city school districts, than it is by the faculties of graduate schools of education. That is hardly surprising, because school districts are under far more pressure to implement strategies to raise student performance than the schools of education are. Thus giving priority to strategies for greatly improving the skills and knowledge of practicing school leaders—as opposed to aspiring school leaders—makes sense in public education right now for all the same reasons that it made sense in business in the late 1970s. They have the greatest incentives to pay attention to the substance of the training. Investing in them is the most efficient strategy, because everyone who is trained will be employed as a school leader (indeed, they are already so employed). And the training will pay off immediately, not years in the future, for the same reason.

But this is no argument for ignoring the initial preparation of school leaders. In the long run, much depends on making strong progress in this arena. Clearly, those who have the resources, the will, and the mandate to focus on initial preparation should do so. But in the rest of this chapter, we will address ourselves mainly to the preparation of those who are already on the job for the challenges they now face. We turn now to the question of design. What should be done and how?

Examples from Abroad

In Great Britain, the challenge of training school leaders has been accorded the highest priority of any social goal. Tony Blair, the prime minister, has personally led a national initiative to address the problem. To ensure that the government had access to the best thinking about school leadership anywhere in the world, Blair directed his staff to benchmark international practices and bring some of the world's leading experts on the topic to London to advise the government. Deciding to bypass the nation's universities, the British government established a national quasi-governmental agency to address the issue and has provided the agenda and operating budget to get it started, as well as a handsome capital budget to house the operation. The government conducted a national competition among its universities for the honor of hosting the new institution. It is still too early to tell whether this approach will produce the results the Blair government has in mind.

The Hong Kong government, equally determined to address the problem, has embarked on a similar course of action.

But each of those governments operates a ministry of education that sets education policy and controls the schools. That function, in the United States, is performed by the states, although no state as yet has all the functions performed by ministries of education in other countries. States could in fact choose to create a quasi-governmental agency to train school principals. States could create not-for-profits to do so or fund existing organizations. Or they could fund the development of state institutions to train incumbent school leaders at their universities, subject to whatever criteria and conditions they choose to impose. Or they could employ any combination of these strategies that seemed appropriate.

First Principles

Whatever strategy is chosen, however, the philanthropies or governments funding the work and setting the rules should, we believe, be guided by certain principles.

First, the focus should be very clear: preparing school leaders to lead and manage schools that can consistently produce steady gains in student performance without substantial increases in school budgets.

Second, no institution should be funded to educate and train school leaders unless it has the same kind of relationships with school districts that the executive development programs in most graduate schools of business have with the major firms that supply their students. The school districts should play a major role in determining who the candidates for training will be, what the form of the training will be, and what the major action projects will be. They should also be responsible for providing mentors and part of the faculty for the training programs.

Third, any program offered should have to demonstrate that it has carefully benchmarked best practices in education and draws widely on the best that leadership and management training in business and the military has to offer as well. Any such program will have to represent a bigger investment in curriculum development than any program of which we are currently aware.

Fourth, no single institution or type of institution should have a monopoly over the provision of programs that individuals or school districts can turn to for the provision of powerful education and training for school leaders. The standards for such education and training should be made clear, and a healthy climate should be established in which the principals' professional societies (see Chapter Ten), other nonprofit institutions, for-profit training organizations, and universities can vie with one another for the favors of this market. One way to establish such a market is to give the money for the training not to the provider institutions but to their customers, the school districts, subject to the kinds of conditions spelled out here. That is basically what happens in business and the military, which is a significant part of the reason that leadership and management training is so much more powerful and relevant in those sectors.

Imagine for the moment that such programs were actually available in many places in the United States. How might they be structured? What teaching strategies would work best? What sort of curriculum might they offer?

Teaching Adults: The State of the Art

Let us look at the way a wide range of other professions go about developing an effective curriculum for the training of leaders and managers, as well as what has been learned from an equally wide range of professions about the most effective ways of teaching adults what they need to know to be effective in their profession (see Chapter Six).

Before the late 1970s, executive education in business was largely focused on the functions of the executive—finance and so on—but is now focused on strategic leadership and organizational change, mainly because the task is not to make steady improvements in a stable organization but rather to cope with a rapidly changing scene in which the prize goes to the firm that reads the situation right, sets the right goals, and comes up with a superior strategy for achieving them (an exact parallel, as we see it, to the current situation in education). At the same time, and for the same reasons, the content of the training is moving steadily toward ever-greater customization to the needs of the individual firm, within the scope of a program that has a core standard curriculum. As we noted, it follows from this that the faculty for the training increasingly includes executives from the firm as well as university academics.

Executive education has been case-based for decades, but it is now adding to the cases the element of action learning, with constant feedback to the participant. This means projects that are an integral part of the training regime but whose topics are set by the firm, not the faculty. And it means feedback on the work of the project as it progresses, by both faculty and firm executives.

It is only a slight extension of these trends to the next one—the idea that the firm will send whole teams to be trained as a group. Allied to this is the idea of training cohorts so that all of those who enter a class stay together through the course of the training and become a support group for one another then and thereafter, within firms and across firms. This simple idea can greatly and quickly increase the organization's capacity to absorb, disseminate, and implement new ideas.

Finally, there is the notion of cascading learning communities, meaning that the people at the top of the firm combine learning with a developing strategy for the firm as the basis for a kind of learning community formed among themselves; each layer of management below them then does the same thing in a way appropriate to the managers' own responsibilities in the organization. The firm, over time, develops an approach to continuous learning in which each of these learning communities takes responsibility for developing the agenda for the community just below it in the hierarchy and coaching its members through that agenda—the cascade.

In this way, the top executives in the firm develop a very efficient method for driving their agenda and strategies for achieving their goals right straight throughout the firm, from top to bottom, using the professional development system as the agent.

From the engineering profession we might take the idea of developing short, modular courses, designed to be intense, organized in time blocks of various lengths. These courses are designed to complement the core curriculum and can be taught in nontraditional settings, as needed, by nontraditional instructors. Many are intended to reflect the practical and human side of engineering. In executive education in public education, much use is made of short courses, but what is often lacking is the close connection to the actual demands of the new accountability-shaped environment and the goals and strategies of the individual districts in which these education leaders work.

It turns out that there is a real ferment in the forms of professional education for the ministry. Of greatest interest to us is that after their initial training, the participants move directly into practice settings, where they access learning materials through technology and design their learning around the work they are doing, with support and guidance from the faculty in the seminary. They rarely visit the campus of the institution offering the instruction; their learning is almost entirely based in the field. Here, too, as in the business realm, there is great interest in the development of cohort learning communities.

There has been a revolution in medical education in recent years, one that has many parallels to the revolution we think is needed in the preparation of education professionals. Medical education used to be almost completely based in the disciplines, moving to a clinical setting only after the discipline-based education was complete. Now, increasingly, professional education in medicine is driven by real problems, as presented by real cases. There are set courses in the curriculum designed to convey core material to the students in a standard lecture format, and these play a very important role in the process, but a substantial part of the available time is taken by students' finding out what they need to know to diagnose and address particular cases presented by actual patients.

Here again, the cornerstone of the design is a small cohort group, which works on cases together. There is extensive use of technology to deliver instruction and assessments.

A lot of attention in this field has been devoted to the design of assessment. In this case, the form that it takes is to ask the participant to respond to questions about cases, generate hypotheses and alternative treatment plans, and respond to factual and conceptual questions in an oral examination. There is a lot about this approach to assessment that appears to have direct application to the education and training of school leaders and managers.

Finally, it turns out that the emerging form of medical education has managed to turn what could have been a big problem into a big asset. The problem is that the sum of the cases that actually present themselves in the problem-based part of the program do not naturally lead to all of the disciplinary knowledge that the beginning doctor ought to have, even after the students have completed the required lecture courses. There are usually big gaps that have to be filled in somehow before the candidate takes the medical boards. The solution? The cohort groups figure out what they do not know and need to know and divide up among themselves the task of finding the answers, which they then teach to each other, with their professors serving in the role of mentors. In so doing, the students accommodate themselves to the notion that no initial preparation will ever give them everything they need to know and therefore to the idea that they have to be prepared to keep learning throughout their whole career. Most important, they are actually required to figure out what they need to know and where and how they can get the knowledge they need. In other words, they have to develop a strategy for learning to learn and for doing it in the company of colleagues who have the same needs. This is a crying need in the education and training of school leaders and managers.

In many of these fields, e-learning is combined with the discipline of instructional design to produce Web-based forms of instruction, typically combined with face-to-face instruction, that both require and merit substantial capital investment. The investment can be spread across many more students than would normally participate in a conventional course.

In this way, carefully developed case studies can be presented in text form and augmented with videos of key actors in the cases as well as tools that can be used to analyze certain aspects of the cases, video commentary on the cases from participants and experts, and links to related cases, articles, and Web sites. Simulations and action projects can also be used to engage the participants and bring them into the world of the practicing professional in powerful ways. Group software makes it possible for groups of participants to learn collaboratively and for teachers and mentors to interact with their students and mentees no matter how separated they might be in space and time.

The e-learning world is clearly evolving very quickly in ways that make it vital for individuals who are providing learning opportunities for tomorrow's school leaders and managers to participate fully.

The High-Performance Curriculum

The points made in the preceding section have mainly to do with pedagogy. But what about curriculum content? We focus here not on what aspiring principals should know but on what the curriculum should be for principals who have some experience, the people on whom the district is most likely to rely to turn around performance in its schools now.[10]

The Educational Challenge

One would think that it would hardly be necessary to explain to the modern school principal the challenge that the principal faces. Who but the principal could be more expert on that point? But we have come to think otherwise. The public opinion research that has been done shows clearly that American educators have only the haziest understanding of the ways in which the rapid globalization of the world economy has dramatically raised the level of academic skills and knowledge needed to lead a life beyond the threshold of economic struggle. Nor do they understand the extent to which educators hold different expectations for wealthy, majority students than they do for those from minority, low-income backgrounds and the corrosive effects that this difference in expectations has on the academic performance of these groups of students.

The starting point for the curriculum, we think, has to be a deep understanding of the circumstances that have led to the expectation that schools will produce greatly improved student performance at little or no increase in cost, a realistic estimate of the specific obstacles that stand in the way of reaching that goal, and an acceptance of the challenge to get every student ready for college without remediation by the time she leaves high school. Absent that understanding and acceptance, it is hardly likely that the principals will be able to produce among the whole school community the moral commitment to the vision that will be needed to achieve it.

Standards-Based Instructional Systems

The federal education legislation passed in the early days of 2002 (HR 1, the "No Child Left Behind Act") makes official the commitment of the nation to an educational policy based on standards-based instructional systems. But few principals have more than a superficial understanding of the nature of such systems or the degree to which they hold the key to producing great improvements in student achievement without significant increases in cost. Principals will need to understand the different kinds of standards and assessments available, the appropriate uses of each, and the relationships among them. Similarly, they will need to understand the structure and function of curriculum frameworks and the ways in which curriculum and instructional materials can be analyzed for fit with the standards. Last and most essential, they will need to grasp the overriding importance of aligning all of the parts of the instructional system to make it internally coherent and consistent and the role of the principal in making that alignment a reality.

The Principal as Strategic Thinker

But understanding the essentials of standards-based systems of instruction will avail little if the principal does not have the skills to think strategically about the challenges he faces and to put together a clear and powerful strategy for addressing these challenges. Educators on the whole think tactically and operationally but rarely strategically. That is no great handicap when tomorrow looks much like yesterday and the challenge is simply to keep school, but when the challenge is to reach a goal that the school has never attempted before, the ability to think strategically may make all the difference. Much of the best literature and best practice in this field comes not from education but from business and the military, and the powerful curriculum that principals now need will have to draw heavily from those arenas.

The Principal as School Designer

Organizing all of the resources of the school to produce high achievement requires looking hard at all aspects of the life of the school and redesigning them so that they all contribute to a powerful and coherent program. Not only does the instructional program of the school have to be fully aligned, but every other aspect of the life of the school must also be aligned with the redesigned instructional program, from the master schedule to the budget to the way before- and after-school programs are configured.

This is what is meant by school design. All schools can be said to have designs, in the sense that something is in place. But those designs are rarely the result of a conscious, deliberate attempt to conceive of how a school might function with all aspects of its program operating in harmony with one another. Rather they are the result of years of incremental decisions, many of them made with little or no consideration of the effect a new program or project might have on the ones already in place, with the result that many end up working at cross-purposes with one another.

So it will be very important to introduce the principal to the essentials of school design, because it is the principal, more than anyone else, who has to have the overall architecture of the school's program constantly in mind as a road map for the work ahead. Whether the school chooses to contract with another organization to provide a design or to come up with one itself, its leaders must know how to recognize a good design, improve one that needs help, and assess the adequacy of the one they already have.

The Foundations of Effective Learning

School design, including all the work needed to achieve high performance, is built on the core principles of teaching, learning, and curriculum. A deep and detailed knowledge of all of the relevant research literature is the result of years of concentrated study, which is well beyond the scope of any program of the sort we have in mind. What is required here is a careful distillation of that literature into a form in which it becomes useful to the practicing principal as a guide to the redesign of the instructional program of her school in the context of the framework provided by the new standards and accountability systems. And it is clear, too, that the new curriculum for principals will have to provide an opportunity for the participants to make these distilled principles of learning, teaching, and curriculum their own, practicing applications in the kinds of situations they actually face.

Leadership for Excellence in Literacy and Mathematics

Principles of the kind we have been discussing are important and valuable, but they are usually couched in a way that is independent of the subject being taught. If the principal is to be a true instructional leader, he will have to be more conversant with the essentials of teaching literacy and mathematics than most principals are today. This is, in the end, what it will mean to be in touch with and in command of the core business of schooling. Principals will need to be able to recognize best practices in literacy and mathematics, to judge the quality of programs (including their own program) and instructional materials in those subjects, and to assess the quality of instruction in the classroom by talking with students, looking at their work, and observing the interactions between students and teachers. They will have to know how to align the other aspects of the way the school functions to support their literacy and mathematics programs and will have to be able to provide leadership for the development of effective literacy and mathematics programs. The analytical skills that principals need to examine and improve their literacy and mathematics programs will be no less valuable when they turn to the other aspects of the curriculum for which they are responsible.

Promoting Professional Knowledge

One of the most important aspects of the new curriculum for principals is promoting the professional knowledge and skill of the faculty. Principals will have to know how to establish a culture in which every professional on the staff is expected to be learning all the time, in which professional development is not simply a personal matter, episodic and random, but is seen by the faculty as the most important tool by which they acquire the skill and knowledge they need to implement the strategies and designs that the school has adopted for improving student achievement. And the principal will need to develop the skills required to design and implement a system for organizational learning that will permit the staff, in a disciplined way, to benchmark best practices elsewhere and to learn from their own practices in the school over time. Much of the adult learning in the school will take place in teams that the principal will need to establish, and the curriculum will have to include the skills needed to establish and supervise effective faculty teams, as well as the skills needed to coach both individuals and teams to ever-greater effectiveness. The principal will also have to learn what to look for as she walks around the school and observes classrooms, mentoring teachers to help them become more effective in a standards-based environment.

The Principal as Instructional Leader

Much of the knowledge and skill needed by the modern school principal to be an effective instructional leader has already been included in the curriculum elements described earlier. But not all. Here the principal stands back from the trees to observe the forest, coming to understand how the job of the school principal in the United States came to be disassociated from the work of teaching and learning and why the same person must now make instructional leadership the heart and soul of the job. Among the topics in this part of the curriculum are ways in which the responsibility for instructional leadership can be shared by the principal with a number of other faculty members, how time can be freed up from other responsibilities for the work of instructional leadership, and how the instructional leadership role relates to other roles of the school principal.

The Principal as Team Builder

As we just implied, the job of leading and managing the school is not something the principal can do alone. But most principals try to do just that. Much depends on their capacity to do what successful leaders and managers in other fields have worked hard at doing—building effective teams. The curriculum here is focused on developing the knowledge and skills needed to define the goals for teams, recruit and select their members, and motivate and coach them to success.

Creating a Culture That Is Ethical, Results-Oriented, and Professional

The principal is above all a moral leader and a builder of culture. Culture is "the way we do things here." Because young people are shrewd observers of adult behavior, if the way we do things here is not ethical, the students will see that right away, and the faculty will lose them right away. Hence this part of the curriculum will need to focus hard on what it means to be a moral leader and how it can be done, as well as how one can analyze school culture and the steps a principal can take to build a school culture that is ethical, results-oriented, collaborative, and respectful of everyone in the school community. Earlier we addressed the need to be results-oriented and to create a school that nourishes the continuing growth and development of the faculty as a community of professionals. Here, too, the leader will fail unless he succeeds in building these goals into the culture of the school.

The Principal as Driver of Change

There is a large literature on organizational change in general and school change in particular. But the literature on managing change to produce results in schools is much smaller. And that is the topic in this part of the curriculum that we recommend. The aim is to provide the principal with the knowledge and skills needed to lead, design, and drive a change process calculated to lead to steady improvement in the achievement of the students in the school. Here the principal learns to analyze the motivations of the various participants in the process, to identify friends and foes, and to maximize the former at the expense of the latter over time, moving steadily from small wins to substantial gains. The principal should also learn how to identify root problems and causes, gather intelligence and formulate a plan on the basis of appropriate data, set performance targets, select strategies, and develop sound implementation plans.

Managing for Results

Here the curriculum pulls together much that has gone before to put the emphasis on the principal's role as the driver for results. This last part of the curriculum begins with a focus on the crucial role of data in the drive for results, from the careful setting of targets to the collection, display, and analysis of implementation and outcome data to the use of data for setting goals, monitoring progress, allocating and reallocating resources, and managing the school program. But it does not stop with data. This part of the curriculum would return to the beginning, reemphasizing the crucial role of the principal in providing a vision of the results worth achieving and keeping that vision constantly in front of the school community, allocating responsibilities to everyone involved for realizing that vision, and holding everyone accountable for doing his part, not excepting the principal herself. It is here that the participant would come to understand that the principal must be the keeper of the flame, the person whose eyes are never off the results that are desired and the results actually achieved.

This curriculum design emerged from our analysis of the role the principal must play in a standards-based system focused on getting all students ready for college without remediation, on the one hand, and from our reading of the literature on leadership and management in the fields of business (see Chapter Four), the military, and education, on the other hand. We offer it for consideration by anyone who wishes to build a modern and relevant program for the training and development of school principals. It is the design that we are using to build the curriculum for the National Institute for School Leadership (see Appendix A).

Reprise

We return here to the question with which we began: Why would anyone want this job? The reason, of course, why good people seek this job and stay in it, despite all the problems we have catalogued, is that, as Jerry Murphy has observed, it always has the potential for being one of the most rewarding jobs on the planet. Few jobs, in fact, provide such great opportunities for exhilaration, learning, personal growth, and the richness of spirit that comes from helping others.

Notwithstanding all the obstacles, we have known principals of schools serving mostly students from low-income families who have led their schools from despair to hope, from 5 percent of their students meeting state literacy standards to 60 percent meeting those standards in just two years. Those principals do not have to go to bed at night wondering whether they have made a difference. They know that students who leave elementary school not reading well account for the overwhelming majority of young people who drop out of school, use drugs, commit crimes, and end up in prison again and again. They know that they have made it possible for the children in their care to turn an enormous corner, to reach for the stars, to succeed.

Not all schools are in such dire shape, and not every case of improvement is quite so dramatic. But much now depends on the creation of a whole generation of what business calls "turnaround artists," people who can walk into their own school or another school and work with its faculty, students, parents, and community to turn it around, make it sing, and enable all of its students to succeed at levels few thought possible before. If the standards and accountability movement succeeds, it will be because the United States has figured out how to make it possible for its school leaders and managers to get the job done.

Notes

1. There are many books that tell this tale well. One that we particularly like, by Gary Jacobson and John Hillkirk, *Xerox: American Samurai* (Old Tappan, N.J.: Macmillan, 1986), describes the challenge that Xerox faced and how its leadership decided to respond to it.

2. This account of the rise of the modern executive development program is based on conversations with faculty members and administrators at the graduate schools of business at
   Harvard University, Stanford University, and Dartmouth
   College.
3. An associate dean at Harvard Business School told us that
   the school typically invests $800,000 in the development of
   a course for its M.B.A. program and an additional $1 million
   to convert the course into a form suitable for Web-based
   delivery. This is exclusive of the cost of the salaries of the
   professors involved. Most of the costs of the development
   process cover the time of the professional case developers. It
   is important, of course, to keep the relative sizes of the
   respective enterprises in mind as we compare the investments made by business schools in executive education to
   those made by graduate schools of education. The average
   size of the Fortune 500 firms is more than *thirty times* that of
   the five hundred largest school districts, and the research
   and development budgets of the largest firms are often as
   large as the entire budgets of comparably ranked school districts. Still, what we are describing is a sea change in the
   structure of business schools in response to the challenges
   business faced in the 1980s, compared to very modest
   changes made to help American schools and districts face
   the leadership challenges of the 1990s.
4. We are indebted to two former provosts and one incumbent
   provost of the National War College at Washington, D.C.,
   who spent hours introducing us to the military's approach to
   executive development. One of these men, Robert Hughes,
   is the coauthor of Chapter Five.
5. Our description of how one gets to be a principal and of the
   training that principals receive is drawn from many sources,
   including Chapters Eight and Nine.
6. This lack of coherence appears to be a distinguishing characteristic of most programs. In our interviews, we asked the

respondents to nominate programs that they believed to be the best school administrator preparation programs in the nation, which we then visited. The one most nominated was taught by a half dozen professors from the distinguished school of education in which it resided, as a series of short courses in an intensive summer session. When we asked the director of the program how the topics to be taught were chosen, he responded, after considering the question as if for the first time, "The topics are chosen by the professors who agree to participate. They can teach whatever they like." It was enough for him, evidently, that these well-known professors had agreed to participate in the program.

7. This description, and much of what follows, is based on extensive interviews with principals and with deans of graduate schools of education. A dean of the graduate school of education of one of America's most prestigious universities concluded our interview by verifying our conclusions and warning us against expecting any changes in the conditions portrayed here for the foreseeable future.

8. As we did in all our focus groups with principals.

9. Some of these programs are described in Chapters Eight and Nine. We identified others in the course of our research.

10. The ideas for curriculum presented here draw heavily on the work of Peter Hill, Tom Sobol, and Marie Eiter, the authors of Chapters Two, Three, and Four, respectively, and on the deliberations of the members of the National Advisory Committee of the National Institute for School Leadership (NISL), whose names appear in Appendix B. The curriculum described here is the curriculum currently offered by NISL to the jurisdictions with which it works.

Part One

Roles of the Principal

Chapter Two

What Principals Need to Know About Teaching and Learning

Peter W. Hill

It is a truism that teaching and learning are the core business of schools and the functions that distinguish education from other fields of endeavor. What is less evident, at least to "outsiders," is the fact that few school principals have deep and up-to-date knowledge about teaching and learning. Indeed, knowledge about the core business of schooling is typically not considered in the appointment of new principals.

Why is this so? The answer is complex and requires an understanding of how schools have developed over time.

A Brief History of Instructional Leadership

When schools were first established, the principal was expected to be the local expert on teaching and learning. Indeed, the principal was the head teacher, responsible for a large class of students and for the supervision and training of one or more junior or pupil teachers. In many parts of the world, including some European countries, this concept of the school leader as the head teacher persists to this day.

At the beginning of the twentieth century, as Taylorism and modern factory methods of mass production began to permeate the economies of advanced nations, schools became larger, and a separation emerged between the role of teacher and school administrator, with the latter focusing increasingly on management and administration. This industrial approach to the role of the principal was reinforced and shaped by prevailing views of the nature of teaching and learning based primarily on models of learning developed in the field of behavioral psychology.

It was also reinforced by real advances in ensuring that all teachers were fully trained and certified and also by the growing strength of teacher unions, which resisted intrusions into the professional work of teachers. It became convenient to assume that teachers, once fully trained, were by definition effective educators and remained so throughout their career. Any intervention by the principal to improve the quality of teaching in the classroom was viewed as an attack on the teachers' professional autonomy and a questioning of their competence. Principals were expected to deal with blatantly obvious cases of incompetence as disciplinary matters. Professional development was to be encouraged by the principal but was viewed primarily as a matter of individual teacher discretion. The principal had only a minimal role in improving the quality of teaching and learning, basically that of facilitator and encourager.

As a consequence, educational administration courses neglected serious consideration of content related to teaching and learning. Because principals are universally recruited from the teaching profession, it was assumed that they already knew enough about teaching and learning to do their jobs effectively. In reality, this knowledge was often tacit or dated, based on increasingly distant memories of a former life in the classroom, and uninformed by new conceptions of teaching and learning.

In the United States, the separation between teaching and school administration that arose during the first part of the twentieth century was deep and enduring, so that to this day there is often little overlap between the roles performed by teachers and principals. A more serious problem is that there is little shared knowledge of the two roles. As Murphy (1999b) recently expressed it, educational administration in the United States has remarkably little to do with education, and schools are run by leaders who know very little about the core business of schooling and devote remarkably little time to its core technology.

Worse still, this separation is reciprocal in that the teaching profession has almost no understanding of school organization and how it relates to school effectiveness. Murphy notes that "organizationally clueless teachers and educationally uninformed administrators provide a poor foundation for school success" (1999a, p. 5).

Historically, moves to reconnect principals to the core business of schools can be dated to the late 1970s and the shift from a focus on inputs and processes to a focus on improving student learning outcomes. This shift was given a particular impetus by the findings of research into effective schools and also by attempts in the early 1980s to conceptualize and promote the view of the principal as an *instructional* leader. Qualitative research undertaken during the late 1970s highlighted the importance of strong leadership in effective schools, and these findings were seized upon by school reformers. According to Hallinger (1992, p. 37), "By the mid 1980s, virtually every state boasted a substantial in-service effort aimed at developing the instructional leadership of principals. School administrators were deluged with a 'new orthodoxy' that reflected an effective schools perspective on leadership."

The new instructional leadership orthodoxy implied that principals should possess very specific knowledge related to teaching and learning, knowledge based on the characteristics of effective schools. This knowledge was then expected to reform their managerial behavior into an instructionally oriented role.

The instructional leadership movement was very much an American phenomenon and did not persist long. It soon became apparent that the findings of effective schools research could not be used as a recipe for school improvement. The research might have accurately described what "good" schools looked like, but it did not provide many insights into how ordinary or failing schools became good schools. Cuban (1984, p. 132) made the astute comment that "none of the richly detailed descriptions of high performers can serve as a blueprint for teachers, principals, or superintendents who seek to improve academic achievement."

Perhaps more significant, not enough attention was given to effective ways of promoting professional learning among principals. As Hallinger (1992, p. 39) points out:

- Relatively few resources were actually allocated for coaching and on-site assistance.

- Principals frequently returned from training centers to work contexts that made it hard for them to exercise instructional leadership (often to a context in which increasing demands on the principal to perform other roles meant that there was even less time to exercise instructional leadership).

- Principals were not provided with technical assistance, adjustments of role expectations, or policies designed to support the use of new knowledge about instructional leadership.

Finally, Hallinger notes that in response to broader changes that were taking place in the economy and in society, the emphasis shifted to the role of the principal as a "change agent" or "transformational leader," reflecting the imperative for schools to respond to ongoing and rapid change in the external environment. Principals were urged to look to business for powerful models of effective leadership, and the writings of management experts were given much prominence.

The concept of "transformational leadership" was promoted in the education context by writers such as Leithwood, Begley, and Cousins (1990), who argued that the notions implied by instructional leadership conveyed only one part of the dynamic and complex role that the modern principal had to perform. Thus, to quote Hallinger (1992, p. 39), "just when the image of the instructional leader gained professional currency, it began to be questioned." And so the emphasis shifted away from specific knowledge related to teaching and learning to a more general body of knowledge concerning the principal's role in leading and managing change.

In English-speaking countries such as the United Kingdom, Canada, Australia, and New Zealand, the notion of instructional leadership received little attention during the mid-1980s. There were, however, other developments with important implications for the knowledge required by principals. Successive governments promoted school reform through a process of simultaneously devolving operational responsibility to the school site level and encouraging parental choice within centralized frameworks and policies governing curriculum, standards, and accountability for learning (Caldwell, 1994; Caldwell and Spinks, 1998).

The thrust toward self-management in these countries had major implications for the role of school leaders but tended to reinforce an emphasis on knowledge to support generic management and leadership capabilities. The critical knowledge required by principals in systems that devolved substantial responsibility to the school level concerned goal setting, planning, budgeting, financial resource management, human resource management and development, the development of information systems, marketing, community and external relations, and compliance with public accountability requirements.

Whitty, Halpin, and Power (1998) claim that there is now clear evidence that these policies shifted energy, funds, and focus away from teaching and learning. This is apparent in various recent attempts to redefine the principal's role in the context of increased devolution of responsibility to schools. For example, the state education system of Victoria, Australia, recently commissioned the Hay Group, international management consultants, to develop a set of competencies or capabilities for school leaders. This parallels the British government's commissioning of Hay/McBer to develop a framework for describing effective teachers. The capabilities identified by the Hay Group as required by school principals in the Victorian initiative are set out in Exhibit 2.1.

The Hay Group concluded that of these thirteen capabilities, all but two ("maximizing school capability" and "big-picture thinking") are also required by leading teachers in schools, indicating the

Exhibit 2.1. Capabilities Required by Principals.

Driving School Improvement	*Building Commitment*
Passion for teaching and learning	Contextual know-how
Taking initiative	Management of self
Achievement focus	Influencing others
Delivering Through People	*Creating an Educational Vision*
Leading the school community	Analytical thinking
Holding people accountable	Big-picture thinking
Supporting others	Gathering information
Maximizing school capability	

Source: Hay/McBer, Victoria, Australia.

generic nature of the capabilities identified by the authors and per-haps also the distributed nature of leadership in schools. More significant, the list of capabilities identified in Exhibit 2.1 is characterized by an emphasis on generic qualities required by knowledge workers in almost any service setting and does little to suggest the importance of specific knowledge about teaching and learning for principals. Of course, it can be argued that while each of the characteristics is stated in a generic way, they all imply specific kinds of knowledge in the school context, but that knowledge is assumed knowledge rather than explicitly stated knowledge. Alternatively, it could be assumed that not much educational knowledge is needed.

In conclusion, in a number of English-speaking countries, the role of principals has changed significantly in recent years. But the direction of the changes has invariably been to cast principals as leaders who are less, rather than more, connected to and knowledgeable about teaching and learning.

More recently, a further change of direction is becoming apparent as new and powerful forces have emerged that do indeed require principals to refocus on the core business of schools and to have a highly structured and very deep knowledge of teaching and learning.

First, across all systems, there has been an unrelenting focus on holding schools accountable for student learning outcomes through ongoing monitoring of achievement linked to explicit standards and performance targets (Marsh, 1999). Particularly in schools serving poor and minority students, these pressures have tended to cause principals to focus more on the bottom line and to seek to learn why some schools are successful in ensuring that most students attain high standards while all too many do not.

Second, following the disappointing results of earlier process-based, content-free improvement and reform initiatives, there has been a growing interest in deliberate, comprehensive, research-based approaches to designing schools that are effective in improving learning outcomes for their students. Sergiovanni (2000, p. 73) describes this as a "change away from a pretentious objective science preoccupied with effective and efficient means to change schools, teachers, and others . . . to a design field." He quotes the systems theorist Simon (1996) in support of the notion that education, like health, law, engineering, and architecture, is centrally concerned with the process of *design*. Reform by design means identifying all of the critical elements of schools and of school systems, working out what needs to change in order for them to operate effectively and in alignment with all the other elements, and then redesigning them accordingly.

In the United States, many model designs have adopted a comprehensive, whole-school approach to improving learning outcomes. Prominent among these are the nine designs promoted initially by the New American Schools Development Corporation (now known as New American Schools; Stringfield, Ross, and Smith, 1996). The implementation of comprehensive school designs calls for principals who possess considerable knowledge of teaching and learning, since such designs typically focus on leveraging change in the classroom. They require leaders with the capacity to integrate each of the elements of a design in ways that generate alignment and synergy of structures and processes in support of effective classroom teaching.

In addition to design approaches to improvement, which have typically been implemented in individual schools rather than across whole systems of schools, large-scale reform initiatives have been mounted in recent years that have a strong focus on teaching and learning. Fullan (2000) gives three examples that have been particularly impressive in scope: the reform initiatives of District 2 in New York City, the Chicago school system reforms, and the British National Literacy Strategy and National Numeracy Strategy. Fullan cites an evaluation by Elmore and Burney (1998) of the decade of reform work undertaken in District 2. Significantly, the authors concluded that principals are the key actors in instructional improvement and that common work among principals and teachers across schools is a source of powerful norms about systemwide instructional improvement as it assists in breaking down the isolation of principals and teachers.

While the adoption of model designs and large-scale reform initiatives can serve to reconnect principals with teaching and learning, a third and more powerful set of forces is also beginning to refocus the role of the principal on the core business. These forces arise from a growing awareness of the significance for schooling of the emergence of the new knowledge society (Leadbeater, 1999; Senge, 1996). Economic globalization and the information and communications technology revolution have led to far-reaching changes in the economy and in society generally. These changes are leading inexorably to a reconceptualization of the goals and nature of public schooling.

At this stage, the transformation is in its early stages, but it is nonetheless apparent that conceptions of teaching and learning in schools will change radically as educators internalize the requirement to educate all students to high standards and to be flexible, lifelong learners. The implications for the knowledge base of principals are potentially dramatic, for principals must be the leaders of efforts to introduce new conceptions of teaching and learning in schools.

To summarize this brief history, the need for principals to have a detailed knowledge of teaching and learning has changed significantly over the past century. There has never been widespread acceptance of the view that principals need *no* knowledge about teaching and learning or that administrators can be recruited from outside the ranks of the teaching profession. Nonetheless, the extent of the disconnection of the role of the principal from the core business activities of teaching and learning during most of the past century has been profound.

On the one hand, over the past twenty-five years, the emphasis on accountability for student learning outcomes and the findings from effective schools research highlighting the importance of the instructional leadership role of principals have served to place a greater premium on principals' knowledge about teaching and learning. On the other hand, the growing complexity of the principal's role has meant that little serious attention has been given to explicating or instilling the required knowledge base. Over the past decade, new imperatives for in-depth principal knowledge about teaching and learning have arisen as a result of internal pressures generated by design-based approaches to improvement and external pressures generated as a consequence of the emergence of the knowledge society.

The Research Base on Instructional Leadership

What is the research evidence regarding the role of the principal in promoting teaching and learning? The short answer is that the research literature provides little guidance in reconnecting principals to the core business of schooling. Heck, Larsen, and Marcoulides (1990, p. 95) summarized the situation accurately when they made the following observation: "In fact, researchers have not really identified what instructional leadership is, nor have they provided empirical evidence to suggest that principals who increase the amount of time they devote to instructional leadership will cause higher academic performance in their schools."

Conclusions regarding the role of principals in promoting teaching and learning range from hugely optimistic assessments to virtually no impact at all. For example, educational leadership has been the most consistently cited characteristic of effective schools in the research literature on school effectiveness and improvement, particularly the American research literature (Levine and Lezotte, 1990). This is especially true of qualitative case studies that have investigated the organizational characteristics of schools that are evidently performing much better than others with which they might legitimately be compared, taking into account their student intakes (known as "effective schools research"). Influential studies such as those of Brookover and Lezotte (1977), Edmonds (1979), and Rutter, Maughan, Mortimer, Ouston, and Smith (1979) concluded that effective schools are characterized by leadership directed at securing a set of agreed goals, increasing the competence and involvement of staff, establishing clear roles and expectations of staff, and developing a school ethos or climate that is supportive of and oriented toward teaching and learning.

Following on from these studies, the concept of instructional leadership emerged in the field of educational administration in the early 1980s. The Hallinger and Murphy (1985) framework for conceptualizing the principal's role in instructional management (see also Greenfield, 1987) identifies three dimensions:

- Defining the school's mission
- Managing the instructional program
- Promoting a positive school climate

These three dimensions flow directly from the earlier findings of the research into school effectiveness. Other writers have proposed variations on this basic conceptualization. Weber (1989) identified five main functions of instructional leadership: defining school mission, promoting a positive learning climate, observing and giving feedback to teachers, managing curriculum and instruction, and assessing the instructional program. Murphy's framework (1990) comprises four dimensions: developing mission and goals, managing the educational production function, promoting an academic environment based on positive expectations and standards, and developing a supportive environment.

A rather different conceptualization of instructional leadership was developed by Scheerens and Bosker (1997) as part of their empirical research into educational effectiveness. They conceive of instructional leadership as one of two aspects of educational leadership, the other being general leadership skills. Their definition of instructional leadership has five components:

- Time devoted to educational versus administrative tasks
- The head teacher as a metacontroller of classroom processes
- The head teacher as a quality controller of classroom teachers
- The head teacher as a facilitator of work-oriented teams
- The head teacher as an initiator and facilitator of staff professionalization

How valid and robust are the findings from effective schools research and the various conceptualizations of instructional leadership? Qualitative studies of effective schools have been unanimous in pointing to the importance of the instructional leadership role of the principal. However, this conclusion has not emerged from quantitative studies into the characteristics of schools in which students make greater progress than expected given their intakes ("school effectiveness research"). In a meta-analysis of international and Dutch research, Bosker and Witziers (1996; Witziers and Bosker, 1997) estimated the overall effect of school leadership on student learning outcomes as 0.05 of a standard deviation, an extremely small even if statistically significant effect. Hallinger and Heck (1998), in their review of research from 1980 to 1995 into the principal's contribution to school effectiveness, concluded that there was little evidence of a direct effect of leadership on student learning, although they found some evidence of indirect effects. Specifically, when leadership was conceptualized as mediated by intervening (teacher or classroom) variables and affected by antecedent variables, a small but nonetheless consistent and statistically significant positive effect of leadership on student learning outcomes was observed.

Hallinger and Heck (1998) go on to refer to weaknesses in terms of conceptualization and methods of analysis in the research literature and in particular a failure to recognize the multilevel nature of questions concerning the impact of leadership. In other words, they imply that principals really *do* have a substantial impact on teaching and learning but that so far researchers have been unable to measure it. Another conclusion one could draw is that most principals really don't exert much impact on student outcomes because they remain disconnected from the core business of schooling and devote very little time to improving teaching and learning.

Knowledge About Teaching and Learning

Teachers and principals, as noted earlier, have always possessed considerable craft knowledge about teaching and learning. But this knowledge is often "intuitive," in the sense that it is frequently uninformed by theoretical knowledge, and "unscientific," in the sense that it is not guided by evidence regarding effective practice. To a large extent, this reflects the fact that the educational research literature is massive, fragmented, and frequently contradictory, with many studies that can be cited to support opposing conclusions. In addition, much of the literature could be described as esoteric and does not lead to obvious implications for teaching and learning in schools.

Over the past decade or more, powerful new methods of summarizing many thousands of studies have been applied to the literature on teaching and learning in a search for more dependable knowledge on which to base school improvement and reform. For example, several quantitative meta-analyses on school and instructional effectiveness have been carried out (see especially Fraser,

1989), and as a result, there is now a much clearer understanding of the factors that are consistently associated with effective learning in schools. In one such study, Scheerens and Bosker, (1997, p. 223) conclude on the basis of meta-analyses of findings and best-evidence syntheses that the basic factors are these:

- Time on task
- Closeness of content covered to assessment instrument
- A structured approach: specific objectives, frequent assessment, corrective feedback
- Types of adaptive instruction that can be managed by teachers

Hill and Crévola (1999) argue, on the basis of the same evidence, that the literature on effectiveness supports just three factors that closely resemble the four factors of Scheerens and Bosker, namely:

- High expectations of student achievement
- Engaged learning time
- Focused teaching

The importance of high expectations and a belief in the capacity of all students to perform to high academic standards, given sufficient time and support, needs little comment. It has become a key principle of the standards movement in education. Time on task is also a well-established concept. One of the most obvious yet profound facts about learning is that it takes time, and individuals need different amounts of time to learn the same things. This essential truth was recognized long ago by Carroll (1963), who proposed a model of school learning in which time is the integrating concept. Considering these two factors together implies that in schools, standards should be held constant while time (and support) should be allowed to vary. All too frequently in schools, the reverse happens: the time and support to learn a task are held constant and the standards are allowed to vary.

The third factor, focused teaching, means ensuring that the purpose of instruction is clear and that the complexity of the task is matched to the needs of the learner. Learning is maximized when a "more knowing other" (such as the teacher) is able to structure learning so that the difficulty of the task is aligned with the individual needs of the learner. The teacher's role, to use Bruner's metaphor, is to "scaffold" the learning of the new task, revealing to the learner how to move from what he or she can currently do with assistance to being able to function independently (Wood, Bruner, and Ross, 1976). Vygotsky (1978) referred to this critical zone in which learning can be facilitated as the "zone of proximal development."

Focused teaching is very commonly observed in interactions between parents and children and is in fact a basic method of human learning. It is also commonly observed in one-on-one situations such as sports coaching or teaching a musical instrument. But as study after study has confirmed, it is uncommon in classrooms. The notion of focused teaching has far-reaching implications for schools and for school principals. The lack of focused teaching is the main reason why so many students fail to make progress. Conversely, the application of focused teaching is a critical ingredient in bringing about accelerated learning (along with high expectations and engaged learning time).

Focused teaching in schools implies constantly monitoring each student to establish starting points for instruction and to match instruction to the student's current ability. It also implies clarity about the purposes of instruction. Finally, it implies that school and classroom organization and teaching strategies employed in classrooms must be capable of responding to the wide range of student abilities found in typical classrooms.

Reviews of the research literature have also begun to make sense of the results of many thousands of studies relevant to specific educational outcomes. Probably the most thoroughly researched area in education relates to early literacy instruction. Early literacy is an issue of enormous significance because it is fundamental to successful lifelong learning. In recent years, some highly influential reviews of the research literature have been undertaken by panels of experts with the express purpose of informing policy decisions as to the kinds of reading programs that governments might fund and schools should adopt. The report by Snow, Burns, and Griffin (1998) on preventing reading difficulties in young children and the Langenberg (2000) report on teaching children to read illustrate a new trend by legislators in the United States to require that funds in education be used to support the adoption of "scientifically based" programs. The findings of these reports are clearly of great significance for principals of elementary schools because they not only provide a distillation of research evidence regarding early literacy teaching but also determine the kinds of programs that get funded.

Research syntheses and meta-analyses of research are inevitably backward-looking and constrained by the kinds of studies undertaken in the past. Principals also need to be aware of emerging understandings. Russell (2000) has characterized new thinking about teaching and learning as focusing on three sets of interacting characteristics, strategies, and skills that students need to help to develop when they are provided with formal instruction:

- Thinking and learning
- Motivation and engagement
- Self-regulation and autonomy

For each set, Russell identifies some overall conclusions that can be drawn from recent research. She reaches the following conclusions:

Thinking and Learning

- Good learners seek depth of understanding and meaningfulness.
- They have strategies, skills, styles, and attributes that enable the achievement of understanding and productive manipulation of ideas.

- They have a cultural and strategic knowledge base.
- They are conscious of and reflect on their own learning and thinking.

Motivation and Engagement

- Good learners have learning goals, expectations, and feelings that enhance involvement in and quality of thinking and learning.

Self-Regulation and Control

- Good learners determine, regulate, and control their own behavior in the service of learning.

In summarizing the supporting literature, Russell (2000) observes that a major conclusion to be drawn from recent research is that learning can no longer be viewed as "cold" cognitive functioning or conceptual change. It must be seen as a dynamic process involving the whole human being—both will and skill are evident in the active, self-regulated functioning of the good student. She quotes the following description by Paris and Byrnes (1989, pp. 192–193) to capture new conceptions of effective learners:

> They know how to make effective plans before engaging in a task, they know how to monitor their own performance, and they know how to review and correct their work. They understand task-specific rules and generalizable heuristics. They know when to transfer strategies and when to seek help. The cognitive and metacognitive skills that they possess enable them to master new and challenging tasks in school. At the same time, these students have positive perceptions of their own competence. They see themselves as the agents of their own learning who have control over the choice of strategies and volition to achieve their intended goals. They are optimistic learners in the goals they set and in their attributions of success to their own efforts and investment of energy in appropriate tactics. They are task-involved and derive a sense of satisfaction and

pride from their own efforts and mastery judged against their personal standards rather than social comparison. Self-regulation is thus enabling and empowering for continued learning.

This description points to an important and rapidly growing knowledge base that is critical to emerging conceptions of education in the knowledge society and has important implications for the role of principals as they seek to create schools that will be successful in adapting to this new world.

What Principals Need to Know

How should the relationship between the school principal and the improvement of teaching and learning be conceived, and what is the knowledge base that needs to inform that relationship? In view of the failure of empirical studies to establish strong evidence of direct effects, it is inevitable that answering this question involves a considerable amount of forward projection of current knowledge. The question can also be approached, however, through a process of backward mapping, as will be explained in more detail.

Taking a holistic view of the work of school principals, it is useful to distinguish between the *roles* they perform, the *qualities* that they need to perform those roles, and the *knowledge* implied by those roles. In the literature, there is a fairly broad consensus that the school principal must both lead and manage and that leadership and management are complementary processes. Fullan (1991, p. 158) argues that "both sets of characteristics are essential and must be blended or otherwise attended to within the same person or team" and that "successful principals and other organizational heads do both functions simultaneously and iteratively." With this in mind and synthesizing the categorizations of a large number of writers such as Kotter (1990), who have come to broadly similar conclusions, it is suggested that the three most important roles of principals are as follows:

- Leading and managing change
- Motivating and managing people
- Designing and aligning systems, processes, and resources

Leading and Managing Change

A prime task of principals is to exercise leadership of the kind that results in a shared vision of the directions to be pursued by the school and to manage change in ways that ensure that the school is successful in realizing the vision. In a world of increasingly rapid change, what is the terra firma on which a robust concept of the principal as a leader and manager of change can be built? Murphy (1999a) has proposed, in a *tour de force* review of the state of educational leadership, that the profession should adopt school improvement as its center of gravity and education as its foundations in a reconceptualization that places a premium on applied (as opposed to practical or theoretical) knowledge. He cites Evans (1991), Foster (1988), and Sergiovanni (1993) in support of the notion that placing school improvement at the center of the profession ensures that the job of the principal is pedagogically and educationally grounded and tied directly to the core business of schooling.

Following Murphy, it is suggested that the principal's role as a leader and manager of change be conceptualized as one of leading and managing school improvement. In this way, the core role becomes one of improving student learning outcomes by improving the quality of teaching and learning within the school. Such a conceptualization of the principal's role immediately privileges theoretical knowledge of the learning process and practical knowledge of the conditions under which students learn in the school setting. It also privileges applied knowledge of educational change and school improvement, drawing on theoretical and practical knowledge of teaching and learning in school settings. In brief, it emphasizes the role of the principal as a knowledge manager with respect to the core business of the school—teaching and learning—in a context of change and the ongoing imperative for improvement.

Motivating and Managing People

There is overwhelming evidence from the literature on school effectiveness and improvement regarding the significance of the principal in establishing a school culture that promotes and values learning and that embodies realistic but high expectations of all students and teachers. To the extent that principals have an impact on student learning, this impact is largely mediated through teachers and classroom teaching. Thus beyond the generic issues involved in motivating and managing people are the more specific issues involved in working with and through teachers to bring about improvement in the quality of teaching and learning as measured by improvement in student learning outcomes.

This focuses attention on the importance of the role of the principal in promoting organizational learning or learning within the specific context of the school and its school improvement agenda. While the school and teams in the school provide the contexts in which organizational learning occur, learning, knowledge, and changes in beliefs, understandings, and classroom practices must take place within each and every individual. This implies opportunities that extend well beyond traditional models of and approaches to professional development and in-service training. Effective professional learning involves intensive, sustained, theoretically based yet practically situated learning, with opportunities to observe good practices, to be involved in coaching and mentoring processes, and to take time for reflection (Fullan, 1993; Hargreaves and Fullan, 1992).

At the same time, as a manager of people, the principal's role must be to ensure that the circle of accountability is complete and that investment in the learning of individual members of staff is reflected in improvement in student learning outcomes. This needs to be reflected in systems of staff appraisal and ongoing processes for evaluating programs and monitoring the performance of the school.

In terms of a knowledge base, the foregoing implies that principals require general knowledge about human resource development and organizational learning and particular knowledge of the sources of professional satisfaction among teachers as they succeed in realizing the educational vision of the school. The latter includes both theoretical and practical knowledge of what it means to bring about standards-based improvement in school learning that simultaneously enhances the motivation of staff and their competence and capacity to engage in a process of ongoing development and improvement.

Designing and Aligning Systems, Processes, and Resources

A key role of the principal is to ensure that each of the elements that contribute to improved student learning outcomes is present, working effectively, and aligned with all other elements. The principal is thus, as it were, the chief architect of the school, the one who has the overview of systems, processes, and resources and how they combine to produce intended student learning outcomes.

This implies that the principal is able to articulate the significance of all key elements, to justify their design and configuration, and to be in a position to make judgments regarding the operational effectiveness of each element and of the total impact of all of the elements as they function in combination. When outcomes are not being realized or when evidence accumulates that particular elements are not working effectively, the principal is responsible for ensuring that the redesign work is carried out. This could mean minor readjustments but in cases of endemic failure to reach required standards is more likely to involve transforming the whole ecology of the school in order to obtain the desired result.

As Wilson and Daviss (1994, p. 22) explain, "The redesign process is the integration of research, development, dissemination, and refinement by which innovations and the procedures that create them are originated, improved, and made affordable. . . . The redesign process is an institutionalized method of strategic, systemic change that works unceasingly to enact a vision of excellence as well as to redefine excellence itself when changing conditions make it necessary." In other words, the redesign process embodies a philosophy about ongoing quality assurance and its role in bringing about improvement.

Most leadership programs for school leaders pay significant attention to the role of the principal in leading and managing change and in motivating and managing people, often drawing from the wider pool of knowledge and experience in preparing leaders of government, business, and industry. As a consequence, principals are often quite knowledgeable about these roles. When it comes to designing and aligning systems, processes, and resources, most leadership programs tend to focus on aligning resources to priorities and in establishing systems for managing resources, especially financial and staff resources, but give little attention to the notion of educational design and the redesign process. This reflects the fact that attention to design is a relatively recent phenomenon and that systematic knowledge about comprehensive approaches to designing educational environments is not widely shared.

A Design Template for Improving Learning Outcomes

There are, however, as noted earlier, a sufficient number of well-documented and externally evaluated designs to provide generalizable knowledge about the kinds of things that principals and other school leaders need to know to create a learning environment that maximizes student learning outcomes. Hill and Crévola (1997, 1999) have described a general design, or design template, that identifies nine critical elements of schools, shown diagrammatically in Figure 2.1. In the discussions that follow, use is made of the notion of backward mapping (Elmore, 1979) to identify the knowledge about teaching and learning required by principals for the purposes of designing and aligning systems, processes, and resources.

Figure 2.1. General Design for Improving Learning Outcomes.

Source: Hill and Crévola, 1977.

Backward mapping involves beginning with the end in mind and mapping backward to identify what should be done.

Beliefs and Understandings

Beliefs and understandings about teaching and learning occupy the central position in the design summarized in Figure 2.1. Principals need a strong theoretical foundation of current knowledge about teaching and learning, practical knowledge of the beliefs and understandings of staff in the school, and applied knowledge of how to bring about development and change in those beliefs and understandings. As noted earlier, the principal has a key role to play in ensuring that the implications of modern conceptions of teaching and learning are understood by teachers and are reflected in the curriculum and in school and classroom structures and practices. The principal and other members of the leadership team need to be involved in disseminating this new knowledge. It is also suggested that they will have to become intimately involved in the following activities:

- Rethinking the curriculum
- Creating larger blocks of time for in-depth learning
- Reducing the emphasis on content coverage while increasing the amount of time given to in-depth learning
- The teaching of thinking skills
- Promoting interdisciplinary studies of issues and problems
- Integrating the new information and communications technologies into regular classroom practices

Up-to-date knowledge of teaching and learning is thus critical if the principal is to create a school culture that embodies high expectations of student achievement and a confidence in the capacity of individual teachers and of the school to realize those expectations.

Standards and Targets

High expectations of student achievement need to be reflected in explicit standards that have been benchmarked against those of other schools and school systems to ensure that they reflect best practices. Standards and associated targets constitute the starting point for redesigning how schools operate so that meeting the standards has top priority in everything that schools do. Principals therefore require a knowledge of the sources of relevant content and performance standards and of processes for setting targets at the school and student levels that reflect community expectations and that are challenging yet achievable.

Monitoring and Assessment

Teaching and learning involve regular monitoring and assessment of students, and the design of this element must ensure that consistent, coherent information is generated, on a regular basis, on the progress of all students and on all key indicators. Assessment is important to determine whether targets have been met. Effective teachers closely monitor their students' progress so as to be sure that each student is always working at an appropriate level of challenge. Indeed, the most important function of monitoring and assessment is to help the teacher develop a profile for each student, to establish starting points for teaching, and to use this diagnostic information to drive classroom instruction. Principals need to be informed about effective strategies for monitoring and assessing students and about appropriate assessment instruments and the information they provide. Principals also need practical knowledge in interpreting assessment data and in monitoring trends in the value-added performance of the school over time.

Classroom Teaching Strategies

Effective teaching is structured and focused on the learning needs of each student in the class. It requires that teachers have detailed understandings of how children learn and that teachers use well-developed classroom routines, structures, organization, and management and an ability to motivate and engage students by employing a wide range of classroom practices and strategies. Principals do not need detailed curriculum content knowledge, nor do they need to be expert teachers themselves, but they do need to be able to recognize good teaching and what it means to effectively implement different teaching strategies in different learning contexts. Scheerens and Bosker (1997) invoke the system-theoretical concept of "metacontrol" to express the overarching control and influence exercised by an educationally or instructionally oriented principal with respect to classroom teaching strategies. As the metacontroller of classroom processes, the principal must work toward the creation of a common school language to talk about and reflect on classroom teaching and the encouragement of a culture that constantly seeks to refine and extend classroom teaching strategies.

Professional Learning Teams

A crucial element in any design aimed at improved teaching and learning in schools is the provision of effective, ongoing, and professional learning opportunities for teachers that promote learning not just among individuals but throughout the organization as a whole. Put in another way, central to a design approach to improving learning in schools is the establishment of a culture and of systems and processes for promoting organizational learning. Professional learning teams function through a mixture of both off- and on-campus learning but principally through a combination of demonstration teaching, mentoring, coaching, and opportunities for the team to debrief and reflect on practices and progress. Principals need theoretical knowledge about organizational learning and applied knowledge about strategies for establishing professional learning teams among cross-grade groups of teachers for the purpose of improving specific student learning outcomes.

School and Class Organization

To maximize engaged learning time and to facilitate teaching that is responsive to student needs, interests, and current readiness to learn, it is necessary to align organizational structures and processes in the school. For example, it is important to ensure that adequate time is devoted to key learning outcomes and that this time is, as far as possible, free from interruptions. In large schools, it is important that structures are in place that promote cohesion, pastoral care, and a sense of identity and do not lead to feelings of isolation and alienation among students. It is also important that classroom organization facilitate focused teaching. Principals need to be aware of the findings of research into such issues as the impact of class size and of different forms of school and class organization, including within-class student grouping practices. These are issues that impinge massively on the resources available in schools and on the capacity of teachers to focus their teaching on the needs, aptitudes, and abilities of their students.

Intervention and Additional Assistance

Even with the best classroom teaching in place, many students fail to make satisfactory progress. Among these students will be those with disabilities and impairments, those who come from homes devoid of books and see no purpose in school learning, those who may have severe emotional blocks that interfere with their concentration, and those who may have frequent absences from school. For such students, the school will need to establish systems and processes to provide support and assistance beyond regular classroom instruction to enable them to catch up quickly to their peers. Without timely and effective intervention, these students continue to fall further and further behind in their schoolwork and experience diminished self-esteem and increased alienation from schooling. For the lowest-achieving students, one-to-one intervention is likely to be the only way to bring these students up to standard. Principals require a knowledge of effective intervention programs and how they can be implemented in a manner that is cost-effective and that supports and complements regular classroom instruction.

Home, School, and Community Partnerships

Linking with the home, with feeder schools, and with the community is important at all levels of schooling. A strong body of research shows that when parents, caregivers, and the community are supportive of the work of the school and involved in its activities, students make greater progress (Booth and Dunne, 1996; Cairney, Ruge, Buchanan, Lowe, and Munsie, 1995; Epstein, 1991). But to be effective, it is not enough to establish links with the home: what is needed is comprehensive and permanent programs of partnerships with families and communities. Principals need a knowledge of the role of the home and the community in supporting school learning and in particular of strategies for establishing lasting partnerships in learning.

Leadership and Coordination

As discussed earlier, studies of effective schools have consistently drawn attention to the importance of strong educational leadership. Good teaching may be possible in a school in which there is weak and ineffective educational leadership, but it is harder. Change and sustained improvement are extremely difficult, if not impossible, without good educational leadership, particularly where whole-school change is sought. Educational leadership and coordination are not the sole responsibility of school principals: they can and should be exercised at all levels of the organization. In particular, attention has been drawn to the crucial role of senior teachers with release time to enable them to coordinate and lead professional learning teams and to act as mentors, coaches, and lead learners. It is nevertheless incumbent on principals to ensure that they are providing leadership and coordination at all levels and that they are allocating sufficient time to that role, relative to other roles, such as administration, personnel management, and student welfare issues. This may require considerable rethinking to enable principals to reclaim the role of educational leadership and successfully delegate other leadership and management tasks to general administrative staff.

Following Murphy (1999a), it has been argued that the principalship should adopt school improvement as its center of gravity and education as its foundation in a reconceptualization that places a premium on applied (as opposed to practical or theoretical) knowledge. This implies an ongoing focus on educational change. Miles (in Fullan, 1991) talks about change as progressing through three phases: initiation, implementation, and institutionalization. During each phase, the principal and the leadership team need to be able to provide an appropriate balance of pressure and support. Pressure is necessary to provide stimulus and incentive to change and improve. Low expectations and complacency are unavoidable consequences of lack of pressure. At the same time, pressure needs to be balanced with the kind of support and assistance that staff need in order to change and improve. Improvement in schools rarely happens simply by raising the level of challenge or by exhorting teachers to work harder or more effectively. It happens because the right mix of pressure and support are in place.

The kinds of roles, capabilities, and knowledge required to exercise educational leadership have been alluded to throughout this discussion. Exhibit 2.2 summarizes what principals need to know about teaching and learning in terms of the three key roles discussed in the preceding sections.

The knowledge base encompassed by Exhibit 2.2 is extensive, and while overlapping with the kinds of knowledge expected of teachers, it covers additional areas that are not typically covered in either preservice or postgraduate courses and programs and are almost completely absent from principal leadership programs.

Exhibit 2.2. What Principals Need to Know About Teaching and Learning: A Summary.

Role	*Knowledge Base*
Leading and managing change	Designing and aligning systems, processes and resources
Motivating and managing people	
Curriculum theory and educational outcomes required by young people living in the knowledge society	The redesign process in education
	Educational standards and target setting
Child development and the learning process, including modern theories of learning and motivation	Monitoring and assessment of student progress
Teaching and learning in school settings	Classroom teaching strategies
	Organizational learning and strategies for promoting professional learning
Educational change and school effectiveness and improvement	School and classroom organization
	Safety nets, intervention, and special assistance
	The role of home, school, and community partnerships in promoting learning

Acquiring the Knowledge Base

How are principals to acquire knowledge about teaching and learning? Traditional methods are likely to be appropriate in providing a grounding in much of the knowledge associated with leading and managing change and in motivating and managing people. However, much of the knowledge associated with designing and aligning systems, processes, and resources appears to call for on-the-job approaches to learning that are not always found in current leadership programs.

Given the focus on leadership for school improvement, it would seem appropriate to consider nontraditional methods such as the use of mentors and coaches to support leaders in training as they go through the process of initiating, designing, implementing, and evaluating improvement projects as a means of obtaining practical experience in educational leadership directed at improving student learning outcomes. It would also seem appropriate to make use of study groups to enable principals to learn together and collectively seek to extend their applied knowledge base of teaching and learning. The establishment of such study groups could provide a much needed boost to the morale of principals at a time when the principalship is widely viewed as onerous and senior teachers are becoming increasingly reluctant to apply for principal positions.

Based on the experience of earlier attempts to promote the instructional leadership role of school principals, it is clear that both systemic support for principals in redefining their role and technical assistance and policies designed to support the use of new knowledge about teaching and learning are critical.

By reconceptualizing the role of the principal by placing school improvement at the center and focusing on the acquisition of an extensive applied knowledge base about teaching and learning, a natural consequence will be that the most valued expertise about school leadership will reside in the leaders within the profession itself and not in the academies and university faculties. This may be a vital step in creating a genuine profession of school leaders.

References

Booth, A., and Dunne, J. (eds.). *Family-School Links: How Do They Affect Educational Outcomes?* Hillsdale, N.J.: Erlbaum, 1996.

Bosker, R. J., and Witziers, B. "The Magnitude of School Effects, or Does It Really Matter Which School a Student Attends?" Paper presented at the International Congress for School Effectiveness and School Improvement, Leeuwarden, Netherlands, Jan. 1996.

Brookover, W., and Lezotte, L. *Changes in School Characteristics Coincident with Changes in Student Achievement.* East Lansing: Michigan State University Press, 1977.

Cairney, T. H., Ruge, J., Buchanan, J., Lowe, K., and Munsie, L. *Developing Partnerships: The Home, School and Community Interface.* Canberra, Australia: Department of Employment, Education and Training, 1995.

Caldwell, B. J. "School-Based Management." In T. Husen and N. Postlethwaite (eds.), *International Encyclopedia of Education.* Vol. 9. (2nd ed.) New York: Pergamon Press, 1994.

Caldwell, B. J., and Spinks, J. M. *Beyond the Self-Managing School.* Bristol, Pa.: Falmer Press, 1998.

Carroll, J. B. "A Model of School Learning." *Teachers College Record,* 1963, *64,* 722–733.

Cuban, L. "Transforming the Frog into a Prince: Effective Schools Research Policy and Practice at the District Level." *Harvard Educational Review,* 1984, *54,* 129–151.

Edmonds, R. R. "Effective Schools for the Urban Poor." *Educational Leadership,* 1979, *37,* 15–17.

Elmore, R. F. "Backward Mapping: Implementation Research and Policy Decisions." *Political Science Quarterly,* 1979, *94,* 601–606.

Elmore, R. F., and Burney, D. *School Variation and Systemic Instructional Component in Community School District #2, New York City.* Philadelphia: Consortium for Policy Research in Education, University of Pennsylvania, 1998.

Epstein, J. L. "Effects on Student Achievement of Teacher Practices and of Parent Involvement." In S. Silvern (ed.), *Advances in Reading/Language Research,* Vol. 5: *Literacy Through Family, Community and School Interaction.* Greenwich, Conn.: JAI Press, 1991.

Evans, R. "Ministrative Insights: Educational Administration as Pedagogic Practice." Paper presented at the annual meeting of the American Educational Research Association, Chicago, Apr. 1991.

Foster, W. "Educational Administration: A Critical Appraisal." In D. E. Griffiths, R. T. Stout, and P. B. Forsyth (eds.), *Leaders for America's Schools: The Report and Papers of the National Commission on Excellence in Educational Administration.* Berkeley, Calif.: McCutchan, 1988.

Fraser, B. J. "Research Synthesis on School and Instructional Effectiveness." *International Journal of Educational Research*, 1989, *13*, 707–719.

Fullan, M. G. *The New Meaning of Educational Change.* (2nd ed.) New York: Teachers College Press, 1991.

Fullan, M. G. *Change Forces: Probing the Depths of Educational Reform.* Bristol, Pa.: Falmer Press, 1993.

Fullan, M. G. "The Return of Large-Scale Reform." *Journal of Educational Change*, 2000, *1*, 5–28.

Greenfield, W. (ed.) *Instructional Leadership: Concepts, Issues, and Controversies.* Needham Heights, Mass.: Allyn & Bacon, 1987.

Hallinger, P. "The Evolving Role of American Principals: From Managerial to Instructional to Transformational Leaders." *Journal of Educational Administration*, 1992, *30*(3), 35–48.

Hallinger, P., and Heck, R. H. "Exploring the Principal's Contribution to School Effectiveness, 1980–1995." *School Effectiveness and School Improvement*, 1998, *9*, 157–191.

Hallinger, P., and Murphy, J. "Assessing the Instructional Management Behavior of Principals." *Elementary School Journal*, 1985, *86*, 217–247.

Hargreaves, A., and Fullan, M. G. *Understanding Teacher Development.* New York: Teachers College Press, 1992.

Heck, R. H., Larsen, T. J., and Marcoulides, G. A. "Instructional Leadership and School Achievement: Validation of a Causal Model." *Educational Administration Quarterly*, 1990, *26*, 94–125.

Hill, P. W., and Crévola, C. A. *The Literacy Challenge in Australian Primary Schools.* IARTV Seminar Series No. 69. Melbourne, Australia: Incorporated Association of Registered Teachers of Victoria, 1997.

Hill, P. W., and Crévola, C. A. "The Role of Standards in Educational Reform for the 21st Century." In D. D. Marsh (ed.), *ASCD Yearbook 1999: Preparing Our Schools for the 21st Century.* Alexandria, Va.: Association for Supervision and Curriculum Development, 1999.

Kotter, J. P. *A Force for Change: How Leadership Differs from Management.* New York: Free Press, 1990.

Langenberg, D. (chair). *Report of the National Reading Panel: Teaching Children to Read: An Evidence-Based Assessment of the Scientific Research Literature on Reading and Its Implications for Reading Instruction: Reports of the Subgroups.* Washington, D.C.: National Institute of Child Health and Human Development, 2000.

Leadbeater, C. *Living on Thin Air.* London: Viking, 1999.

Leithwood, K., Begley, P., and Cousins, B. "The Nature, Causes, and Consequences of Principals' Practices: An Agenda for Future Research." *Journal of Educational Administration*, 1990, *28*(4), 5–31.

Levine, D. U., and Lezotte, L. *Unusually Effective Schools: A Review and Analysis of Research and Practice.* Madison, Wis.: National Center for Effective Schools Research and Development, 1990.

Marsh, D. D. (ed.). *ASCD Yearbook 1999: Preparing Our Schools for the 21st Century.* Alexandria, Va.: Association for Supervision and Curriculum Development, 1999.

Murphy, J. "Principal Instructional Leadership." In L. S. Lotto and P. W. Thurston (eds.), *Advances in Educational Administration: Changing Perspectives on the School.* Vol. 1. Greenwich, Conn.: JAI Press, 1990.

Murphy, J. "Reconnecting Teaching and School Administration: A Call for a Unified Profession." Paper presented at the annual meeting of the American Educational Research Association, Montreal, Apr. 1999a.

Murphy, J. "The Quest for a Center: Notes on the State of the Profession of Educational Leadership." Paper presented at the annual meeting of the American Educational Research Association, Montreal, Apr. 1999b.

Paris, S. G., and Byrnes, J. P. "The Constructivist Approach to Self-Regulation and Learning in the Classroom." In B. J. Zimmerman and D. H. Schunk (eds.), *Self-Regulated Learning and Academic Achievement: Theory, Research, and Practice.* New York: Springer-Verlag, 1989.

Russell, V. J. *Enabling Learning: The Crucial Work of School Leaders.* Camberwell, Victoria, Australia: Australian Council for Educational Research, 2000.

Rutter, M., Maughan, B., Mortimer, P., Ouston, J., and Smith, A. *Fifteen Thousand Hours: Secondary Schools and Their Effects on Children.* Cambridge, Mass.: Harvard University Press, 1979.

Scheerens, J., and Bosker, R. J. *The Foundations of Educational Effectiveness.* New York: Pergamon Press, 1997.

Senge, P. "Leading Learning Organizations: The Bold, the Powerful, and the Invisible." In F. Hesselbein, M. Goldsmith, and R. Beckhard (eds.), *The Leader of the Future.* San Francisco: Jossey-Bass, 1996.

Sergiovanni, T. J. "Organizations or Communities: Changing the Metaphor Changes the Theory." Paper presented at the annual meeting of the American Educational Research Association, Atlanta, Apr. 1993.

Sergiovanni, T. J. "Changing Change: Toward a Design Science and Art." *Journal of Educational Change,* 2000, *1,* 57–75.

Simon, H. *The Sciences of the Artificial.* (3rd ed.) Cambridge, Mass.: MIT Press, 1996.

Snow, E., Burns, M. S., and Griffin, P. (eds.). *Preventing Reading Difficulties in Young Children.* Washington, D.C.: Committee on the Prevention of Reading Difficulties in Young Children, National Research Council, 1998.

Stringfield, S., Ross, S., and Smith, L. (eds.). *Bold Plans for School Restructuring: The New American Schools Designs.* Mahwah, N.J.: Erlbaum, 1996.

Vygotsky, L. *Mind in Society: The Development of Higher Psychological Processes.* (M. Cole, V. John-Steiner, S. Scribner, and E. Souberman, eds. and trans.). Cambridge, Mass.: Harvard University Press, 1978.

Weber, J. "Leading the Instructional Program." In S. C. Smith and P. K. Piele (eds.), *School Leadership: Handbook for Excellence.* (2nd ed.) Eugene, Ore.: ERIC Clearinghouse on Educational Management, 1989.

Whitty, G., Halpin, D., and Power, S. *Choice and Devolution in Education: The School, the State and the Market.* Melbourne, Australia: ACER, 1998.

Wilson, K. G., and Daviss, B. *Redesigning Education.* New York: Henry Holt, 1994.

Witziers, B., and Bosker, R. J. "A Meta-Analysis on the Effects of Presumed School Effectiveness Factors." Paper presented at the International Congress for School Effectiveness and Improvement, Memphis, Tenn., Jan. 1997.

Wood, D. J., Bruner, J. S., and Ross, G. "The Role of Tutoring in Problem Solving." *Journal of Child Psychology and Psychiatry,* 1976, *17,* 89–100.

Chapter Three

The Principal as Moral Leader

Thomas Sobol

Consider the following scenarios:

Whom Do You Work For?

Juan Ruiz tilted back in his office chair and stared idly at the banner. "*Somos Uno,*" it said. "That's a laugh," he thought. He remembered the day the kids had tacked it up—they were so proud and happy. Not just the banner but the whole world seemed to be coming down.

Juan was halfway through his second year as a junior high school principal. He was surprised when he got the job, because he had no prior experience as a principal. But his superintendent, Tony Mercado, had stuck his neck out for him. "Juan is OK," he told the board. "He's great with kids, and he's completely loyal." Juan closed his eyes. "That's another one," he thought.

Located in a rundown, violent city neighborhood, the school had been a problem for years. Teachers put in their time and left early; fights broke out often; test scores were low. Juan had been—and still was—determined to turn it around. Intuitively, he knew he had to connect with the kids and make them feel that they counted for something; he also knew he had to find the teachers who hadn't given up and give them some tangible reason for hope. The first year, he spent a lot of time listening to people and finding small things to do to show both kids and teachers that he was paying attention. Slowly, the atmosphere began to change. Then, last

September, they started the "*Somos Uno*" campaign, and even the burned-out teachers began to get enthusiastic about the place.

The campaign was a set of activities designed to bring people together and help them feel pride in themselves and their school. It included a multicultural festival for students and families, an "English-plus" approach to bilingual education, and "community meetings" to hash out school problems. Juan himself was surprised at how well it all worked. But the test scores didn't go up—in fact, the midyear eighth-grade reading and math scores, already low, declined a bit. The superintendent, whose job was on the line, had told Juan that he had to scrap the "*Somos Uno*" program in order to devote more time to test preparation. When word reached teachers and parents, they raised the roof. They told Juan that if he wanted their respect as a principal, he'd better defend their program against the superintendent and that ignorant board of education.

Juan had tried. In fact, he had just come back from Mercado's office. Mercado himself had seemed troubled, but in the end, he had said, "Juan, what do you want from me? You want me to tell my wife and kids that I'm out of here? Drop the program, and leave me alone."

Juan rubbed his eyes and looked at the banner once more. What should he do? Should he drop the program as ordered? Should he organize a community appeal to the board of education? Should he pretend to drop the program while actually continuing it? Should he ask for a transfer or look for another job?

Mostly, he wondered, to whom did he owe loyalty? The superintendent who had hired him? The staff and parents? The kids, whom he loved? His own parents, their silent voices telling him from beyond how proud there were of him and how they wanted him to be strong? His own conception of personal and professional integrity? And if he got himself in trouble, how would that be for his wife? Didn't he owe loyalty to her? Where were these questions, he thought, in Education 101?

Who Gets the Money?

Money was always tight in Big City, but this year it was even tighter. The board and the superintendent had waged a successful campaign for a bond issue, and now some of the most decrepit buildings would receive long-needed repairs. But that left precious little money for program improvement. The superintendent had made that clear at the administrative council meeting that morning, and Sondra Young still hadn't figured out what to do.

Sondra, principal of the Lincoln Elementary School, had been working with her school planning team for weeks to try to establish budget priorities for the coming year. The team, which consisted of teachers and parents elected by teachers and parents, was only in its third year and still trying to find its way. But Sondra took it seriously, because she knew that she could accomplish much more with the team's support than without it. She nurtured the team along and almost always took its advice.

Recently, the team had identified two budget priorities for the coming year. One was the school's new program of "inclusion." A number of students with special needs had been assigned to regular classes so that they could learn in a more "normal" situation. Money was needed, the team said, to provide teacher aides, special instructional materials, and professional development for the regular classroom teachers who would be working with these children. The second priority was the school's effort to raise standards and achievement for all its students, in keeping with a statewide and national push in that direction. If test scores were to rise, the team said, money was needed for new textbooks, staff training, and special tutorial help for any student who needed it.

Sondra agreed with these priorities. The problem, however, was that she had just been told in no uncertain terms that there would not be enough money for both. (Of course, she could pretend to do both by sprinkling a little bit of money in both places, but she was experienced enough to know that doing so would make little difference anywhere.) A difficult choice would have to be made. And to make matters worse, she knew that she and the planning team would not agree on what that choice should be. The team would want the money to go to the standards and testing program (where it would presumably do the most good for the greatest number), and Sondra's gut told her that the funds should be spent on the inclusion program (where the children were most in need).

Sondra took her time driving home and tried to work it out. What was the right thing to do? She really did believe that the neediest kids should be helped first. But she had to admit it would be hard to argue with the team members if they said that fairness required an equal share for all. Besides, did she have the right to impose her own views on the team? Hadn't she promised to be guided by them unless they proposed something absolutely wrong? But as soon as she began to think that way, another question arose: Did she have the right to ignore what she truly believed to be in the neediest children's best interest? Wasn't her whole professional training and job premised on doing that right thing for the needy children, according to her best professional judgment?

Sondra turned on the car radio and listened to the traffic report, trying to push the questions out of her mind.

Doesn't Thirty Years Mean Anything?

As a high school principal, Emily Jones had always felt in the middle—but never more so than today. "Look," the superintendent had said, "I know she's your friend. I know you've known her forever. I know you feel sorry for her. I even feel a little bit sorry for her myself. But this isn't a club we're running—it's a school. The kids come first. If she's not helping the kids anymore, she's got to go. The parents are going crazy. And I've about had it with phone calls from board members asking me when I'm going to do something about it. Start building the case against her and get her out of here—*now!*"

Emily left the superintendent's office angry, and truth be told, feeling a bit sorry for herself. But she was a strong, mature woman, and on her drive back to the school, she tried to sort things out. What were the facts?

Emily had known Susan Stern for thirty years, the last fifteen of them as her high school principal. For over two decades, Susan had been one of the stars of the district. In a community that prided itself on the superiority of its schools, Susan was the ultimate symbol of teaching excellence. Her students loved her class, they all did well on tests, and their parents lobbied for their children to be assigned to her. She was also active in extracurricular matters, advising the staff on the yearbook and helping with drama productions. But over the past few years, things had changed dramatically. Susan had gone through a stressful divorce and now lived alone. Both her son and her daughter had dropped out of college and were living somewhat unconventional lives. Her health was failing; she had lost much of her energy and was frequently absent. A spell of counseling, undertaken as part of the district's employee assistance program, hadn't made much difference. Students no longer liked working with her, and many parents had complained about her lackluster teaching. When new ideas or programs were discussed in faculty meetings, Susan would invariably criticize them in a cynical and negative manner.

Emily sighed. Obviously, it would be better if Susan were to retire. But Emily knew that Susan needed five more years of teaching to qualify for her full pension in order to make up for the years when she had stayed at home to raise her small children. There would be no way to persuade her to leave on her own—she would have to be forced out somehow. Did Susan deserve that? Clearly, the students deserved competent teaching, but shouldn't twenty-plus good years count for something?

And what about the personal side of it? Emily and Susan were not close friends, but they had worked together for a long time and shared many ups and downs. Did being a professional educator mean that you stop being a person? Emily knew what she had been told to do, but right now she didn't much like it. She had parked the car in the lot and made it all the way back to her office without deciding what she was going to do.

What can we say about these scenarios? What do they have in common, and what do they tell us about ethics in educational leadership?

First, they are not unusual. Principals and other school leaders face such decisions all the time. In a human organization such as a school, decisions about personnel, about who gets what resources, and about who owes what to whom are unavoidable.

Second, they are not especially dramatic. In fact, to many of the people involved, they may seem like "no-brainers." If the teacher is not performing, fire her. If the test scores are down, drop everything else and prepare for the test. But to the protagonists in these scenarios, the choices do seem difficult, and more seems to be at stake than the issue itself. Each choice raises such questions as "What kind of person am I?" and "What kind of place is this, anyway?"

Third, although each issue can be looked at pedagogically or politically or legally, each can also be looked at ethically—and it is the ethical component that is the hardest for the protagonists to deal with. Juan Ruiz understands the politics of his situation thoroughly; his question is not what is the smart thing to do but what is the *right* thing to do and which he should choose. Emily Jones knows the laws in her state concerning teacher dismissals; what she finds hard is weighing her obligations to her students against her obligations to a friend. This ethical dimension of administrative decision making is much more pervasive and stressful than many people realize.

Fourth, in none of the situations is there a clear right or wrong path to take. The choices the protagonists must make are not between right and wrong but between right and right—for example, the right of all children to academic support versus the right of the neediest children to be helped first. No matter what choices the protagonists make, the results are likely to leave the decision makers feeling soiled and uncomfortable. And the fact that some people will not like either decision does not help at all.

Fifth, because so many of these choices are between right and right — or sometimes between wrong and wrong — there are no clear rules for making them. The laws and regulations may help, but they do not address all situations. Further, the law sometimes seems to conflict with morality, as history has shown us again and again. Religion provides broad principles and an ethical context, but not even religion can tell Juan Ruiz whether to drop the "*Somos Uno*" program. In many situations, schoolteachers must make decisions and choose courses of action guided only by their gut and their mind — and this often happens when they are feeling pressured from all sides, when political and practical considerations seem paramount, and when the ethics of the situation seem lost or forgotten in the fray.

Is it not odd that in these circumstances, most school leader preparation programs make little or no provision for dealing with ethical issues? One thing that most students and teachers and parents want their school principals to be is "fair." In fact, a principal's effectiveness often depends on whether he or she is seen as fair or not. But how can you be "fair" if you do not know what "fair" is in a given situation? How do you choose between two "fairs"? What kind of help can we give Juan and Sondra and Emily so that they can deal more effectively with the ethical dimensions of their job?

Why Study Ethics?

Why should school leaders study ethics? For some people, the answer to this question is not obvious. People who want to lead school systems have to know and be able to do a lot, and most of it seems more fundamental and pressing than ethics. Especially in schools and systems that are dysfunctional — places where students are not learning, where nothing seems to work — the pursuit of ethics sounds "soft" and elitist. In this view, the job is to clean up the mess and get the kids learning. Ethics we can worry about later.

This chapter argues just the opposite. It argues that morality and values are at the very core of education. Those troubled schools where equity and justice are absent and where the duty of care seems to be ignored are precisely the places in which ethical thought and action are most needed. Indeed, dysfunctional schools cannot be improved without sustained attention to their ethical dimensions.

The reasons for studying ethics lie in the nature of education, of schools, and of leadership. Education is an inherently moral matter. It is moral because people develop (or fail to develop) morally as well as physically, emotionally, and intellectually. It is moral because teaching—helping to shape other people's minds, sensibilities, and capabilities—raises deep questions of purpose, values, and responsibility. It is moral because it involves the relationship between one generation and another, a relationship that helps determine the direction and quality of human life.

Schools and schooling are inherently moral as well. Not only are they charged with the moral purpose of education, but as social institutions, they constitute a rich soup of human relationships and interactions through which children learn a moral code. For most children, school is life, not just preparation for it. And children learn from the lives they lead, not just from their lessons. If we want our children to lead ethical lives, their schools and the adults in them should model ethical behavior.

Educational leadership raises the moral stakes. Educational leaders have the power and the duty to influence the education of large numbers of students. Moreover, they work in organizations and complex political environments wherein competing values and beliefs must be moderated toward wise and just ends. Such enterprises cannot be conducted well by administrative technique and politics alone; they must be informed by a larger sense of purpose and guided by clearly delineated ethical considerations.

Furthermore, educational leaders have power—information, positional authority, control of resources. How they use that power is a profoundly moral matter. As Tom Sergiovanni (2001, p. 346) has written:

> Whenever there is an unequal distribution of power between two people, the relationship becomes a moral one. Whether intended or not, leadership involves an offer to control. The follower accepts this offer on the assumption that control will not be exploited. In this sense, leadership is not a right but a responsibility. Morally speaking, its purpose is not to enhance the leader's position or make it easier for the leader to get what she or he wants but to benefit the school. The test of moral leadership under these conditions is whether the competence, well-being, and independence of the follower are enhanced as the result of accepting control and whether the school benefits.

There is yet another reason for paying attention to ethics. The moral nature of leadership is a largely unrecognized and untapped source of motivation for the education profession. Most of the people who become teachers or school administrators do so because they want to help children. The draw and the rewards are those of the helping professions—a sense of moral purpose and commitment, of being part of the larger cause, of doing good for others. Inevitably, as time passes, these original motives become partly buried beneath the baggage of other human needs—esteem, recognition, variety, power, material success. But the core values and motives remain; and precisely because education cannot compete with Mammon on Mammon's terms, it is to this core that we must appeal if we wish our education leaders to remain committed to their profession. We must recognize the moral nature of the education enterprise, and we must honor those who see their work as a calling and act accordingly. Few people can be energized for a lifetime by the pursuit of higher test scores. Many are hungry for an opportunity to be part of a moral cause. The policymakers who advocate financial incentives for improved performance are off target. Of course, the able teachers and administrators will take the money if it is offered—they are not stupid. But what they really want is to make their lives meaningful by serving others. We need to learn how to tap into this deep well of human motivation.

Does the Public Want Ethical Schools?

America's public schools serve a vast and diverse constituency. People differ in their aspirations, their attitudes, their values, and their sense of how things should be done and how people should behave. Given these realities, is it right for the public schools to impose a uniform ethical vision? Is there sufficient agreement among the public on ethical matters to justify preparing educational leaders to think and act ethically?

Such questions are not as difficult as they may at first seem. We believe that there is a core of civic values to which most people in our society subscribe—democracy, the rule of law, majority rule, minority rights, and so on. The schools need not shrink from asserting such values. Similarly, there is a core of personal virtues most people prize—virtues such as honesty, integrity, responsibility for one's actions, and respect for property and for life. At a high level of generality, these virtues are not in dispute. On broad and basic matters such as these, where most of the public is in full agreement, the public schools and their leaders have not just the right but the duty to take a positive ethical stand.

The problem arises when one digs beneath that level of generality. What seems clearly right or wrong in the abstract may be difficult to unravel in particular circumstances. Indeed, part of the educational leader's job is to sort through the facts and figure out how general principles are best applied. When you get down to cases, judgment is involved, and reasonable people may differ. Does the public want its educational leaders to exercise such judgment? For us, the question is moot. The fact is that principals, superintendents, and other education leaders must make decisions with moral consequences all the time. There is no other way to operate the schools. The question, it would seem, is whether leaders can make such ethical decisions ethically. In our democratic society, the role of the educational leader is not to impose a personal vision of morality on others. It is to act ethically in one's own terms and to foster a dialogue through which differing conceptions of ethics can be expressed and considered in the course of shaping a shared ethical vision. In our democratic society, the leader is not a high priest, preaching the gospel; he is a member of a community, teaching others and learning from others and shaping his own attitudes and behavior, as well as those of others. Some writers describe the role as "leader as servant." If one understands the word *servant* in its most exalted meaning, that sounds right.

Of course, the public is divided on larger issues as well. Vast differences exist on such matters as vouchers, high-stakes testing, educational equity, and desegregation—not to mention abortion, sexual identity, race, socioeconomic status, and whether teachers should wear neckties. Where important matters are in such dispute it would seem wrong for public school officials to take a unilateral stand. Here again, the role of the leader is to foster and participate in a public dialogue wherein all the issues may be debated vigorously. In the public system, ethics sometimes consists of maintaining the fairness and integrity of democratic processes.

All of these considerations argue for ethical schools and ethical school leaders. In the end, advocates of ethical schools have history on their side. From the days of the New England Primer and McGuffey's Readers on down to the present, Americans have almost always wanted their schools to produce character as well as competence. Ask parents what they want for their children; yes, they want them to do well on tests, go to college, get good jobs. But almost universally, they also want them to become decent people and responsible citizens—to lead good lives. And they believe that the schools should play a role in helping them do so.

What Does Being Ethical Mean?

As has been noted, there is no guidebook, no simple set of principles or rules to answer this question. In much of what they do, educational leaders must work hard to discover what being ethical means in the specific situations that confront them. However, we know enough from the writing and experience of wise and thoughtful people who have preceded us to be able to describe the general landscape. Here are some of the features of that landscape, presented not from the lofty standpoint of a philosopher but from the perspective of an on-the-ground education practitioner.

Being ethical and acting ethically do not mean simply keeping your nose clean. The conventional view (and the gist of most codes of ethics) is that ethics means not doing wrong. Ethical leaders, in this view, should not lie, cheat, steal, goof off, or hurt people. That is good advice, as far as it goes. Leaders should not lie, cheat, steal, loaf, or hurt people. But avoiding wrong is not enough.

The moral imperative for educational leaders is to do right. People who are entrusted with the education of children and young people have an affirmative duty of care. They are responsible for the education and welfare of the students in their charge, and this responsibility must be carried out through positive action. They must create an environment in which effective teaching and learning can flourish; they must develop and sustain wholesome and productive relationships with their students and their staff; they must draw on their knowledge and experience to guard their charges from harm and to create new opportunities for growth. All of this requires proactive, sustained engagement with the life and activity around them. Carol Gilligan (1993) writes about the importance of "stepping in" as opposed to "stepping out." All people, but especially those charged with a duty of care, must "step in" to the confusion and messiness of human life, forging relationships with all kinds of others and making a positive contribution to their lives. Retreating to the office and staying out of trouble is not ethical. Making good things happen for people is.

Making good things happen for people is not always easy. It requires skill, knowledge, courage, and persistence. Leaders must be both ethical and competent. A leader who is pure of heart but ineffective on the job is not of much use. As Sergiovanni (2001, p. 351) has said, "The challenge of leadership is to make peace with two competing imperatives, the managerial and the moral." Consequently, leaders have an obligation to develop their skills and expand their knowledge as fully as possible. Avoidable ignorance, where it affects children's education, is unethical.

So is incompetence. In his book *Defining Moments*, Joseph Badaracco (1997) writes about *virtue* and *virtu*. According to Badaracco, "*Virtu* was Machiavelli's word for the moral code of public life. The word is not an antiquated version of virtue, for it means something quite different. Virtu is a combination of vigor, confidence, imagination, shrewdness, boldness, practical skills, personal force, determination, and self-discipline" (p. 108). To discharge their responsibilities ethically, educational leaders must have both qualities. Being good without being effective does not help much. Being effective without being good can be awful. The two must go together. As James O'Toole (1995, p. 35) has written, "While morality is a necessary ingredient of leadership, it is not sufficient. The Rushmore Standard of Excellence is the two-fold ability to lead change both morally and effectively."

Being ethical also means more than choosing right instead of wrong. As we have seen, in the complex world of schools, the choices that need to be made are often between right and right (or wrong and wrong—"the lesser of the two evils"). Being ethical in such cases means being alert to the ethical dimensions of a situation, reflecting on these ethical implications, and choosing as wisely as possible. It also means knowing when to bend and when to draw the line. Leaders cannot wage a to-the-death fight on every issue, even if they are in the right. (Don Quixote is an appealing figure, but he would be a disaster as a superintendent.) But neither should they sell out—"go along to get along." Perhaps this sounds like equivocation. It is not. It is real life. Being ethical means knowing when to take a stand and when not to. Sometimes it is easy; some-times it is not. There is no absolute standard to guide you. But every ethical leader knows deep down what choice is called for in these defining moments, as Badaracco calls them.

Sometimes such defining moments can shape a leader's career. But there is more to being ethical than choosing wisely on the grand occasions. What also counts is who you are and how you act from day to day. Education leaders interact with scores of other people daily, and the quality of those interactions becomes part of the fabric of school life. How does the leader relate to peers? To superiors? To students? To the rank and file of the staff? To the woman who answers the telephone, the man who sweeps the floor? Are these people valued for themselves, or do they merely serve some end? In Noddings's terms (1984), do they fall within the leader's circle of care? And then there is the leader's "own" work. How responsibly is it done? What standards of quality does the leader meet at those inevitable times when one is tired and no one is looking? We all get tired, and only the saints can do their best on every occasion. But ethical leaders are more consistent than others. If you will pardon a sports analogy, the ethical leader not only hits the October home run but also plays hard on the humid, late-August afternoon when the team is out of the pennant race and few fans are in the stands.

So far the focus has been on the behavior of individual leaders themselves—their ethical awareness, their attitudes, their choices, their relationships, the consistency and quality of their "own" work. This focus is important because no organization can be ethical without ethical leaders. But principals and superintendents are responsible for more than their individual behavior. They must also create and lead organizations that are themselves ethical in their design and operation. Schools and school districts are never value-neutral. They inevitably foster some values and slight or suppress others, and they often privilege some groups above others. How is the school organized and run? Who spends time with whom? Who makes what kinds of decisions? Who gets the resources that are needed, and who goes without? What kind of behavior is rewarded?

What kind is punished or discouraged? The answers to these and hundreds of similar questions determine the nature of the school's ethical environment. A school that does not respect the worth of all its constituents is not an ethical school. A school that preaches equality and discriminates against poor students is a decidedly unethical school. And so it goes. Leaders must attend not only to their own behavior but also to the effects of their behavior on the ethical quality of the institutions they serve.

This distinction between "microethics" (the leader's individual behavior) and "macroethics" (the ethical qualities of the organization, for which the leader is largely responsible) extends beyond the school. Schools and school systems are embedded in social, economic, and political contexts that have their own ethical (or unethical) properties. Sometimes injustices are obvious, as when poor children are not given the resources they need to do what we require of them. Sometimes the schools are caught in the conflicts between competing values, such as liberty (let families choose whatever schools they wish) versus equity (make sure that all students have equal educational opportunity, even if free family choice would produce other results). Educational leaders may not be able to eliminate such injustice or resolve such tensions. But at the very least, they should be aware of the ethical dimensions of such situations and should bring this awareness to bear on the matters within their purview. The individuals charged with education's heavy moral mission should be among the first to bring that mission to the fore.

One of an education leader's foremost macroethical obligations is to unite the organization's members behind a shared vision grounded in basic values. Of course, all organizations have purposes (or once had them), and effective leaders in any setting must help define a vision and bring people together behind it. But because of the moral nature of education, the tasks take on a moral dimension in the schools. As Sergiovanni (2001, p. 345) says, "The school must move beyond concerns for goals and roles to the tasks of building purposes into its structure and embodying these purposes in everything that it does with the effect of transforming school members from neutral participants to committed followers. The embodiment of purpose and the development of followership are inescapably moral." In this view, educational leadership is necessarily moral leadership as well.

Finally, being ethical means maintaining a lifelong habit of reflection on education's moral purpose and on one's own developing moral sensibilities. One is not born with moral certitudes, nor do the seeming certitudes of youth always survive lived experience. Some people find that secure moral guidance, while broadly helpful, must be fine-tuned to meet the specifics of the complex human situations we encounter. We need to draw continually on what we have learned, what we have come to feel, and what we have synthesized from our own experience if we are to understand ourselves and bring our wisdom to bear. In the crunch times, it is not to external sources that we turn for answers—we must look within. The ancient commandment was to "know thyself." This we can do only through experience and reflection. And as we reflect, we come to understand that the road to moral wisdom is not through applying abstract principles but through raising honest questions.

How Should We Teach Ethics?

A century or more ago, the teaching of ethics was an accepted part of the curriculum in colleges and professional schools. It was common for the president, as the senior scholar of the faculty, to teach seniors a course in moral philosophy as the capstone of their college experience. Ethics was not something superficial, like frosting on a cake; the very purpose of the university was not only to create and disseminate knowledge but also to make students wise and good.

Over the course of the past century, this custom fell away. Discussions of the "just" and the "good" came to seem as out-of-date as fustian draperies and tub-thumping speeches on the Fourth of July. Ethics and morals were relative, contextual, personal; the role of the university in the modern age was to develop and inculcate knowledge that would stand up to rational, scientific inquiry. Ironically, two great wars that were in part a moral crusade ushered in a world in which all the old codes and credos were called into question. Moral compasses were to be set individually, not collectively, and they did not all point in the same direction.

In the past quarter century, this trend has begun to change. The fading civil rights movement, the Vietnam War, and a succession of political scandals has called attention to the absence in our civil life of a shared moral vision, or at least a set of principles by which we can guide our public decisions and acts. In recent years, issues of ethics and morality have been receiving increased attention — not only in education but also in business, in the military, and in the society generally.

In the schools, people as dissimilar as Michael Apple (1996), William Bennett (1992), Amy Guttman (1987), Tom Lickona (1992), Nell Noddings (1984), and Tom Sergiovanni (2001) — along with an army of just plain parents and citizens — are raising important questions of purpose and values. In higher education, the work of Derek and Sissela Bok and of Daniel Callahan, among others, has charged the academy with neglecting this important part of its historic mission, eliciting an active, albeit uneven, response. Many professional schools of educational administration now require their students to complete courses in ethical studies.

In preparing educational leaders to meet the ethical challenges of today's (and tomorrow's) world, it is important to distinguish between thinking about ethics and thinking ethically. We need the latter. School leaders do not need to become moral philosophers, nor need they intellectualize brilliantly about ethical theory. They do need to be alert to the ethical dimensions of their work, to cultivate the habit of thoughtful reflection on them, and to develop the will to think and act ethically.

Sermons and exhortations to do good avail little. Our purposes call for learning experiences in which prospective leaders examine the ethical issues that arise in educational practice. There are many ways to provide such experiences. Case studies of ethical issues, drawn from the professional literature or from students' own experiences, offer rich possibilities. Students can examine the ethical properties of the organizations of which they are a part. They can reflect on the ethical behavior they see modeled by the leaders in their lives. Many university leadership programs now offer full courses in ethical issues. Many others deal with such issues as part of their regular coursework. Whatever the form or the activity, what is important is to pay explicit and sustained attention to the ethical dimensions of educational experiences, wherever they arise.

Students can also be made to see the ethical implications of the work or other studies in which they are involved. One cannot discuss, say, education finance or "special education" intelligently without raising moral questions, as well as pedagogical, political, and administrative ones. One cannot develop the instrumental skills of leadership without considering the purpose for which they are to be employed—that is, without asking to what use one is to put to them. In addition to the educational and social science readings conventionally found in university leadership training programs, we can draw from the entire realm of literature and the humanities, from history and current events, and from students' own personal and professional experience. Martin Luther King Jr.'s "Letter from Birmingham Jail" says more about the relationship of the law to morality than most legal textbooks. Robert Penn Warren's *All the King's Men* (1946) teaches more about personal responsibility and the corrupting nature of political power than most political science writing. Mark Twain's *Huckleberry Finn* illuminates the tension between personal integrity and social convention more powerfully than any academic study. People who aspire to become educational leaders should know such works and should reflect on them and should apply them to the situations and relationships that develop in their professional lives.

Moreover, such reflection should not cease once leaders are appointed to their jobs. At present, most public school principals, superintendents, and other administrators have few opportunities to discuss the ethical content of their experience with professional peers. Time is limited, getting together is hard, and there is no tradition (as perhaps there is in independent schools) of public discourse about such matters. As a result, most leaders hear little about the experience of their peers and are left to make sense of things on their own, with only their minds and moral compasses to guide them. We need to establish real and virtual communities that nourish leaders' continuing professional growth in matters ethical as well as academic and political. Moral reflection should not always be a solitary pursuit.

Conclusion

This chapter has argued that education is intrinsically moral and that educational leaders must be prepared to deal with its moral dimensions. It is as important for school principals, superintendents, and other leaders to be morally responsible and effective as it is for them to be pedagogically skillful and politically astute. For that reason, all professional and educational leadership training and licensing programs should have an ethical component, and provision should be made as well for continuing discussion of ethical issues throughout an educational leader's career.

The foregoing pages have asserted the case for such a recommendation. But one reason has been reserved for the end.

The children and young people whose education we have been discussing pass through our hands and our lives but once. Our influence on them can be profound or scanty, benign or destructive. We only get one chance. In the blink of an eye, the child entering kindergarten is leaving high school, diploma in hand. I have seen it again and again. If there were world enough and time, we could be casual. We could fix tomorrow what we broke today, make up next week the missed chances of last month. The harsh truth that we cannot do so requires us to do well whatever we can do today. Thus do time and mortality make moralists of us all.

Alfred North Whitehead (1929) has said it best:

> We can be content with no less than the old summary of educational ideal which has been current at any time from the dawn of our

civilization. The essence of education is that it be religious. Pray, what is religious education? A religious education is an education which inculcates duty and reverence. Duty arises from our potential control over the course of events. Where attainable knowledge could have changed the issue, ignorance has the guilt of vice. And the foundation of reverence is this perception, that the present holds within itself the complete sum of existence, backwards and forwards, that whole amplitude of time, which is eternity.

References

Apple, M. W. *Cultural Politics and Education*. New York: Teachers College Press, 1996.

Badaracco, J. J., Jr. *Defining Moments: When Managers Must Choose Between Right and Right*. Boston: Harvard Business School Press, 1997.

Bennett, W. J. *The De-Valuing of America: The Fight for Our Culture and Our Children*. New York: Summit Books, 1992.

Gilligan, C. *In a Different Voice: Psychological Theory and Women's Development*. Cambridge, Mass.: Harvard University Press, 1993.

Guttman, A. *Democratic Education*. Princeton, N.J.: Princeton University Press, 1987.

Lickona, T. *Educating for Character: How Our Schools Can Teach Respect and Responsibility*. New York: Bantam Books, 1992.

Noddings, N. *Caring: A Feminine Approach to Ethics and Moral Education*. Berkeley: University of California Press, 1984.

O'Toole, J. *Leading Change: Overcoming the Ideology of Comfort and the Tyranny of Custom*. San Francisco: Jossey-Bass, 1995.

Sergiovanni, T. J. *The Principalship: A Reflective Practice Perspective*. (4th ed.) Boston: Allyn & Bacon, 2001.

Warren, R. P. *All the King's Men*. Orlando, Fla.: Harcourt Brace, 1946.

Whitehead, A. N. *"The Aims of Education" and Other Essays*. Old Tappan, N.J.: Macmillan, 1929.

Part Two

Best Practices in the Training of Leaders, Managers, and Other Professionals in Business, the Military, and Beyond

Chapter Four

Best Practices in Leadership Development

Lessons from the Best Business Schools and Corporate Universities

Marie Eiter

Increasing technological change, greater global competition, the deregulation of markets, and the changing demographics of the workforce have prompted an explosion of interest in leadership development both within organizations and among business schools that support these corporations with new M.B.A. talent and through executive education. In both the business schools and companies, seven key dimensions of leadership have taken on increased importance: the leader as strategic thinker, the leader as driver of change, the leader as having a teachable point of view, the leader as coach, the leader as creator or champion of culture, the leader as decision maker, and the leader as driver for results. In this chapter, I will explore each of these dimensions and review sample curricula for each. I will also focus on the content of the programs and on teaching pedagogies such as the case study, business simulations, and action learning. Finally, I will discuss other leadership development activities that support all of the corporate programs, including assessment and feedback, coaching, mentoring, and the use of development assignments.

For the past two decades, John Kotter of the Harvard Business School has promoted our understanding of the phenomenon of leadership. Kotter was among the first to articulate a significant distinction between management and leadership. Management is about coping with complexity. Its practices and procedures are largely a response to the emergence of large, multinational organizations. Good management brings a degree of order and consistency to key dimensions like the quality, timeliness, and profitability of products. Leadership, by contrast, is about coping with change. Part of the reason that leadership has become so important in recent years is that the business world has become more competitive and volatile. Faster technological change, greater global competition, the deregulation of markets, and the changing demographics of the workforce are among the many factors that have contributed to this shift. The net result is that doing what was done yesterday, or doing it 5 percent better, is no longer a formula for success. Major changes are more and more necessary for businesses to survive and compete effectively. More change always demands more leadership.

This set of events has prompted an explosion of interest in leadership development. My purpose in this chapter is to highlight the leading-edge practices in leadership development in both corporations and business schools. In selecting these practices, several aspects of leadership were not included. Beyond the scope of this chapter are the tasks of the global leader—developing a global mind-set, understanding the global economic environment, and developing cross-cultural competencies. Also not included is a discussion of the more traditional management practices of planning and budgeting, organizing and staffing, controlling, and problem solving.

In addition to addressing the content of leadership development programs, I will review useful pedagogies such as the case method, business simulations, and action learning, that are used by both companies and schools to engage the learner and enhance the learning process.

Finally, it is important to note that virtually all of the corporate programs are supported by a systems approach to leadership development that goes beyond the classroom experience to build skills through assessment, coaching, mentoring, and development assignments. I will provide a brief description of these nonclassroom development activities.

Leadership Dimensions

The Leader as Strategic Thinker

In any organization, an executive's role falls into three arenas. The first is to manage the present, the second is to selectively forget the past, and the third is to create the future. In a survey I recently conducted at the Tuck School of Business at Dartmouth, fifty-five executives reported that they spend over 85 percent of their time managing the present. These managers admitted spending most of their time finding ways of reengineering core processes to lower costs, instituting total quality management processes, and developing just-in-time production systems to improve their ability to be competitive in the marketplace. While these executives are well versed in strategic planning, their strategic plans tended to be more about today's problems than tomorrow's opportunities. What was lacking was the ability and willingness to think strategically about the future in ways that were fundamentally different from the past.

The concepts of strategic intent, strategy as stretch rather than fit, and strategy as revolution, introduced by C. K. Prahalad at the University of Michigan and Gary Hamel of the London Business School, among others, have reframed the concept of strategy. These concepts emphasize the leadership quality of strategic thinking rather than the traditional management process of strategic planning.

Strategic intent envisions a desired leadership position for the firm. It is inspiring and motivating because it focuses on the value of the company's product or service to the customer, not the financial rewards to shareholders. It is challenging because it cap-tures the essence of winning. It provides direction without being overly prescriptive.

Whereas the traditional view of strategic planning focuses on the degree of fit or congruence between an organization's existing resources and current opportunities, strategy as stretch implies a deliberate misfit between resources and ambition. Current capabil-ities and resources will not suffice, thus forcing the organization to be more inventive and to make the most of limited resources.

The concept of strategy as revolution challenges the reduction-ist methods of traditional strategic planning processes. It advocates a radical rethinking of the company's approach to products by chal-lenging the traditional price-performance relationships. It redefines market space and resets consumers' expectations about accessibil-ity. This type of imaginative strategic thinking requires the input of managers at all levels of the corporation, in which the hierarchy of experience is supplemented with the hierarchy of imagination.

These approaches to strategic thinking are reflected in many corporate leadership programs. Motorola's Global Organization Leadership Development Process (GOLD), Abbott Laboratories' Leadership Development Program, and Lucent's LEAD program all place increased emphasis on setting a vision and developing a strategic intent. Participants are exposed to the concept of strategy as stretch and strategy as revolution and discover how it differs from resource allocation models.

Abbott Laboratories, one of the most diversified manufacturers of health care products in the world, defines its strategic intent as continuously creating the capability to improve people's lives. Abbott defines the leadership competency of strategic thinking in the following way (Linkage, 2001, p. 19):

- Create and deliver a vision of the future that improves cus-tomers' lives.

- Establish and commit to strategies and a course of action to accomplish that long-range vision.

- Communicate a clear vision of the desired future state to employees, customers, and suppliers and other stakeholders.

The Linkage study (pp. 19–29) identifies the following skills that support this leadership competency:

- A leader understands trends, their implications, and opportunities in the global environment (customer, technical, health care, regulatory, and so on).
- A leader gathers information from multiple sources, including customers, peers, staff, and external experts.
- A leader looks to the future, using the global marketplace, technology, and business knowledge to identify emerging opportunities and then seizes them.
- A leader balances opportunities, resources, and investments to maximize growth.
- A leader effectively communicates the business vision and strategies to align the organization with the strategies.
- A leader effectively translates the business vision and broad strategies into concrete actionable strategic plans and goals.

The Leader as Driver of Change

Managing current performance while innovating for the future is a crucial task for leaders and their teams. Ultimately, it is the leaders' action or inaction that determines the fate of their organizations. Industry leaders who focus solely on the present rarely enjoy enduring success. Those who remain successful, by contrast, do so by managing short-run excellence as they drive long-term innovation and change.

The primary goal of the Harvard Business School executive program Leading Change and Organizational Renewal (http://www.exed.hbs.edu) is to explore ways that organizations can transform themselves. The program draws from the work of Harvard professors Clayton Christensen, David Garvin, Rosabeth Moss Kanter,

Charles O'Reilly, and Michael Tushman in addressing the difficult issues of leading change, innovation, and organizational renewal. The program focuses on the senior team's role in leading change and the in building the organizational architectures that drive both incremental and disruptive innovation. Participants learn to anticipate shifts in competitive demands, respond proactively to change, and effectively manage innovation for both today and tomorrow. The program also provides participants with an integrated set of concepts and tools for leading innovation, change, and organizational renewal. These tools are directly linked to specific cases and the experience of practicing managers in a number of companies.

Curriculum topics include the following:

- Building organizational architecture for short- and long-term success

    Strategy objectives and vision

    Organizational arrangement

    Human resource capabilities

    Work process and task interdependencies

    Fit and congruence

- Understanding the dynamics of innovation and organizational change

    Why organizations often fall victim to past successes

    Roots of organizational inertia

    Role of industry standards and dominant designs on firm performance

    Role of technological substitution and disruptive technologies on firm performance

    Effect of technological cycles on organizational evolution and drive innovation

- Adapting leadership styles

    Managing contradictions: stability versus experimentation, continuous improvement versus revolutionary innovation

Important levers to shape organizational capabilities for short-term advantage and long-term renewal

Proven management processes for getting things done

Role of the senior team in managing change

Role of leadership styles and behaviors in shaping innovation, learning, and change

- Developing competencies to play the dual management game

    The efficiency game: aligning strategy, structure, people, culture, and processes

    The game of organizational renewal: knowing when and how to initiate revolutionary innovation and change

Companies such as Johnson & Johnson, Hewlett-Packard, Merck, 3M, Procter & Gamble, and Motorola all have enduring core values that remain fixed while their business strategies and practices endlessly adapt to a changing world. These companies understand the difference between what should never change and what should be open to change. This rare ability to understand how to manage continuity and change is addressed in the Stanford executive program, Leading and Managing Change, directed by Professor Jerry Porras (http://www.gsb.stanford.edu/exed). Within a research-based framework, the program gives participants critical insights to help them understand the complex processes of change and key leverage points that will help them achieve the necessary changes to drive their organizations into the future.

The Leader as Having a Teachable Point of View

According to Professor Noel Tichy of the University of Michigan, a teachable point of view is a clear explanation of what a business leader knows and believes about what it takes to succeed in his or her own market. It identifies why a person approaches work as he or she does; it lays out his or her assumptions and beliefs about the business.

Executives who attended General Electric's Crotonville Leadership Development Institute over the past ten years might have found their teacher to be none other than Jack Welch, the former company CEO. Welch spent an enormous amount of time taking the hot seat in question-and-answer sessions, and he also spent a significant amount of time teaching. He taught a variety of modules critical to the development of leaders at GE. He considered such sessions essential and was proud of his commitment. On numerous occasions, Welch cited the importance of his frequent visits to Crotonville to interact with new employees, middle managers, and senior managers.

In *The Leadership Engine*, Tichy (1997) also cites Andy Grove, former CEO of Intel, as a frequent visitor to the classroom to teach Intel executives how to lead in an industry in which the product (microprocessors) doubles in capacity every eighteen months. Grove's teaching sessions focus on the role of leaders in detecting and navigating the turbulent industry shift in fast-clock-speed industries such as telecommunications and computers.

The Ford Motor Company has systemized teaching as a means of driving change through the organization. In an interview in the *Harvard Business Review* (Wetlaufer, 1999), Ford CEO Jacques Nasser maintained that Ford had to change its fundamental approach to work and that teaching was the best way to do that. At Ford, Nasser and his team created what they called their "teachable points of view." These leaders shared their teachable points of view with the next level of executives. After debate and discussion, those executives were trained as teachers and shared their teachable points of view with their direct reports. Within three years, Ford trained fifteen hundred leader-teachers who have in turn reached fifty-five thousand employees with the message of how Ford needs to change to survive.

In the University of Michigan's executive education program, Building the Leadership Engine (http://execed.bus.umich.edu), Noel Tichy and the program faculty work with managers to develop their own teachable point of view. A leader engages other people by translating his or her points of view into a dynamic story. Based on these stories, people at all levels take actions that transform their organizations. During the program, participants are coached in how to create a compelling story of where their organization is headed and how it will get there.

Tichy maintains that there are two reasons why the concept of a teachable point of view creates better leaders. First, the very act of creating and testing a teachable point of view forces executives to step back from the day-to-day fray of the business and reflect on their knowledge base. Implicit knowledge becomes explicit and can then be questioned, refined, and honed to both the leader's and organization's benefit.

Second, the teachable point of view engages leaders in one of their most mission-critical tasks in today's organization: developing people. Leaders tend to develop other leaders by example. This can take a long time and leave many insights unarticulated. The teachable point of view gives leaders an explicit body of knowledge to impart. They construct a framework for their own ideas and then transfer those ideas in a systematic way to others (Tichy, 1997).

Having worked with a number of successful companies such as Ford, General Electric, Allied Signal, PepsiCo, and Intel, Tichy argues that what these companies have in common is leaders who place a high value on teaching and creating a culture within the organization that to be a leader one must also be a teacher of others.

The Leader as Coach

In the past, the keys to a corporation's success were its control of physical and financial resources. Today and in the future, it will be the control of knowledge. In the past, the worker needed the company more than the company needed the worker. Today, these roles are reversed: the company needs the knowledge worker far more than the knowledge worker needs the company. The "organization man" has been replaced by the "free agent." For many of America's most successful companies, the most important task of the leader is retaining and developing the next generation of talent. This problem is exacerbated because many of these major corporations are facing a demographic crunch. A large number of experienced leaders are nearing retirement age, and there are a dwindling number of experienced leaders "in the wings" waiting to take their place.

Recognizing the fact that superior talent will be tomorrow's prime source of competitive advantage, companies like GE, Allied Signal, Motorola, Ford, and Colgate are now focusing on the role of leader as coach. As part of this emphasis on coaching, line managers are being held more accountable for the development of their people.

According to Marshall Goldsmith, a leading authority on the development of leaders as coaches, coaching is a "how to get there" process, not a "where to go" process. If the organization is headed in the wrong direction, behavioral coaching will not make it change course. Goldsmith maintains that the role of coach does not come easily to many leaders. "One reason," says Goldsmith (2000, p. 21), "is that leaders, like most people, want to be liked. Leaders are often afraid that confronting people about poor teamwork or other behavioral shortcomings will cause them to be disliked." It is ironic that leaders shy away from the coaching role while the field of executive coaching—the practice of hiring coaches to improve the skills of senior executives—is the fastest-growing area of management consulting.

Goldsmith has crafted an eight-step process to train managers in the role of consultative coaching. Before beginning the coaching process the person being coached must

- Be willing to make a sincere effort to change
- Have the intelligence or functional skills to do the job
- Be working in an environment that provides an opportunity for change
- Be working in an organization that has a fundamentally sound mission and strategic objectives

Goldsmith maintains that in the process of becoming effective coaches, executives become better leaders because they are providing people with honest feedback and helping them in their development. When people improve, their self-confidence is enhanced, resulting in a more positive, responsive, and cohesive organization.

Goldsmith's coaching process is taught in a number of leadership development programs in companies, such as Motorola's GOLD program, and also in executive leadership programs in business schools such as Tuck's Global Leadership 2020 program.

The Leader as Creator of Culture

Truly great companies understand the difference between what should never change and what is open to change, between what is immutable and what is not. The task of the leader is to articulate and preserve the core culture of the organization while stimulating progress toward more immediate goals.

In the article "Building Your Company's Vision," Collins and Porras (1996) define *core ideology* as a consistent identity that transcends product or market life cycles, technological breakthroughs, and management fads. It is the glue that holds an organization together as it grows, decentralizes, diversifies, and expands globally. This core ideology, in turn, consists of two distinct parts: core values—a system of guiding principles, and core purpose—the organization's most fundamental reason for existence.

Collins and Porras (1996) maintain that companies tend to have only a few core values, usually between three and five. Strongly held and consistently practiced core values give culture its power.

As a result of downsizing and an unprecedented number of merged and acquired companies, there is a great need in organizations today for cultural leadership. Deal and Kennedy (1999) identify a series of steps leaders must take to revitalize many of today's weakened cultures.

First, the leaders must look inward to find their own personal values and beliefs. Leaders who seek to rebuild the cultures of the companies and to recapture superior performance must hold strong beliefs and be willing to stand up for them. Culture is about embracing deeply held beliefs about what it takes to succeed and to excel.

The next step is to find out what other managers and employees think the company stands for. Deal and Kennedy (1999) suggest a "walking the halls" exercise to find out what employees think is really at the heart of the business.

Step 3 is a collective process to pinpoint or hammer out a set of shared core values. Hewlett-Packard's *HP Way* and Johnson & Johnson's *Credo* are examples of documents that set out core values.

The Leader as Decision Maker

Today's leaders must be equipped to handle information overload, a data-intensive environment, and profound ambiguity. To succeed in this environment, managers must be trained in a sound process for framing problems and making decisions. The University of Pennsylvania's Wharton School program Critical Thinking: Real World, Real Time Decisions (http://www.wharton.upenn.edu/execed) provides a set of models for framing problems and making decisions. Led by Professor Paul Schoemaker, the program helps managers separate the merely incidental event from the systematic pattern, convert expert yet conflicting opinions into useful insights, and identify acceptable risks in alternative decisions. The program presents the following six key frameworks through which managers discover the key elements of effective decision making.

- *Decision framing* provides strategies for framing problems. Framing highlights what is important and what is not and identifies the boundaries drawn around the problem, the reference points used to define success and failure, and the yardsticks used in measurement.
- *Thinking framing* identifies the biases or predispositions that an individual carries around automatically by virtue of education, occupation, or culture.

- *Intelligence gathering* examines the decision biases of overconfidence, availability, and recency in making decisions. It examines how to use the available information and how to recognize when additional information is needed.
- *Making choices* identifies systematic approaches to weighing options and explores decision rules and linear models.
- *Group decision making* provides a strategy for avoiding groupthink and identifies where in the four elements of a decision (framing, intelligence gathering, coming to conclusions, and learning from past cases) the group can make the greatest contribution.
- *Learning from experience* avoids the human bias to claim credit for successes and rationalize away failures by improving feedback loops and by analyzing not only the outcomes of past decisions but also the processes that produced them.

Many companies are turning to spreadsheets and computer models to gain critical insights into the decisions they face. Managers today are asked to make fast, effective decisions of economic consequence to their firms. The problems they face are challenging and beyond routine, requiring creative but analytically sound approaches and solutions that can be explained in simple terms. Both the Tuck School of Business at Dartmouth and the University of Pennsylvania's Wharton School offer executive programs in modeling for decision making. These programs teach managers how to design, build, and test effective spreadsheet models and use influence diagrams for problem structuring and prototyping for model development.

The Leader as Driver for Results

To be effective, the overall goal of leadership development within a company must be linked to the marketplace and to the firm's long-term strategic goals. The companies investigated in this research all focused on the accountability of the leader to achieve business goals in a timely manner. A key theme throughout all the company programs was to gain competitive advantage in the marketplace. The focus on the leader as a driver for results was evident in case studies, business simulations, and assessment inventories that were administered prior to attending a leadership development program.

In many companies, leaders are assessed against a set of key performance dimensions before attending a program. The content of the programs is linked to these key dimensions. Senior executives focus on the company's strategy and competitive pressures of the external market, while program faculty speak knowledgeably and with insight about the organization, its strengths and weaknesses, its vision, business challenges, and the strategic issues facing the firm.

The following is an example of the "leader as driver for results" dimension as applied in two successful companies as reported by Linkage, Inc. (2001).

Abbott Laboratories: Drive for Results

- Collaboratively set challenging goals.
- Keep self and others focused on key performance indicators.
- Set short-term objectives that drive toward long-term goals or strategies.
- Support staff with necessary resources to meet objectives.
- Hold self and others accountable for delivering high-quality results.
- Regularly evaluate self and staff on goal attainment.

Colgate-Palmolive: Taking Responsibility for Results

- Take responsibility for the performance of all key accounts.
- Evaluate all business plans continuously.
- Deliver on commitments.

Whereas all of the companies conduct evaluations to determine the impact of their leadership programs, Colgate focuses on the key accountability aspect of the program.

Useful Pedagogies

The Case Method of Instruction

The case method is one of the principal methods of instruction used by leading business schools and most internal corporate leadership development programs. Long identified with the Harvard Business School, the case method is known for its active, discussion-oriented learning mode, disciplined by problems drawn from the complexity of real life.

A case is a statement of conditions, attitudes, and practices existing at some particular time in a company's history. It usually describes a situation in which the company is facing or has resolved a challenging problem or problems. A case differs from a problem in several respects. A case typically contains several problems. Some of these problems may be self-evident, but more frequently the key problem or problems must be identified. One of the very real benefits of the case method of instruction is the extent to which it forces the learner to identify problems.

A case provides some, but not all, of the information that was available to executives at the time they had to resolve a challenging problem. It frequently includes data on alternative courses of action. Because it is an attempt to reconstruct a real-life situation, a case is purposely written in a manner that requires the rearrangement of facts and interpretation of these facts, including the evaluation of opinions, behaviors, and intentions. Many of the facts may be relevant to the solution of the problem presented in the case, but some may be irrelevant. This arrangement of the descriptive material, in a somewhat unstructured way, in itself simulates experience. Data available for the solution of a problem are never presented in an orderly and systematic manner.

It should be emphasized that the case method does not provide "the answer." In most case discussions, several viable "answers" are developed and supported by various segments within the group. An instructor may or may not suggest the pros and cons of various alternative actions. What actually happened or what any one person thought ought to be done is of no great significance; what is significant is the analytical process that the learner follows in developing one's own solution.

Business Simulations

A business simulation experience puts managers in the position of operating businesses in a competitive environment. The goal is for participants to learn by doing. Working in small teams, participants first read and analyze the simulation situation that describes the business and industry, as well as supporting materials and reports describing the industry and competitive forces. Using this information, participants in the simulation develop a strategy and make business decisions in key areas.

Because the computer can condense time, participants are able to see the future impact of their decisions on performance and on customer retention. A computer-based simulation provides the complexity of multiple time horizons. During a typical simulation, the members of a team run their business for several years so that they can learn the risks of making shortsighted decisions. They experience the difficulties of operating with restrained resources in a changing environment. Simulations are detailed enough to provide for strong competition and realism. Many participants observe that it is the best way to experience how all the various functions in the corporation are interrelated.

Simulations allow a manager to experience the role of leader in realistic terms. Often in leadership development programs, simulations allow participants to examine their leadership styles while addressing strategic actions within teams. Such programs have been found to result in improved attitudes toward self-development and more effective transference of concepts into practice. The classroom setting provides an opportunity to debrief these behaviors and provide immediate feedback. The purpose of the debriefing is to gain self-awareness. How did the team function? How did each participant function and perform as part of the team? How were problems resolved? How were decisions made? The approach is inductive. Managers start by examining their own behavior in the simulation and then go on to lessons about leadership that they then can apply when back on the job.

This activity has proved to be an extremely effective way to induce behavioral change in individuals. Learning is an iterative process of action and reflection that takes place over time. In a business simulation, participants have the opportunity to gain valuable insight into their own behavior and discover areas that need improvement.

Action Learning

Action learning extends the learning process beyond the classroom walls by providing the opportunity to apply concepts learned in the classroom to an issue of major importance to the corporation. It places classroom training in context and enhances the transfer of skills and knowledge. In most leadership programs that incorporate action learning, participants bring an individual or team project they are working on to class to use as an example to which to apply newly learned skills and knowledge.

In many companies, the composition of the action learning team is structured so that team members represent different geographies, functions, and lines of business. On average, an action learning team has five to eight members. A typical team might have a marketing manager from Texas, a business development manager from Singapore, an engineer from Germany, a human resource manager from Illinois, and a quality director from Mexico. This mix reflects the nature of global work teams today, in which leaders no longer have the luxury of working with a team located in the same building or even the same country.

In all of the companies interviewed, participants did not choose their action learning project — the project was selected by a senior executive who then became the project sponsor. These senior executives were advised to select a strategic business issue that "kept them awake at night."

Here are some examples of typical action learning projects:

- Creating and establishing a pervasive brand identity and dominant market presence in China
- Developing a global supply chain management process
- Identifying the expectations of on-line shoppers and opportunities for competitive advantage in the "e-tail" experience

Prior to attending the program, the senior sponsor briefed the team on the nature of the project and the expected outcomes. Faculty with expertise in the area were available to the team as resources. Teams had to find time to make progress on the action learning project between the program sessions. Since the team's action learning project was in addition to each individual's regular managerial responsibilities, team members had to schedule conference calls and project review meetings over and above the normal work activities. This is consistent with the belief that outstanding leaders must find ways to achieve outcomes despite time and resource constraints.

In summary, the characteristics of a typical action learning experience include an emphasis on learning by doing, a team approach to learning, a focus on an actual and substantive company issue that puts participants into problem solver roles, and the requirement that the team learning is formalized into a presentation to senior management.

Leadership Development: A Systems Perspective

The most successful leadership development efforts in corporations take a systems approach that extends beyond the classroom experience. In these companies, leadership skills are augmented through

360-degree assessment and feedback, coaching, key development assignments, and mentoring.

360-Degree Assessment and Feedback

Assessment is a commonly shared element in the leadership development process of the companies studied. Corporations have taken to heart the idea that leaders must "know themselves." Because managers find themselves in multiple roles as bosses, subordinates, colleagues, and participants in client relationships, the use of 360-degree assessment provides managers with feedback from multiple levels in the corporation as well as from customers outside the company. Among the most commonly used assessment inventories are Benchmarks, a product of the Center for Creative Leadership, and Profilor, a family of assessment inventories developed by Personnel Decisions, Inc. for different levels of management.

Both the Center for Creative Leadership and Personnel Decisions, Inc., along with a number of other management consulting firms, offer professional, experienced consulting staff to work with individual managers to enable them to build on their strengths and identify their development needs. In some organizations, assessment precedes the design of the development program and drives the selection of the program content. In other instances, where the content of the program is driven by current business issues, assessment and coaching are used as parallel development initiatives.

Executive Coaching

Today, executive coaching is one of the most popular vehicles used for developing leaders. Coaching bridges the gap between what managers are being asked to do and what they have been trained to do. Managers use coaches to help employees understand the new work environment. As companies shift away from a traditional top-down, command-and-control organization structure, coaches teach managers how to motivate rather than command, as well as how to communicate with workers and elicit their opinions.

Managers at all levels, experiencing a void in mentoring and advising from inside the company, are enlisting coaches for guidance on how to improve their performance, boost profits, and make better decisions about everything from personnel to strategy. Organizations are so lean today that often managers do not have time for some of the traditional roles of advising, motivating, and training. "You're paid for what you produce, not for time you spend developing people," observes Karen Cates, assistant professor of organizational behavior at Northwestern's Kellogg Graduate School of Management (Morris, 2000, p. 146). The nature of work today differs so greatly from the past that you cannot turn to your gray-haired mentor and ask, "From your 30 years of experience, how does one handle a dot-com?" remarks Barry Mabry, a partner at Ernst & Young. "Nobody on earth has experienced this kind of business environment" (p. 146).

There is not much consensus about what kind of business experience or academic training qualifies someone to be a corporate coach. Coaches come from many different backgrounds. Some are organizational psychologists; other have backgrounds in consulting or sales. Rather than any type of credentialing, managers choose coaches primarily through word-of-mouth recommendations from colleagues.

Sun Microsystems pays particular attention to coaching its more than one hundred vice presidents in its Leadership Development Program. Each vice president's assessment profile is reviewed, and individual coaching is tailored to his or her needs. As Sun rapidly evolved from an entrepreneurial upstart into a $12 billion organization, executives found themselves in bigger jobs than they had ever imagined. Many of these executives had to be developed on the job through coaching.

Key Development Assignments

Although development is most commonly thought of as what occurs in training programs and much of what corporations describe as development takes place in the classroom, most of the development described by successful executives occurs through on-the-job experiences. In their groundbreaking study, *The Lessons of Experience*, McCall, Lombardo, and Morrison (1988) documented the power and effectiveness of job assignments as a tool for leadership development. In interviewing executives about events that had a significant impact on the way they lead and manage their companies, these executives described challenging experiences, which for the most part occurred outside the classroom.

As a result of this research, five kinds of job assignments were identified as having unique development opportunities: start-ups, turnarounds, leaps in scope, task-force assignments, and line-to staff switches. Each type of assignment teaches a unique set of skills. For instance, start-ups require a leader to bring something new into existence. The leader has to learn the art of identifying what is really important out of the myriad of tasks that need to be done and then how to select team members and organize them to get the job done. Often this is with minimal direction from above. By contrast, in a turnaround situation, the leader is sent in to fix an operation besieged with difficulties. Here the leader must work with demoralized and perhaps hostile or incompetent subordinates and untangle the complexities that underlie the faulty operation. From these experiences, leaders learn how to diagnose organizational problems, build or redesign control systems, and make tough decisions that inevitably result in human pain.

Unfortunately, using experience for development is not as simple as it may appear. When an organization has to quickly put a new start-up in place or confront a failing operation, it usually looks for someone who has successfully done that before, not someone for whom this is a learning experience. In other words, the pressures of the business tended to override the leadership development needs of the individual. Despite the obstacles, companies recognize that leadership skills are developed through certain experiences. No one is born knowing how to fix a troubled business or make the successful transition from a technical manager to a general manager. These skills are learned on the job, and successful companies provide both learning opportunities and on-the job-support for learning as an integral part of their leadership development process.

Mentoring

The lessons learned from relationships are an important balance to the lessons learned from assignments. If assignments teach what needs to be done in certain situations, it is from mentors that leaders learn to form the values that guide their actions. Through the process of mentoring, the norms and values of the organization are passed on to the new members.

As aspiring executives move into upper levels of the organization, there is another culture that they must be acquainted with— the culture of institutional leadership. In making the transition to senior management roles, managers must learn to think differently. Mentors can help ease this transition to senior management roles. The primary role of the mentor at this level is to help the rising manager develop his or her own vision. Mentors also provide immediate and practical help to their mentees in such areas as how to negotiate a union contract, the most humane way to close down a plant, or the best way to navigate the organization's informal political system.

Summary

Globalization, information technology, and the deregulation of markets have created a more volatile and more competitive business environment. Companies attempting to compete in this environment have recognized the need for talented leaders who are capable of driving large-scale organizational change. This has led to an explosion of interest in leadership development both in organizations and in business schools.

In the research conducted for this chapter, considerable overlap was found to exist in the content of the leadership development programs used by corporations and business schools. The leader as a strategic thinker, driver of change, person with a teachable point of view, coach, creator of culture, and driver for results are the focus of both university-based programs and those developed by corporations.

In terms of pedagogy, university programs are still more centered on lectures and case studies, while corporate programs place greater emphasis on business simulations, action learning and assessment, and coaching. University-based programs, with a focus on the individual, can be viewed as a broadening experience and a way of preparing individuals for positions of senior leadership in the corporation.

Company programs are more tied to the unique needs of the corporation. For example, GE uses the leadership development programs at Crotonville to transform the organization. Motorola uses the Global Organization and Leadership Development Program to address key business issues the company faces. Ford uses leadership development to drive change within the organization. The individual is developed in support of organizational goals. All of the company programs took a systems approach, going beyond the classroom experience to build skills through job assignments, mentoring, and coaching.

The development of future leaders continues to be a challenge faced by all successful organizations. As the pace of change continues to increase, the need for leadership at all levels grows more critical. No single approach to leadership development is best; the combination of dimensions and the relative weight given to each dimension vary with the needs of the organization and change over time. Likewise, the leadership development field is not static; it is always changing and incorporating new concepts and applications in response to changes in the marketplace. Perhaps the best approach to developing future leaders is to continually reexamine leadership development efforts in light of best practices in corporations and groundbreaking research at the top-ranking business schools.

References

Collins, J. C., and Porras, J. I. "Building Your Company's Vision." *Harvard Business Review*, Sept.-Oct. 1996, pp. 65–78.

Deal, T. E., and Kennedy, A. A. *The New Corporate Cultures: Revitalizing the Workplace After Downsizing, Mergers, and Reengineering.* Reading, Mass: Perseus Books, 1999.

Goldsmith, M. "Coaching for Behavioral Change." In M. Goldsmith, L. Lyons, and A. Freas (eds.), *Coaching for Leadership.* San Francisco: Jossey-Bass/Pfeiffer, 2000.

Linkage, Inc. *Linkage, Inc.'s Best Practices in Leadership Development Handbook.* San Francisco: Jossey-Bass/Pfeiffer, 2001.

McCall, M. W., Jr., Lombardo, M. M., and Morrison, A. M. *The Lessons of Experience: How Successful Executives Develop on the Job.* New York: Free Press, 1988.

Morris, B. "So You're a Player. Do You Need a Coach?" *Fortune*, Feb. 21, 2000, pp. 144–151.

Tichy, N., with Cohen, E. *The Leadership Engine: How Winning Companies Build Leaders at Every Level.* New York: HarperBusiness, 1997.

Wetlaufer, S. "Driving Change: An Interview with Ford Motor Company's Jacques Nasser." *Harvard Business Review*, Mar.-Apr. 1999, pp. 76-88.

Chapter Five

Professional Military Education

A Serious Enterprise for Leaders

Robert C. Hughes, Richard Haney

No profession in the United States values education and professional development more highly than the military or puts more of its resources there. This emphasis begins in the first days of the enlisted person's experience, as it does with officers, and it continues for the entire period of his or her service, be it a few years or an entire career. Here we shall focus on officers, however, and shall select from the educational strategies designed for them those aspects of military training that may be equally useful in preparing men and women to be principals of schools from kindergarten through the twelfth grade.

An interlaced system prepares officers at every level, from cadet to general, building strengths and skills one step at a time. Such an ambitious system must be elaborate, of course, and substantial bureaucracies are needed to administer it. Nonetheless, it is equally important that the system remain flexible and robust, or it will fail the people it proposes to engage. Each new commander brings unique perspectives and skills, just as new teachers and classes of students do, and as people constantly move from staff and operational assignments to directed study and back again, their practical experiences help keep the programs fresh and relevant to the tasks they will expect to perform in the field.

Six features of military education and skills training are particularly germane to the challenge of preparing school principals:

1. Ideally, the system evaluates a person's potential for leadership, provides the education to realize that potential, and then measures performance in order to determine how far and fast he or she advances. Obviously, no two experiences will be exactly the same, even when they are equally successful, but the arc from first to last is roughly similar.

2. People are given responsibilities and attain ranks that correspond to their experience and education. Each level builds on competencies developed in the preceding level and employs an evolving mixture of professional learning, leadership opportunities, and work, whether done individually or in groups.

3. When everything works as it should, the training and education programs are geared to the particular tasks and missions that service personnel will encounter professionally. Some ways of learning are more useful than others in reaching certain given objectives, just as different people learn in different ways. But mentoring by the profession's "graybeards" is usually effective, and so is role playing. Case studies in the classroom can provide the basis for investigating the ways decisions present themselves and judgments are made. Situations of ever-increasing complexity can be used to initiate students into the process of exploring more and more intricate problems and learning how to go about breaking them into their various components and ultimately solving them. Students will eventually find their own levels, and only the most astute and determined will be able to reach the heights of synthesis and evaluation. Nonetheless, valuable experiences will be gained along the way, and flashes of insight and truly fresh thinking invariably depend on the hard analytical work that has preceded them.

4. The entire educational system is subject to constant review and periodic recertification. Sometimes this is done by academic accrediting agencies, sometimes by organizations within the Joint Chiefs of Staff or even by committees of Congress. Always the key questions are whether the system is achieving its stated objectives and whether it is meeting its approved standards.

5. Accountability is the system's watchword and applies at every level, from the Joint Chiefs to the basic programs of instruction and the teachers responsible for them.

6. Finally, the key to success rests always with the individual officer. He or she is responsible for taking advantage of what the system offers, for seeking new opportunities and accomplishing ever more difficult tasks, and for performing well and getting results. From this process our leaders emerge.

A congratulatory letter like the one in Exhibit 5.1 is commonly received by an officer when he or she is promoted or has performed well in a given assignment. It demonstrates how closely senior officers connect promotion with education, as well as how clearly promotion is about the possibilities of the future as much as it is about the accomplishments of the past. Furthermore, performance is imagined primarily in terms of leadership, the ability to communicate, and a mastery of problem-solving techniques.

In fact, we want to underscore the truth that leadership is by no means the exclusive province of senior officers. Quite the contrary, it is critical also at the initial stages of officer education. The Army and the Marine Corps, in particular, operate on the assumption that leadership skills can and therefore must be taught early, and so leadership training assumes an important place in the cadets' formative years in every service academy. While academics are often tapped to "teach" leadership to individuals from a theoretical point of view, in military training programs at places like the Air Force Academy, officers design field exercises that reinforce various concepts of leadership, among other ways by emphasizing team building. They may also draw on historical examples of "great captains," and of course they themselves model leadership as they mentor the cadets.

In the pages that follow, we shall examine the ways military education links education and promotion to leadership and management, tracing their evolution from the beginning of a career through years of service up to retirement. At the same time, we

Exhibit 5.1. Congratulatory Letter.

DEPARTMENT OF THE AIR FORCE
HEADQUARTERS UNITED STATES AIR FORCE
WASHINGTON, D.C.

Captain Robert C. Hughes   16 JUN 1980
AF/XOXLL

Dear Captain Hughes

Your recent promotion to Major and selection for Intermediate
Service School is indicative both of your past performance and a
measure of your future potential. I wish you continued success
and many more years of distinguished Air Force service.

My warmest congratulations to you and Mrs. Hughes on this
important occasion.

Sincerely

CHARLES A. GABRIEL, Lt Gen, USAF
Deputy Chief of Staff
Operations, Plans and Readiness

shall highlight the "best practices" that are equally germane to producing school principals who can lead their faculties; oversee the development of high-quality curricula; marshal, manage, and apply their available resources effectively; and perform their duties at a high level of excellence.

Leadership and Management

Leadership and management skills are obviously central to the military system, focusing as the system does on preventing war at the same time it educates people to prepare for, prosecute, and terminate war. A high percentage of the men and women selected to be officers are already well educated, and a striking proportion of their careers will then be devoted to further education and training. Typically, officers spend between a quarter and a third of their time in schools, either as students or as instructors, but when we add less formal kinds of training like self-development projects, that figure may well increase to half.

From start to finish, the system is designed to develop leadership. For example, in its Policy Directive 36-23 on military education, the Air Force asserts that its programs "improve warfighting knowledge and skills and prepare officers to assume higher levels of command, staff, and operational duties and responsibilities." Only the best-qualified officers are chosen for advanced training, and the highest standards prevail.

Fundamental questions are periodically revisited. For instance, are managers and leaders the same? Are leaders made or born? The answers to such questions are the keys to shaping the military's approaches to developing and advancing future leaders. But terms like *leadership* and *management* clearly overlap, even though *leadership* typically denotes one person's influence on others while *management* refers to marshaling and administering resources.

The Department of Defense currently defines management inclusively as "a process of establishing and attaining objectives to carry out responsibilities. . . . Management consists of those continuing actions of planning, organizing, directing, coordinating, controlling, and evaluating the use of men, money, materials, and facilities to accomplish missions and tasks."

Management is therefore somewhat broader than leadership, in that it deals with people as well as other resources. As a 1988 Defense Department pamphlet, *The Armed Forces Officer*, puts it, "People are led, and things are managed. . . . Management, like politics, is the art of consensus and accommodation to the possible. Leadership is the art of creating a willing followership for a common cause that may appear impossible. An Armed Forces officer will find need of both skills. Only a few will become 'great captains,' but all can be 'leaders.'"

No definition of leadership prevails across the military spectrum, and even within one service, definitions may vary. In 1948, for instance, the Army called leadership "the art of influencing human behavior through ability to directly influence people and direct them toward a specific goal." More recently, however, it officially defined leadership as "influencing people—by providing purpose, direction, and motivation—while operating to accomplish the mission and improving the organization."

The conclusion, however, is that leadership makes success possible, however success may be defined in each particular instance. Officers lead their subordinates and staffs, and junior officers are commonly expected to train sergeants and petty officers below them. Except in purely technical specialties, leadership skills determine selection and advancement.

Therefore, the military answers the question "Are leaders made or born?" by concluding that they are both: most people have some innate leadership qualities, and these can be developed and improved. *The Armed Forces Officer* states, in fact, that the military "will provide ample opportunity for both academic and hands-on development. Being a junior officer involves primarily learning, developing skills, and being afforded the opportunity to demonstrate enough proficiency and knowledge to be given greater responsibility." At the same time, not everyone can be a leader, and the Marine Corps' mission flatly states that "those who do not show the potential to develop the leadership qualities we have come to expect of Marine officers must not be commissioned."

Of all the services, the Army has perhaps the most fully articulated program for developing leaders, and its model is grounded on three interlocking pillars:

1. *Institutional training and education.* Progressive courses instruct officers in the skills, knowledge, and requisite abilities to capture leadership positions in Army organizations. School commandants are responsible for designing and developing curricula to support this overall goal.

2. *Operational assignments.* Experience in staff positions allows Army officers to be proactive and to hone their skills at the same time they are broadening their experiences and preparing themselves for increasing responsibilities. Commanders are charged with setting an example for their subordinates while inspiring and guiding them. Many conduct more formal programs that involve reading and study and offer certification, and their assessment of junior leaders commonly helps the latter improve their performance while identifying those most likely to advance to the highest levels.

3. *Self-development.* All officers are expected to maximize their strengths as leaders, minimize their weaknesses, and continually assess themselves to measure their progress. Commanders, peers, and even subordinates can offer feedback that will assist this process. Leaders are expected to seek increasingly challenging assignments and to develop personal plans for self-improvement.

For optimal success, all institutional leadership training and education must, of course, be integrated with operational and staff assignments, as well as with individual plans for self-development.

Officer Professional Military Education

The single most important document to set out the overall objectives, policies, and responsibilities for officer professional military education is the March 1, 1996, Chairman of the Joint Chiefs of Staff's Instruction 1800.01.[1] Overriding the different services' individual systems, no matter how comprehensive, this document defines objectives and specifies "the fundamental responsibilities of the major educational participants in achieving those goals."

It focuses specifically on "jointness"— on requirements for the "broad, multi-service education for U.S. military leadership." Here the Chairman formulates policies designed to coordinate and integrate the armed services' military education and training programs. Furthermore, it specifies the standards to be achieved and the subject matter to be mastered, lists procedures that will ensure the highest-quality education, explains the review and certification process, and describes the charter and mission of the Chairman's own National Defense University as well as its components. Finally, it offers guidance to both students and faculty members who make up the learning communities in each institution.

The document assumes that joint professional military education is a careerlong effort and focuses primarily on the intermediate and senior levels, which is to say on ranks major through colonel— a period that may include a career span of ten to thirty total years of active duty. It also underscores the significance of leadership across the spectrum, from precommissioning through the intermediate grades to senior levels, emphasizing each service's responsibility to bring its officers to the level of responsibility where the need for interservice cooperation becomes obvious. That is to say, each officer must become proficient as an airman, sailor, soldier, or marine and master a whole range of appropriate skills before he or she reaches the level of intermediate and senior education. Needless to say, the requisite training for specialties within each service, such as the infantry or artillery, is complex and demanding. For example, officers must be prepared for command positions; specialists in nuclear weapons, submarine warfare, and biochemical defense must be highly educated; and foreign-language instruction, to be effective, may take several years of intensive work. (Exhibit 5.2 illustrates a typical career path for an infantry officer in the Army, indicating his or her rank, formal schooling, and operational assignments.)

Above all, however, the Chairman underscores the importance of the mentor role, insisting that "officers share responsibility for ensuring the continued growth of themselves and others." More and more, the services emphasize mentoring as an instructional methodology. At the Air Force Command and Control Training and Innovation Group in Florida, for instance, as well as at Air

Exhibit 5.2. Typical Career Path for an Army Infantry Officer.

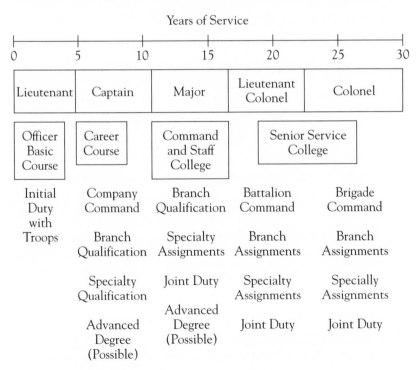

Years of Service

0	5	10	15	20	25	30

Lieutenant	Captain	Major	Lieutenant Colonel	Colonel

Officer Basic Course	Career Course	Command and Staff College	Senior Service College

Initial Duty with Troops	Company Command	Branch Qualification	Battalion Command	Brigade Command
	Branch Qualification	Specialty Assignments	Branch Assignments	Branch Assignments
	Specialty Qualification	Joint Duty	Specialty Assignments	Specially Assignments
	Advanced Degree (Possible)	Advanced Degree (Possible)	Joint Duty	Joint Duty

University in Alabama, newly retired general officers with a storehouse of experience are brought in to teach courses for a week or two at a time.

Finally, the Chairman establishes a mandate for close coordination between the training and education communities in order to focus on common goals and "develop the best possible leadership for the U.S. Armed Forces." One link between these two communities is the Universal Joint Task List, which specifies functions that "might have to be performed by a joint force."

The interconnectedness of the military education system is so basic that it is often spoken of as having a "strategy-to-task" grounding. Important but implicit connections between theory and practice, between knowing and doing, are often not articulated and over the years may in fact have been lost. They are, however, fundamentally important to the military itself and to the aspects of it that may be germane to developing principals who can lead their schools to increasingly impressive levels of achievement.

Framework for Officer Professional Military Education

The Chairman of the Joint Chief's Instruction includes a three-level framework for officer military education. The primary level includes lieutenants and captains; the intermediate focuses on majors; and the senior, on lieutenant colonels and colonels. At each level, the principal focus is calibrated on the major levels of war—tactical, operational, and strategic; the progressive and sequential flow from simpler to more complex tasks; and the distinctions between individual service schools and joint schools like the National War College.

For the purposes of this discussion, we want to underscore once again the fact that the entire military system is composed of smaller interlocking systems, and Exhibit 5.2 demonstrates the essentials of intensive, sequential, and progressive education. The primary stage proceeds from accession through the first five years of service; the intermediate stage generally affects majors with ten to fifteen years of service; and the senior, lieutenant colonels and colonels with fifteen to twenty-two years of service. For the most part, each level is linked closely to the relevant leadership responsibilities and a pattern of gradual advancement based on accumulating skills.

There are significant variations, of course, between individuals, as between different career paths and the separate services. The Navy, for instance, seems to put less stock in mandating sequential levels of military education on the basis of an officer's grade and on occasion in the early 1990s sent very junior officers to senior war colleges. Furthermore, it shows little reluctance to pull officers from schools to undertake operational assignments.

As another variation, a major who receives an early promotion to lieutenant colonel or the equivalent in the sea services may never attend the intermediate-level school with a curriculum designed for majors. Over the past twenty years, the Air Force has periodically insisted on sending its "best" lieutenant colonels and colonels to the Air War College at the Air University rather than to the National War College or the Industrial College of the Armed Forces at Fort McNair — the foremost joint colleges in the system. At other times, however, there has been no such pattern.

Courses at the primary level may vary from nine to forty-three weeks, depending on the service, for the duration and curricula of the different primary-level schools have been less standardized than they are at the higher levels. Indeed, the Chairman's Program for Joint Education begins seriously only at the intermediate level. Nevertheless, the emphasis on leadership and management remains constant, since leaders who don't begin to develop early are likely not to develop at all.

Student Selection and Mix

On the one hand, each service has its own policies and procedures to choose students for its own schools at whatever level. Each also decides who will go to the other services' schools, to joint schools, to academic programs at selected colleges and universities, and to international institutions like the NATO Defense College in Rome. On the other hand, the Chairman requires that seminars in individual service programs include "at least one officer from each of the two nonhost Military Departments." For example, seminars at the College of Naval Command and Staff at Newport, Rhode Island, should include at least one Air Force officer and one Army officer. At senior-level colleges, at least 20 percent of the student body should be made up of nonhost officers. In addition, provisions have been made to include international students as well as civilians from the Department of Defense and other government agencies.

Student-Faculty Ratios

Congressional interest in the late 1980s and early 1990s spurred the military schools to maintain excellent student-to-faculty ratios. At the intermediate level, the goal is four students to each member of the faculty, while at the senior level, the goal is a ratio of 3.5 to one. When the faculty are experienced and highly qualified, the students have exceptional access to superior learning.

Active Learning

The military education system emphasizes the virtues of active learning, by which we generally mean seminar discussions, role playing, case studies, joint projects, war game exercises, simulations, oral presentations, research and writing, and regional studies overseas in selected schools. Lectures, however, do not have to be passive experiences, and the best ones are anything but that.

Especially over the past ten years or so, the military has hired civilian faculty members with excellent research backgrounds as well as teaching skills, and such men and women have enhanced the quality of its overall faculty. Many teachers at senior institutions like the National War College come from a variety of government agencies, a fact that has also helped diminish the need to bring in outside lecturers: since the 1970s, the number of lecturers has dropped from nearly two hundred annually to about ninety at National. Nonetheless, Washington, D.C., is home not only to the federal government but also to many experts in foreign and security affairs at think tanks, as well as foundations, and it only makes sense to take advantage of the very best talent available for lectures and guest seminars.

The National War College

The National War College, also known simply as National, was founded in 1946; its sister college, the Industrial College of the Armed Forces (ICAF), was founded in 1924. Both are components of the National Defense University at Fort Lesley J. McNair, the oldest active Army post in continuous existence, and together they represent the pinnacle of the professional military education system. Large numbers of their military and civilian graduates have held or now hold high diplomatic, military, and political leadership positions both in this country and abroad. More important for our purposes, however, is that the ways these institutions approach teaching may be applicable to the education of school principals in the United States.

National's mission has not essentially changed in more than fifty years. Noting that its graduates would most likely exercise great influence over national and foreign policy in both peace and war, the board president who recommended that the college be established explained that it would be "concerned with grand strategy and the utilization of the national resources necessary to implement that strategy." In restating its mission for the twenty-first century, again the institution emphasized the preparation of future leaders, whether for the armed forces, the State Department, or other civilian agencies. Leadership, after all, is the exercise of great influence over human endeavor in whatever field.

The curriculum and teaching practices at ICAF are somewhat different from those at National, for it focuses, by mandate of the Chairman, "on the resource component of national power, with special emphasis on materiel acquisition, joint logistics, and their integration into national security strategy for peace and war." Historically, ICAF's approach to senior leadership development has therefore been more direct, detailed, and discrete than National's.

The ICAF core course on strategic leadership and decision making has been complemented by opportunities for the student body, their families, and the faculty to undertake self-assessments as well as to engage in a self-directed program of executive development. Students who get to ICAF are already highly motivated and developed as leaders, of course, and to prepare for their next ten or fifteen years of service, they take a candid inventory of their skills and strengths.

Early in the academic year, students are presented with a series of tools to assess their strengths and weaknesses and to determine their behavioral preferences. Test instruments like the Myers-Briggs Type Indicator and the Strategic Leader Development Inventory help students do their own assessments. Subsequently, they explore possibilities of steps they might take in various areas, either to become more aware of their own ways of doing things or to strengthen good points or modify aspects of their behavior with which they are not wholly satisfied. At the same time, at both National and ICAF, students do rigorous exercises and take treadmill tests and medical exams to obtain a personal physical profile. Ample opportunities are provided for students to discuss and undertake changes in their diet, to learn how to stop smoking, and to try different ways of managing stress more effectively. Each student is encouraged to formulate "individual plans to guide their development" during the school year and beyond and to build into those plans periodic future reviews.

The National War College, by contrast, has steadily deemphasized the development of executive skills in its program as a whole and since the early 1990s has relegated such skills assessment to the periphery. Working on the assumption that its students have already taken similar inventories and made necessary accommodations in forging their personal leadership styles, National focuses more effort on decision making at the highest levels of government. This focus requires that students understand the role that policy plays or can play, explore the intricacies of bureaucratic politics, study various kinds of dominant leadership personalities, examine the components of raw power, and engage in sustained rational deliberations on the nature and application of natural power.

Seminars analyze examples of leadership within specific decision-making contexts. The curriculum proceeds from beginning to end, or "strategy to task," to examine what senior leaders might be called on to do as they conceptualize, implement, and evaluate policy while operating in conjunction with others. In the process, students explore ways they might refine their own capacities to act at the highest levels within their own specialties. In short, National regards leadership more as an art than as a science, while ICAF approaches leadership more nearly like a business process.

The core curriculum at both colleges introduces students to a variety of leadership roles simply by way of the faculty's choice of adult methods of learning. Seminars typically have about thirteen students, for instance, who are reshuffled five times a year into different seminars, exposing each student to approximately one-third of the study body in such settings. Each seminar has a student leader, and students introduce the lecturers, lead discussions, and from time to time give briefings. At one time or another, each student plays various principal and subordinate roles while doing case studies, projects, and exercises.

Twice a year, both National and ICAF hold a special ceremony to acknowledge the best essays a faculty committee has selected from those submitted to it and takes notice of whatever special research or other outstanding work has been done during that period. The War College publicly awards five to eight seminal books to each winner of its writing contest — an exercise that is part of its ongoing effort to foster a lifetime of reading, professional development, and personal enrichment.

Lessons for K–12 School Principals

Two aspects of the National War College lend themselves particularly to the preparation of school principals: its organization and the structure of its curriculum. As for the former, its commandant has typically been a two-star general or admiral, while the dean of faculty and academic programs is a colonel or the equivalent with strong academic credentials. Although the commandant is responsible for the success of the entire college, he serves best in a mentoring and supportive role to the deans, the faculty, and the students. The operation of the college itself rests largely with the dean of students; the educational program, with the dean of faculty. The commandant assumes the primary role, however, in external relations outside the college and with the university and its president, who is a three-star general or admiral. This ordering of responsibilities has stood the test of more than five decades at National while variously gifted people of uneven caliber as commandants and deans have occupied each position. The structure survives because it is simple and its leadership parts can be held accountable, and therefore it may provide a paradigm of governance for K–12 schools.

The second remarkable dimension of the National War College that may be useful in preparing school principals is the structure of its curriculum. Each student takes a set of core courses, usually in the mornings, and supplements these with electives that are generally offered in the afternoons. (Ideally, no student should have more than thirteen hours a week of "seat time," time spent attending lectures, seminars, and electives.) The core consists of several large interwoven blocks of study that provide a grounding in national security strategy. This includes a section on international economics, a study of joint force capabilities, a review of the foundations of military thought and strategy, an analysis of the national security policy process, a survey of regional analyses and methodologies, and preparation in overseas studies programs.

Like military officers, principals in executive development programs should have a solid core curriculum. At the same time, a program of special courses tailored to the kinds of schools they may lead or expect to lead would be nearly as valuable, for elementary schools will be different from high schools, just as those in rural areas will be different from urban or suburban schools and large schools will differ from small ones. Finally, special needs schools are in a category of their own. Fundamental to every educational venture we've described, however, is the fact that commitment and passion can determine the success of any serious enterprise.

Self-Development and Assessment

Self-development programs for officers in each service vary in design but not in intent, for each officer is responsible for increasing his or her value to the institution. Self-assessment, for the most part, is an informal and continuous process that depends on feedback from superiors, peers, and subordinates, and it is an important tool to which the Army, for one, refers as "the key to success." Unit inspections, organization exercises, and other officers' performance of assigned missions give each officer opportunities for comparison and therefore the chance to see how his or her leadership measures up.

Based on that self-assessment, officers design their own plans for reinforcing strengths, remediating weaknesses, and achieving professional goals. These plans typically include professional development reading programs, in which books and articles published by senior military officers and leaders in other fields play a large role. They may also feature correspondence courses or off-duty civilian schooling, which the service often pays for. Finally, officers keen to advance will almost certainly seek challenging assignments and increasingly demanding responsibilities.

Recommendations on the Preparation of Principals

Certain interlocking institutional parts are indispensable to a strategy for grooming effective leaders, no matter what the job, and these include a clear and progressive system of professional preparation, a regular program for performance assessment, and a strong, coherent promotion system.

Any professional development system *must* be designed in relation to the specific missions and tasks its participants can expect to confront and the results they hope to attain. To keep a system focused on its objectives, it will need a process of frequent review and recertification, and accountability should be the watchword throughout. Everything depends on the individual who aggressively works at self-development, engages seriously in programs of instruction, completes progressively complex assignments, gets results, and continually improves his or her leadership skills. Finally, the measures of success and failure must be clear.

We do not believe that the military system itself always lives up to these unforgiving goals, especially in relation to performance appraisals. Both the preparation of warriors and the education of children depend, however, on such appraisals' being taken with the utmost seriousness. To prepare principals of K–12 schools, we draw on our military experience to recommend the following:

1. *Establish a national task force of subject-matter experts to make strategy-to-task analyses of the common functions expected of K–12 principals.* The military equivalent is the Universal Joint Task List, which analysts use to create a master training guide.

2. *Create a plan of instruction based on a master list of tasks that a principal must perform.* A plan of instruction is created on the basis of the master training guide that sets out topics and methods of teaching appropriate to the required areas. With this plan in mind, curriculum developers then create lesson plans that teachers and trainers will turn into instruction, whether in schools or as part of distance learning programs. A combination of self-development processes, schoolhouse studies, and distance learning courses may be ideal for principals. The prime focus must be on the school's mission, a high-quality curriculum, a competent faculty, and the particular needs of the specific learning community. (A new and revised structure should relieve the principal of obligations toward

the physical plant, student affairs, security, and mundane administrative tasks.)

3. *Involve a small number of universities in this process, or even better, create a model institution to demonstrate what is possible to the education community and its related bureaucracies.*

4. *Examine the organizational structure of professional military schools like the National War College for applicable models and useful lessons.* We are not suggesting that there could be a wholesale application of all features.

5. *Develop a national standard for a principal's career path, moving, perhaps, from classroom teacher to committee chair, from department chair to assistant principal, and finally to principal.* This progression should include a number of sabbaticals of six to twelve months, during which the aspiring or sitting principal goes into industry, business, or the public sector to discover new ways of doing things and to assess other priorities. (The system may lose some good principals this way, but the gains outweigh the risks.) In our opinion, such a program can be most effectively tried at the state level or in the more than fourteen thousand school districts.

6. *Establish a formal mentoring program at the school district and the state level, looking particularly to retired school principals to act as mentors.*

7. *Set up a national certification program to make the objectives and standards of professional development for principals clear and measurable in order that they may be met.*

8. *Create at the district level a suggested reading list for principals, and hold professional development sessions with the superintendent on the materials read.*

9. *Where necessary, revise the annual principal appraisal process to emphasize leadership and management skills and to stress the importance of ranking leadership potential in teacher evaluations.*

Professionals share distinctive qualities and commitments, whether they are military officers or school principals. Among these are a devotion to learning and free inquiry, an ability to perform characteristically with excellence, and a belief in improving and enriching the lives of others through their leadership. Above all, they have both passion and reason involved in all that they do.

Note

1. Instruction 1800.01 has been revised since this chapter was written.

Chapter Six

Models of Preparation for the Professions

Implications for Educational Leadership

Gary Sykes
with Cheryl King and Jeannie Patrick

This chapter explores trends in education for the professions as one basis for rethinking the preparation of school leaders. The American version of professionalism features a unitary model with three elements: a body or base of expert knowledge around which to rationalize practice; a code of service that requires the professional to place the interests of client, patient, or service recipient ahead of self-interest; and a primary role for the guild or professional reference group in regulating practice and conduct. While this general model has had pervasive influence in American society from the Progressive Era onward, it has evolved in a variety of profession-specific ways within those occupations that have sought the professional designation. In particular, the nature of expertise and the means of inculcating practitioners with requisite knowledge, skills, and dispositions varies in important ways across such fields as law, medicine, engineering, and the ministry. While these and other professions share certain characteristics such as the central importance of the university-based professional school, they differ in significant particulars and so constitute a rich set of cases for study.

Our analysis begins by examining the problem of school leadership, placing preparation into a larger set of issues. Next we introduce some assumptions that must accompany any descriptions or prescriptions about professional preparation. We then explore four frameworks for professional preparation, followed by the range of available alternatives for managing the transition from study to practice. Next review contemporary innovations in professional preparation, looking at how various fields have attempted to reform their approaches, and conclude with implications of the analysis for the preparation of school leaders.

For this analysis, we focused on the professions of medicine, engineering, law, architecture, the ministry, and business.[1] We reviewed the literature, contacted professional associations for their newsletters and journals, examined Web sites for information, and interviewed selected professional educators. In many instances, reforms in professional education have been stimulated by grants from the Fund for the Improvement of Post-Secondary Education (FIPSE), with individual schools and institutions introducing new approaches.

Any curriculum is defined as much by what it leaves out as by what it includes, because the knowledge and experience regarded as useful preparation inevitably exceed the time available to provide them. This generalization holds as true for English literature in the liberal arts sequence as for the rudiments of medical or legal practice. Reform of professional education in all fields is a dialectical process in which initial attempts to codify knowledge and establish training routines provoke criticisms about what has been overlooked or underrepresented, which in turn stimulate new developments. We frame this dialectic in terms of four models. We illustrate how each of the fields we examined embraced one or another of those models and then initiated reforms by turning, often implicitly, to the omitted models. The challenge for leadership preparation in education, then, is to effect a workable synthesis among these models that draws on the strengths and advantages of each, rather than selecting one or another as the dominant approach.

At the same time, use of the word *synthesis* glides over a defining tension in program development — the tension between breadth and depth. As we will see, criticisms often chastise coverage models of curriculum for neglecting the depth dimensions of learning, particularly when learning requires transfer to new situations and applications in novel and fluid contexts. These design challenges bear with similar force on all complex fields, not least leadership preparation in education.

Defining the Problem of Educational Leadership

The problem of educational leadership may be framed in terms of inadequate preparation for the role, but that is not the only alternative under discussion. This chapter concentrates on improvements in preparation as one means of addressing the problem of school leadership, but at the outset we acknowledge other ways of framing the problem. Multiple strategies may be needed that include but extend beyond reforms in preparation. We can discern at least four other problem frames in the reform discourse: role restructuring, rewards, personnel management, and nontraditional recruitment.

Role Restructuring

The principalship today may be unmanageable as constructed (see Sykes and Elmore, 1989). According to this frame, the task is not to prepare individuals for impossible work but to alter the role and work environment so that individuals may succeed and find satisfaction in the job. Some observers argue that the demands on the job have escalated to such an extent that without superhuman effort and ability, the job has become unworkable. Listen for a moment to a veteran elementary school principal reflecting on the qualities needed in her work. The scene is a university classroom for a graduate course on school administration taken by aspiring principals. She writes:

The professor is making his list of the qualities of a good principal. The eager aspirants are giving input. Democratic, visionary, decisive, energetic, calm, dispassionate, objective, approachable, intelligent, firm, supportive, honest, organized, disciplined, friendly, healthy, courageous, having a sense of humor, broad liberal education, excellent management skills, knowledgeable about the latest research in education, good judge of character, able to relate to students, imaginative, creative, clear-thinking, wise, determined, patient, kind, respecting . . . [Carmichael, 1985, p. 312].

She is coteaching this course with the professor, and as she watches him scribble this list on the board, she reports:

I suddenly felt a wave of electrical panic flow through my body. My God! That list is horrendous! I hardly have any of these qualities. I have some of them, but only some of the time. Tomorrow it would be my turn to present myself before the class and impart information about the "good" school administrator. Six months from now I would return from sabbatical to my school and faculty and have to play this administrator role. Role, hell; it was a suit of armor [p. 312].

Such testimony will resonate with many school principals. The role is a suit of armor protecting the principal, perhaps, but weighing her down, rendering her inflexible and slow to respond. As the multiple demands proliferate and intensify—building manager, instructional leader, buffer to the external environment, entrepreneur and fundraiser, central office subordinate, policy implementer, community organizer, service broker—it may be that role restructuring rather than (or in conjunction with) reformed preparation will be necessary.

Rewards

The rewards of the job may no longer compensate for its demands and stresses. Working hours have increased, salaries have compressed relative to teachers and other education workers, and the pressures to produce instant, measurable results have intensified dramatically. Just as teacher shortages across the country call forth salary increases as the most direct response in a labor market, it may be that substantial salary increases and other rewards for principals will be necessary to attract a requisite supply of highly qualified individuals.

Personnel Management

District processes of recruitment, selection, induction, and continuing education may not adequately identify, groom, and support school principals in their work. Today, for example, teacher professional development is widely regarded as a critical ingredient of educational reform. If school principals are the chief agents of school improvement, why would *their* development not be a vital issue for human resource management? Likewise, if moves are made to increase the pool of applicants via enhanced rewards, the identification of promising administrators becomes critical. For example, how important is evidence of exemplary teaching or of leadership in teaching as a prerequisite to administrative leadership? Is this factor equally important at elementary and secondary levels? And how good are districts at managing initial induction, mentoring, and evaluation of new principals?

Nontraditional Recruitment

Regulatory restrictions to entry may prevent talented individuals from other walks of life from becoming principals. According to this view, managerial expertise is broadly generalizable. Potential recruits may be available in industry, the military, and elsewhere but cannot gain entry without undertaking cumbersome reeducation due to state and district restrictions. This frame questions whether school leadership is inextricably bound to deep knowledge of education grounded in classroom practice. Programs that waive requirements in order to attract nontraditional entrants may be worth pursuing because the relationship between prior educational experience and school leadership is ambiguous and contested.

A comprehensive approach to the problem of school leadership will depend on how that problem is defined. Arguably, though, reformed preparation is one strategy for improvement, which is unlikely alone to produce large effects without change on other fronts.

Assumptions Underlying Program Design

Three issues logically arise prior to questions about program design for educational leadership. Or to put this another way, program designs depend on assumptions about these issues.

1. *Goals of leadership.* What are the aims or goals of education around which leadership takes shape? What we can note generally is that the goals of education and hence of educational leadership are plural, contested, and in conflict with one another. They include public and collective aims such as education for democracy and citizenship, for contributions to economic prosperity, for justice and greater equity, and (arguably) for multicultural understanding, acceptance, and amity. They include private and individual aims for liberal and vocational learning, for social and economic advancement, and for continued learning. We would argue, then, that one requirement for program design is to be clear about its stance toward the aims of education and of leadership.

2. *Nature of practice.* Program designs also rely on assumptions about the nature of administrative practice. What is the work for which preparation is offered? Here too are a variety of choices. For example, analysts commonly distinguish management from leadership, calling for greater attention to the latter (see, for example, Bolman and Deal, 1994). Other commentators, however, have argued that elementary competence is a neglected virtue. Good leadership is associated as strongly with doing a lot of little things well as with heroic visions (see March, 1978, who memorably described school administration as "a train schedule with footnotes by Kierkegaard"). Again, it is incumbent on program designers to

surface their assumptions about the nature of the role and of the work as a basis for preparation.

3. *Theories of learning.* Program designs also depend on assumptions about the nature of professional learning. How is the practice of leadership learned? William James famously noted that theories of teaching cannot be derived from theories of learning, but programs build in assumptions about how learning takes place that can be more or less explicit, more or less formalized within some body of theory. The theory-into-practice database, for example, contains descriptions of fifty theories relevant to human learning and instruction. The literature on professional education is filled with references to ideas derived from Vygotsky, Dewey, Gardner, Bruner, and others. New developments in cognitive psychology, particularly associated with the varieties of constructivism (Phillips, 1995; Sfard, 1998) and with adult learning, offer promising leads for the design of instructional environments and activities. Part of what drives reform in professional education are developments in our understanding of human learning that have rich implications for instruction. Rigorous program design calls for theoretical anchoring in some set of assumptions about the nature of learning even when, as Schwab (1978) argued, programs draw eclectically on multiple principles.

Elements of Program Design

A complete treatment of program design treats five sets of influences, each involving complex choices and trade-offs. These are the content of the curriculum, instructional formats and methods, program features, institutional arrangements, and regulatory framework. We wish to concentrate on the second of these influences but shall comment briefly on each.

Program Content. The matter to be learned constitutes the first building block of a program, and the field of educational administration has developed several versions of content that may be represented in topics, standards, assessment matrices, and other textual devices. In the appendix to this chapter, we present two prominent versions of content: one developed by the National Association of Elementary School Principals (1997) and the other developed by the National Policy Board for Educational Administration (Thomson, 1993). These tours of the knowledge terrain can be formidable. The latter document, for example, presents twenty-one domains in 550 pages as developed by a team of 107 authors. Such compendia raise questions about how and how much of such content ought to be represented in a program of initial preparation and how to reconcile multiple versions of the knowledge terrain. One area for development, then, is to review such documents and related materials to reach a workable consensus on the knowledge and skill territory.

Instructional Formats and Methods. Linked to conceptions of the content are considerations of pedagogy and of instructional format. To the question "What is to be learned?" we add the question "How is it to be learned?" Although these can be separated conceptually, in practice they can only be answered together. We shall review a range of instructional approaches in professional education, exploring options and exemplars that have arisen in other fields. The design task, however, requires joint attention to content and method, so our discussion should be regarded as a partial and limited resource for the complex activity of program development.

Program Features. Another set of elements includes attention to programmatic elements. How are individuals recruited, selected, and supported financially for professional study? What kind of practice community is formed in the program? For example, does cohort formation play a major role? Does the program contain explicit standards for evaluation and advancement? Who are the instructors in the program, and how are they selected? What are the requirements for completion of the program, and how much variation is permissible in fulfilling requirements, standards, and other elements? Practical questions of this sort are likely to play an important part in defining approaches to professional education in conjunction with the other elements.

Institutional Arrangements. A less obvious but critically important influence on professional learning is the institutional context in which it takes place. Since the early decades of the twentieth century, professional education in the United States has been institutionalized progressively in the modern university with its numerous professional schools. The traditional model of apprenticeship has given way to formal programs, credentialing schemes, interlocking associations, a full-time professorate, and related developments. One consequence is that theory has enjoyed pride of place in the professional studies sequence, typically represented as foundational to practice in many fields. At the same time, criticisms have emerged, provoking reforms of various kinds. Schön (1983) has provided the most cogent cross-professional critique on this point, arguing that *rigor*, defined in terms of theory, has trumped *relevance*, defined in terms of practical know-how that can be applied on the job. He contrasts the high, hard ground of theory with the swampy lowlands awash in ambiguous problems of practice. How, he asks, might professional education prepare practitioners to negotiate their way in the swamp?

The bias toward theory in professional education may be reckoned an outcome of institutional choice. The press within the university to emphasize theory is strong and has had a powerful influence on university-based professional schools. Reforms, therefore, may seek to alter the institutional arrangements that shape programmatic decisions and emphases. Institutional choice theory (Clune, 1987) stresses two factors: distrust and comparative advantage. Recourse to alternative institutions is typically motivated by distrust of prevailing arrangements. Should schools or school districts be given a greater role in preparing principals in light of the evident failure of universities to do the job? On the one hand, many observers distrust the willingness and capacity of universities on this score, judging that the dysfunctions of leadership preparation programs are deeply rooted in institutional tropes. On the other hand, what are the comparative advantages of other institutions in our society to manage professional preparation effectively? We might argue that changes in program content and method will be insufficient and that new institutional choices also will be necessary; then we must critically interrogate the capacities of alternative institutions, seeking their comparative advantages.

Regulatory Framework. A final resource for shaping professional education is the regulatory frame that influences individual and institutional behavior through processes of licensure, certification, and accreditation. Reform projects in professional education often begin with isolated institutional experiments. The Harvard medical school launches its "new pathway in general medical education"; Georgetown University Law Center radically restructures the first year of legal education. These and other examples typify the course of reform, stimulated by grants from public and private sources. But how do such reforms propagate, coming to exert broad influence on a large set of institutions? How might the reform of professional education "scale up," other than through processes of voluntary imitation and gradual diffusion? The sociologist David Reisman characterized American universities as a "snakelike progression": elite institutions such as Harvard are at the head; all others follow. Change may come courtesy of the prestige hierarchy and the power of influence networks, but this naturally occurring process is slow and uncertain.

Another answer resorts to the framework of regulation as a powerful instrument for institutional change. The motto here might be, "If you want it taught, test it; if you want the program to cover it, require it." The professional model features strong guild influence over standards of various kinds, including those required by the state. The path of influence, then, is through the governance process, as represented in requirements to practice and standards for programs. To influence the preparation of school principals on a broad scale leads directly to questions about licensure requirements and program accreditation standards, together with mechanisms for oversight and compliance. Furthermore, "the profession" might seek to influence these processes indirectly by establishing voluntary certification standards for advanced or specialized practice, which eventually shape other kinds of standards. This strategy is prominent in the teaching field with the rise of the National Board for Professional Teaching Standards and its extensions to the INTASC project to reform initial teacher licensure.

Our observations to this point draw attention to the limited scope and ambition of this chapter. Thoroughgoing efforts to improve the quality of school leadership will depend first on a comprehensive analysis of the problem, which is likely to include the changing nature and demands of the role, the rewards and incentives that are provided, the personnel supports managed by employers over the course of careers, and the prospect of enlarging the pool of talented individuals who are willing to undertake leadership of schools. Improvements in leadership preparation, our subject here, take their place alongside these accompanying reforms.

Designs for new preparation programs rely on several assumptions that must be articulated: about the aims of education and leadership, the nature of practice for which preparation is prerequisite; and ways of acquiring that practice in light of contemporary theories of learning.

Powerful influences on programs include specification of the content to be learned, the instructional formats and methods that convey the content, program features and institutional choices within which programs are structured, and the regulatory framework that introduces standardizing elements across programs. Within this nexus of issues, we next provide a survey of models for professional education as one basis for rethinking similar aspects of leadership development.

Models of Expertise and the Preparation of Professionals

In her superb review of professional expertise, Kennedy (1988) clustered approaches under four headings, which we will use. This chapter, then, might be regarded as an update on this prior synthesis.[2] Her distinctions are technical skill, application of theory or general principles, critical analysis, and deliberate action. Kennedy also sets forth a typology of transitions to practice, which we shall also review.

Model I: Technical Skill

Every profession employs some set of discrete skills on some set of routine tasks that define the nature of professional work. Skillful performance is an important aspect of professionalism, and the work of the professional may be represented via a task analysis that lays out what the professional does. Furthermore, there is a reasonably well regarded model for skills learning that has broad applicability. Not surprisingly, this model derives from coaching athletes and performing artists. Joyce and Showers (1988) identify a four-step sequence: introduce the theory and rationale for the skill or skills; demonstrate their use; provide opportunities for the student to practice the skills in a protected setting with feedback; then transfer skill usage to the practice setting with continued coaching that gradually fades out.

Elements of this model have been influential in education for nurses, doctors, teachers, and engineers, among others, but in recent times, disenchantment has set in. Nursing education, for example, has moved away from task-analytic approaches to the "nursing process" model, and the engineering field has turned away from technique to place greater emphasis on the principles and concepts on which technique is based. A number of difficulties emerged in efforts to organize a professional curriculum around technical skills. In most fields, "competencies" (skills) tend to proliferate madly and to become unworkable as guides to learning. Lists of competencies also provoke disagreements among analysts and lack empirical validation with reference to outcomes. Furthermore, the problem of transfer tends to plague skills-based approaches. In practice, the weakest element of the Joyce-Showers model is follow-up in the practice setting, where application and use of skills take place. Finally, the technical skills account of professional practice has been criticized for its lack of attention to other important aspects, including theory and principles, analytic capacity, and judgment and wisdom.

Professionals must not only acquire skills but also learn about whether, when, and how to employ them in complex, problematic situations. Most skills training regimens have been very weak on these aspects of professional practice. Nevertheless, professional preparation that overlooks skills entirely is evidently inadequate. An exchange between two noted researchers captures this point. Writing about Lee Shulman's work on the cognitive aspects of teaching, Nat Gage claimed that Shulman's emphases on knowledge, understanding, and decision making portray teachers "lost in thought." In response, Shulman replied that Gage's behaviorist conception leaves teachers "missing in action." A focus on observable behavior alone overlooks the intentional aspects of practice, the complex cognitive processes that underlie teaching activity. Clearly, then, attention to both thought *and* action have a place in professional preparation. (Of note is the extension of the Joyce and Showers model to "cognitive coaching"; see Costa and Garmston, 1994).

Model II: Application of Theory or General Principles

A second familiar model begins with the theory that underlies practice or the general principles thought to inform practice. Practitioners in all fields face problems and work on cases, variously construed, but the intellectual equipment they bring to tasks and activities consists of theories and principles. This approach is strongly associated with university-based education and with codified bodies of knowledge such as reside in the disciplines.

Traditional approaches to medical and engineering education clearly exemplify this approach. The usual sequence of study begins with theory as foundational, then proceeds to some form of clinical training. The traditional medical curriculum, for example, features two years of basic science—anatomy, physiology, pharmacology—followed by two years of clinical work. Engineering students may likewise begin with courses on physics or mathematics before engaging in issues related to engineering work. However, not all relevant principles derive from the sciences. Early on, for example, architecture provided training in engineering but gradually shifted emphasis to principles of design. More recently, the field has shifted again from design principles based on social science constructs to inventive, aesthetic principles (Guttman, 1985).

Concentration on theory and principles has the advantage of parsimony over skills training. Rather than elaborating long lists of skills to master, the professional curriculum can identify a core body of knowledge thought to have broad applicability to cases and situations of use. Business schools, for example, had to confront the many positions in the commercial enterprise, each with myriad skills. Individual schools could specialize in a subset of positions or design curricula around broad principles, assuming graduates would learn job-specific skills on the job. Equally important, though, an emphasis on theory and principles provides broadly usable guidance to practitioners who confront ambiguous situations within which they must make decisions and solve problems. Learning to use theory in practice, then, is a critical aspect of professional work that may encompass skills within a larger frame of action.

However, the theory-and-principles approach has suffered its own deficiencies, chief among them the problem of application. Students often have difficulties in connecting general principles to the particular situations they encounter in practice. And equipped with multiple theories and principles by their education, they have problems figuring out which to apply to specific cases, especially when principles conflict with one another. As an investor, which maxim do you follow, "Look before you leap" or "He who hesitates is lost"? Kennedy (1988) writes, "So the general-principles definition of expertise eventually stumbles on the same problem that besets expertise-as-technical-skill: principles provide rules of thumb intended to guide practice, but there are no rules of thumb for how to select the appropriate rule of thumb. Cases do not present themselves to practitioners as examples of general principles, but instead force practitioners to ferret out the principles from the case" (p. 142).

This criticism of the general-principles approach is perhaps the most common complaint about the abstract, distanced quality of university-based professional education. It is associated with ivory-tower types who have little experience with or concern for the genuine problems that practitioners encounter and who employ dusty theories year after year with little concern for whether or how a practitioner might use such knowledge to inform practice. How, the critics ask, does general theory help practitioners decide what to do? A better approach to professional education would transform the practitioner into someone equipped to respond to professional tasks and problems in effective ways.

Model III: Critical Analysis

A third model seeks to supply practitioners with a paradigm for the analysis of situations, which blends substantive knowledge with methods of analysis and interpretation. Legal education most clearly reflects this aspiration. The standard curriculum of the law school is notable for excluding both technical skills and basic sciences as the foundation for preparation. The classic ambition of the law school is to prepare individuals to "think like lawyers." Learning to master legal reasoning is the aim of law school, and the method for this has become well established. In the late 1800s, the Harvard Law School dean, Christopher Columbus Langdell, instituted the case method as the primary teaching approach, and most other law schools soon adopted it (Stevens, 1983). Working on appellate cases, law professors use a question-and-answer format similar to Socratic teaching methods. While students pick up knowledge of precedent cases, the major aim of instruction is to teach active reading and interpretation of cases for which there are no right answers. By immersing students in case-based discussions, law schools transform students into analysts adept at applying the paradigm of legal reasoning to new cases.

Business schools copied law schools in this approach as well, although two varieties have emerged. Some business schools also use the case-analytic paradigm, while others employ a quantitative-analytic model (Schlossman and Sedlak, 1985), in which students learn to apply mathematical models from such disciplines as economics and statistics. (W. Edwards Deming, of Total Quality Management fame, was trained in statistical quality control.) These approaches differ from one another, but each reflects the same pedagogical aim: to teach students to use the paradigm in professional decision and choice making.

Kennedy (1988) reviews a number of criticisms that have emerged over the years concerning the character of legal education. Unrelieved emphasis on analysis of appellate decisions leaves students unprepared for the routine tasks of lawyering, to which law schools reply that these are skills better learned on the job. Elite law schools in particular refuse to "vocationalize" what they perceive to be the intellectual rigor of their curriculum (the better schools also make little effort to prepare students for the bar exam, judging that this is the student's business, not the professional school's). The case method has also been criticized for its failure to convey general principles or to provide access to a body of codified knowledge. Furthermore, by emphasizing analytic process over content knowledge, the Socratic method does not provide students with "right answers." As one commentator notes, "It is hardly surprising that lawyers and legal educators admit they have no clear idea of what the student is supposed to be learning to do" (Cardoza, 1977, p. 48).

Employers of young lawyers also complain that law school may transform students into case analysts, failing to prepare them to act on cases. Appellate cases, after all, treat judgments that have been made already. Students consequently get little idea of how ambiguous issues and conflicts get converted into legal precedents and decisions or of how personalities and unexpected events shape outcomes. (This is similar to research methods courses that portray research as a "narrative of conclusions" rather than as a "logic of inquiry," in Schwab's phrase. Reading research reports fails to uncover for students the messy, indeterminate process that makes up the actual conduct of research.)

We might conclude, then, that the virtues of legal education are also its defects. Kennedy (1988) summarizes: "Its disadvantages are that it can fail to provide students with codified knowledge, where such knowledge exists; it can lead students to become so analytic that they are unable to act; and it can narrow the scope of the students' analytic powers to the point where, as professionals, they are unable to view cases from any perspective other than that of their paradigm" (pp. 146–147).

Model IV: Deliberate Action

A final model assumes that professionals must analyze complex situations, to frame both problems and solutions. But it also assumes that such analysis must occur in the context of action, where the practitioner must reflect on his or her own actions and their consequences. Although this model is not clearly associated with any of the major professional schools, one of its chief explicators, Donald Schön, derived it from close study of architects, town planners, psychotherapists, and organizational managers. In learning settings such as design labs or studios, practitioners engage in structured sequences of action and reflection around projects, where instructor and students interact in relation to student work products and processes. A central element in such professional learning is an ambiguous task on which students must frame the problem, take into account multiple and at times conflicting criteria, consider both means and ends, and try out alternative problem frames and possible solutions. This description might apply to an architectural problem, a town planning dilemma, or a complex clinical case in the human services field. In the context of real or simulated experience, such learning has another feature, which is some sequence of planning, actions, reflections and evaluations, and new actions. Such sequences allow for learning to occur in action and to draw on real or simulated experience as a powerful source.

Schön (1987) describes three methods that teachers use during such learning sequences: "follow me," which involves direct imitation; "joint experiments," in which they assist students in developing alternative analyses and courses of action; and "hall of mirrors," in which they reflect students' thinking in ways that clarify their deliberations and actions. Learning from experience is a time-honored method that this model takes advantage of, but the key to its success may be the instructional mediation because considerable research suggests that inductive reasoning often suffers biases and other deficiencies. Merely supplying experiences together with opportunities to talk about them does not guarantee that professional learning will result. Instead, the result can confirm prior suspicions and prejudices, insofar as people not only believe what they see but also see what they believe. Individuals are also prone to "superstitious learning," making faulty inferences from particular situation-bound experiences.

Nevertheless, in relation to much administrative work, this model has some advantages, including its emphasis on analysis of one's own actions and experiences, attention to problem selection and framing rather than just solution, and joint consideration of purposes as well as strategies. At the same time, professional education built around this model may also suffer some of the problems associated with critical analysis, including lack of attention to codified knowledge and general principles and ambiguity about what exactly is learned during such experiences. As with much constructivist teaching, this model requires considerable skill in instructors if substantial learning is to result from sequences of action and deliberation.

Transition to Practice

Over the years, professional fields have relied on a number of arrangements to manage the transition from preservice study to practice. Some fields, such as the law, continue to rely on what might be termed *immersion*. Students go directly from legal education into practice, with few organized field experiences other than what the student arranges during summers (work in local law offices, clerkships in various courts). In some respects, immersion is a default option that simply defines the absence of a carefully staged or managed transition. Immersion comes close to characterizing the status quo in educational administration, with some exceptions. Teachers may first occupy assistant principal positions before moving into principalships, so that some staged entry is the common norm. Some districts also have developed programs where teachers can work alongside administrators to learn the job or receive mentoring assistance in a first assignment. But no fieldwide practices have emerged.

A second time-honored approach is *apprenticeship*. Prior to the rise of university-based professional schools, this was the major means of entry into such fields as the law or architecture. All professional learning took place on the job, under the tutelage of an experienced practitioner, and elements of this approach survive today in such fields as social work, where individuals must log a certain number of hours of apprentice experience as part of certification requirements. Under such modern arrangements, it is up to the student to secure the apprenticeship. Initial licensure allows the student to begin practice, but advanced certification requires that the student undertake a modified apprenticeship. Graduating engineers, for example, take the Fundamentals of Engineering Exam to obtain a license to practice. After four years of working under the supervision of a professional engineer (PE), they take the Professional Engineering Exam, which in combination with signoff on paperwork by the supervising PE grants rights to the title. A similar sequence structures the architectural field.

Immersion and apprenticeship are essentially under the control of the employer or employing organization, and this is both a strength and a weakness. These first two options allow the practitioner to begin working for salary and to acquire on-the-job skills that are specific to particular work settings. However, immersion with no benefit of guidance can foster the development of bad habits and narrow ways of thinking. Likewise, apprenticeships can feature haphazard, incomplete, and situation-bound learning that overlooks underlying principles and theories. Furthermore, each of these options contains little quality control because each apprentice is judged only by his or her master.

All the remaining options arose in some sense to replace the tradition of apprenticeship, and each operates primarily in the context of university-based education. First, universities can offer *laboratory experiences* in which students can practice technique or observe concepts and principles presented in coursework. Labs are time-honored activities in engineering and medical schools, as well as elsewhere. They provide options for practice in controlled settings, where the cost of mistakes is low, but they fail to supply the multidimensional complexity of real-world settings. Nevertheless, they have evident advantages for novice practitioners at the early stages of learning.

Closer to practice are *simulations* of various kinds that universities can design and offer. Kennedy (1988) distinguishes simulations from lab experiences by noting that the latter present tasks with fixed, predetermined outcomes, while the former engage students in tasks that may be open-ended and may have multiple possible outcomes. Nearly all fields include some attention to simulations, and these may be organized around problems or projects of various kinds.[3] As with lab experiences, simulations allow for protected and mediated experiences with low-stakes outcomes, under conditions in which the instructor can intervene at various points to promote learning. With modern technologies, simulations can be virtual as well as real, and many fields are developing new applications.

Another option, *clinical experiences*, involves real situations rather than faculty-designed projects or problems. However, the settings for clinical experiences are still protected in that the professional school exercises some control over them. Furthermore, such experiences involve a balance of aims between service to clients or patients and emphasis on the learning of the novice. The university-affiliated teaching hospital, with its clerkships and residencies, is a primary example, but teacher education also has a long tradition of "practice teaching" in real schools that enjoy some loose affiliation with the university-based teacher education program.

Finally, the professional school can arrange for students to participate in full- or part-time *internships*, which are analogous to apprenticeships. Interns may have local mentors whose role is similar to that of the master in an apprentice relationship, but an internship also implies formal attention to the learning of the intern, typically in relation to the model of expertise enacted in the program. Internships have the same financial advantages of an apprenticeship in that an employing institution provides primary supervision, but such arrangements raise questions about the preparation of mentors and their attention to intern learning. In the worst case, internships can degenerate into immersion, as occurred in the early years of nursing education, when student nurses simply became sources of cheap labor for hospitals, almost completely sacrificing the goal of professional learning. Internships can also limit learning if restricted to one setting because interns then cannot explore the principles, theories, skills, and analytic processes that must be adapted to particular settings and situations.

All fields today provide some form of transition experience, and its character will be related to the underlying model. For example, mastery of critical analysis in law school requires relatively little transition into practice because the paradigmatic form of reasoning has already been practiced and acquired. Other forms, though, require experience, either to practice and master technical skills, apply general principles and theories, or learn to deliberate in action under real conditions. Each kind of transition experience also leaves some aspects of practice to be learned elsewhere, typically on the job. In this manner, professional schools define the appropriate preservice curriculum by what is included and by what is excluded. Concentration on general principles, for example, may omit attention to technical skills; focus on deliberation and analysis may slight codified knowledge.

The four models outlined here might provide occasion for choice or for combinations in the design of leadership preparation. A number of broad intellectual trends establish the context for contemporary designs that might draw on these traditions. Sykes and Bird (1992) characterize an ongoing reconfiguration of social thought in the following terms:

> Educational work [today] reflects a set of connected (and relative) trends, from a law-seeking to an interpretive aspiration in inquiry; from a concern for universal principle to a concern for particular relationships; from the positivistic stance of an observer on the scene to the pragmatic stance of the actor in the situation; from authoritative transmission to mutual exploration of knowledge; from conditioned behavior to meaningful action as a model for teaching and learning; from a cooler appraisal of teaching as knowledge and technique to a more passionate consideration of teaching as moral agency; from vision as the metaphor for knowledge to speech as the literal means for constructing knowledge; and from lecture to conversation as the mode of interaction between professors and teachers [p. 465].

These broad intellectual currents have influenced the nature of reforms in professional education and may also influence the effort to reform leadership development. While the typology of transitions to practice covers the available options, new technologies may augment the possibilities along with new institutional arrangements (virtual universities, for example). Next we examine a number of reforms to the traditions of professional education.

Reforms in Professional Education

A variety of unflattering analogies caricature efforts to reform university education: "It's like moving a graveyard"; "It's like trying to herd cats." But there has been a surprising degree of ferment. Professional education in most fields includes a variety of reforms, some incremental, some far-reaching. We shall highlight a small sample of such reforms. Our selection is meant to be provocative, not representative; we proceed from the least to the most radical.

Design Projects in Engineering

One commentator has pointed out that 80 percent of the engineering curriculum is comprised of the "-ics"—physics, mathematics, dynamics, electronics—but that engineering practice consists of "-ings"—consulting, designing, planning, and evaluating, to name a few. He wonders whether a professional education program might usefully be required to certify that its graduates can competently perform the tasks of engineering (Harrisberger, 1985).

One response in many engineering programs is to introduce multidisciplinary, team-based projects into the curriculum to give students more experience with leadership roles and teamwork. Design projects and so-called engineering enterprises, often cosponsored by businesses and industry, set unique design problems and challenges for students to work out. Examples are such challenges as the "car of the future" or the concrete canoe. Teams often mix students across schooling levels (for example, sophomores, juniors, seniors, graduate students), and from various engineering specialties. Seniors and grad students may become "CEOs" of an enterprise after serving as team members in prior years. Businesses find this kind of activity promising because it encourages innovation early, supplies links between the university and corporate worlds, assists in recruitment, and provides a simulation that includes such practical elements as teamwork, leadership, and problem solving under constraints of time and other resources.

In addition to these integrative simulations, where peer learning plays a significant role, engineering schools also are beginning to introduce new topics into their curricula to reflect the practical and human side of engineering practice. One method for doing this involves offering single credit modules of short, intense duration, supplied in various time blocks such as on Saturdays or in the evenings over six to eight weeks. Such modules complement the traditional curricula with topics such as leadership, communication, and business practices. Another feature of these modules is that they can be taught in nontraditional settings by nontraditional instructors. For example, a local corporation might send a team on two Saturdays to work with students on how to set up a production line. In this manner, the practice of engineering is gradually making a stronger appearance in the curriculum. The "-ics" have not been abandoned, but they are increasingly supplemented in various ways by the "-ings."

The First-Year Law Curriculum

Legal education in America has remained largely unchanged since the early decades of the twentieth century, and it is remarkably uniform from school to school. As we have described, the case method, organized around appellate court decisions, has been the reigning paradigm, with its aim of teaching students to "think like a lawyer" and to acquire the skills of critical analysis. Efforts have been made over the years to alter this dominant model of legal education, without much success.

One contemporary reform has sought to restructure the first year of legal education. The traditional focus in most law schools has been on a set of common law topics such as property, torts, and contracts that are treated as sharply separated subjects. This curriculum features little integration and scant attention to the broader context of legislation and regulation. Furthermore, students learn little about the economic, social, political, or philosophical context of laws and get no practice with the "lawyering process"—what lawyers actually do.

To remedy these defects, the Georgetown University Law Center instituted a reform that restructured the curriculum around a new set of courses and learning experiences. The aim was to provide deeper acquaintance with foundational issues without sacrificing attention to the essential basis of legal doctrine, procedure, and argumentation. New course titles suggest the move to an enlarged conception of the law: "Bargain, Exchange, and Liability," "Democracy and Coercion," "Legal Justice," "Governmental Procedure." In addition, the program also includes a small-section seminar that deals with jurisprudential topics that transcend the boundaries of other courses. For example, students evaluate contemporary intellectual movements such as legal process theory and critical race theory. Pedagogical methods continue to rely on cases and on skills preparation around legal writing, for example, but the seminars and new courses also provide scope for broader discussions, reading material, and student assignments.

Put in terms of our analysis, the first-year law curriculum has tended to ignore both technical skills and theoretical principles in favor of critical analysis. The Georgetown reform introduces elements of these other two models into the introductory year of legal education.

Cluster Concept in Preparation for the Ministry

A role in our society just as demanding as the school principalship is the ministry. Members of the clergy are similar in many respects to school principals. They must lead an organization, respond to external demands from constituency groups and formal hierarchy, balance secular with "spiritual" (or educational) concerns, and juggle multiple responsibilities that include fundraising, dispute resolution, pastoral counseling, charismatic leadership, and management of the physical plant. Many denominations today face a crisis in recruitment to the ministry as the stresses of the position have escalated and the rewards have diminished. Divinity schools have long been criticized for failing to equip future ministers with the practical know-how required to run a parish. A recent survey of senior pastors of mainline denominational churches revealed that of fifteen essential skills, the majority of respondents regarded their preparation as inadequate in several, including staff building, financial planning, and time management. In other areas, such as counseling, communication, and interpersonal skills, they felt better prepared (Naman and McCall, 1999). An interview study with a sample of priests and ministers also identified six developmental themes: control, burnout, role confusion, isolation, mixed messages, and inadequate seminary preparation (Brillinger and Pocock, 1993). Most school principals would sympathize.

The typical curriculum for a master of divinity degree[4] might include a set of courses on Bible study, history of Christianity, doctrine and theology, interpreting and confessing the Word, leadership for mission, and discipleship. Within the leadership concentration are courses on "telling the story," music and hymnody, preaching, and pastoral care. In addition, most schools require a yearlong internship in a church. Not surprisingly, divinity schools have stressed the sacred or spiritual aspects of the profession over the secular requirements associated with leading a parish or church. The resulting disjunction between preparation and practice is understandable. How, though, might education for the ministry be reformed to provide a better practical basis for the work?

One option under consideration in the Baptist church is to rely more heavily on a cluster of learners to provide a community for education (see McNeal, 1988). This idea of a learning community relies on peer learning and on connections among churches and seminaries for acquisition of practical know-how. Multiple options for implementing this idea are visible; for example:

- A student opts for residential study. After a year of multidisciplinary study, the student selects a small group of colleagues with whom to complete seminary education. This cohort forms a learning community, taking charge of significant aspects of subsequent study and assisting one another in the learning process.
- A student takes one year of core interdisciplinary courses on campus and then moves away to assume a provisional position with a church. Her remaining education is conducted in the field in a learning cluster. Students access material through CD-ROM or compressed video technology. Members of the learning team design their learning around ministry venues they are involved with already, with support and guidance from seminary faculty who also certify acquisition of core competencies and knowledge.
- A student never or rarely visits the campus to pursue a seminary degree. He forms a cluster with students who are also nonresident. Distance learning technology assists in maintaining connections among cluster members and faculty, including use of the Internet, teleconferencing, and CD-ROM library.

Other options are possible, but the primary features of this proposal are to create a learning community among students, giving them substantial voice in the construction of a curriculum; to base more of the learning in the field and in the context of the work of ministry; and to use distance learning technologies to supplement or complement residency-based professional education.

Transformation of Executive Education

"Twenty years ago, education for [business] executives consisted primarily of university-based programs or seminars offered by specialized training organizations. Participants learned the latest theory and techniques for effective management largely by studying cases and listening to classroom lectures by notable academics. Training content was decided by university faculty who offered courses on strategy and functional skills such as finance and marketing. Many programs essentially were abridged MBAs. For the attending executive, the experience itself was seen as both a reward and as preparation for . . . promotion to senior levels" (Conger and Xin, 2000, p. 76). So write several students of the business field in the introduction to a survey of business leaders on trends in the practice of executive education. This work surfaced a set of trends beginning in the 1980s and continuing to the present. New topics such as globalization, e-commerce, employee diversity, and organizational learning are part, but not all, of the story. Older emphases on general or functional knowledge have given way to newer emphases on education as a lever for promoting organizational change. The authors of this study summarize their findings in six trends.

1. *Learning needs—a shift from functional knowledge to strategic leadership and organizational change.* In most large companies today, the central issues are change management and strategic thinking. Specialized knowledge will continue to have a place in executive education, but the new emphasis will be on strategy, leadership, and change. Distributed leadership will become paramount, drawing line as well as staff workers into leadership training. Prior training was good for routine problem solving, planning and budgeting, and policymaking but relatively weak at developing strategic vision, communicating, motivating, and inspiring. These new emphases must be diffused throughout the organization rather than residing at corporate headquarters alone.

2. *Learning content—a shift toward ever-greater customization.* In the past decade, executive education has relied increasingly on learning materials customized to individual company and industry conditions. Action learning projects today are built around company issues rather than generic cases from distant firms. This has led to a shift in the locus of education from universities and business schools to companies and business consortia. One study reckons

that 75 percent of all U.S. executive education dollars now go into customized programs (Conger and Xin, 2000).

3. *Pedagogy—a shift toward action learning and feedback pedagogies*. The general trend is toward greater learner involvement, especially through action learning projects, which often use team-based experiential exercises aiming to solve real-life problems with immediate relevance to the company. "For example, a company division might be contemplating new markets in Malaysia or leasing its products rather than selling them. These decisions become the learning initiatives" (Conger and Xin, 2000). A development to watch is the use of new technology such as the Internet and CD-ROMs; business does not yet make widespread use of these new tools.

4. *Participants—a shift to learning in executive cohorts*. As corporations flatten hierarchies, they need greater coordination across the organization. Change efforts implicate all members of an organization so that teams or cohorts of executives participate together in training.

5. *Integrating mechanisms—a shift toward the cascading of learning experiences*. "Cascading" means a sequence of activities that follow up on training and draw a widening circle of employees into new initiatives. The idea is that if a group of senior-level executives undertakes a strategic-planning or vision-setting seminar, its members follow that up with parallel experiences throughout the organization so that all leaders in an organization, at all levels and in all divisions, participate in a common process over time, sustaining momentum for change and learning efforts.

6. *Instructors—a shift toward greater use of executive teachers*. Increasingly, companies are relying on a diversity of instructors, including outside consultants and trainers, university faculty, company executives, managers with specialized knowledge, and corporate trainers from within the organization. The shift, however, is toward increasing use of company executives in training, perhaps reflecting the new emphases on leadership for change and on broad, organizational management issues.

This example describes education or training supplied by employers and integrated into the ongoing work of the organization. The new realization is that corporate training is not separate from organizational development but is a critical resource for it. There is a close parallel here to a case in the education field, describing how Anthony Alvarado, superintendent in New York City's Community District 2, dissolved the boundary between teacher professional development and administrative leadership (Elmore and Burney, 1999). An emerging lesson may be that investment in professional learning must become tightly coupled to organizational improvement and must be conceptualized as a primary resource for corporate effectiveness and the management of change.

Harvard Medical School's New Pathway to General Medical Education

A celebrated case of reform took place in Harvard University's medical school beginning in 1982. Known as the "new pathway to general medical education," this reform dramatically reorganized the four-year curriculum of general medical education and tested the new model alongside its traditional counterpart. A general sketch of this far-reaching reform reveals some provocative themes and ideas that may carry into other fields.

Daniel Tosteson, the dean who spearheaded the reform, describes its essence quite simply: "The two essential components of the New Pathway methodology are student and problem" (1994, p. 10). By this he meant that the new approach places greater responsibility for learning in the hands of the students themselves and orients more of the learning around actual problems of practice. In the first two years of medical school, the lecture as dominant pedagogy is replaced (but not eliminated) by problem-based learning exercises, which students must complete in small groups. The weekly schedule features more unstructured time for work on these problems, with lectures occupying a reduced and more strategic role in the overall learning regimen (see Figure 6.1 for a comparison of instructional methods between the traditional and the new curriculum). Cases are developed by faculty from actual medical records and are collected in casebooks, which are continually updated. Here is a case description from the Harvard case catalogue, listed under "Chemistry and Biology of the Cell":

The Concerned Adolescent

Diane is a 15-year-old girl who presents to her physician with a series of complaints: increased acne, darkening of her knuckles, irregular periods, hair loss and excessive facial hair. Tests and a physical exam reveal androgen excess. Fasting insulin is also abnormally high. She and members of her family are found to be insulin resistant. Further genetic testing reveals the existence of a single dominant disease-causing allele.

(18 pages) Endocrinology, Genetics, Gynecology, Molecular Biology

The cornerstone of learning is the student tutorial group, which works on cases of this sort. "The students begin with medical cases in all their complexity, richness, and humanity. The experience is initially overwhelming. The students' first response is to rush to medical textbooks, to try to be a 'doctor.' But they realize rapidly that they must first learn some basics (what's inside the chest?)" (Armstrong and others, 1994, p. 75). Rather than organizing the foundational years of medical education by the basic sciences underlying practice, the new curriculum embeds study of underlying science within problematic cases that are studied in small groups (tutorials),

which produces an environment of peers in which it is safe to admit ignorance. Because the faculty group leader also cannot know all there is to know about the case and does not control the agenda for discussion, she or he must also admit ignorance, contributing to, role-modeling, the safety. The group must discuss and agree on

Figure 6.1. Student-Faculty Contact Time in the New Pathway and Traditional Curricula.

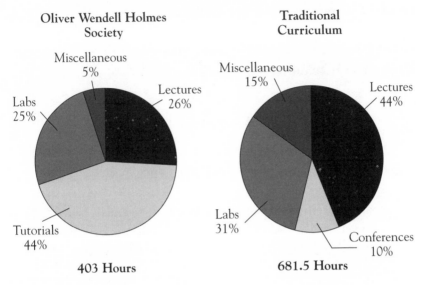

Oliver Wendell Holmes Society

Miscellaneous 5%
Lectures 26%
Labs 25%
Tutorials 44%

403 Hours

Traditional Curriculum

Miscellaneous 15%
Lectures 44%
Labs 31%
Conferences 10%

681.5 Hours

Source: Adapted from Tosteson, 1994, p. 41.

goals and develop common meanings. This process allows students and teachers to define what they don't know and what they need to know. The group must prioritize these needs, set agendas, and explore study strategies. Differences arise immediately and must be negotiated; the necessity fosters appreciation of the richness offered by difference. This process of group formation is exquisitely complex and occurs at different rates for different groups [Armstrong and others, 1994, p. 75].

The New Pathways curriculum made modest changes to years 3 and 4 of medical education, retaining the basic rotation of clinical clerkships in surrounding hospitals. However, the new program added several clerkships—for ambulatory care and for women's and children's health issues—and continued study of the basic sciences via a two-option requirement: either a student thesis reporting a research project or an advanced basic science course.

Other elements of the new program featured more extensive use of technology, including electronic mail and information search capabilities; organization of students and faculty into a series of "societies"; new curricular content in the early years, including a course titled "Patient-Doctor," which served to explore the human, interpersonal, and ethical dimensions of practice, even in the context of basic science learning; and new methods for assessing student learning. For example, the old multiple-choice, short-answer, and essay examinations were supplemented with a new form of assessment known as the "triple jump" in which students first read a case and then respond to questions under exam conditions. This emphasizes hypothesis generation and alternative treatment responses. They research issues related to the case for the rest of the day and then undergo an oral examination given by one or two expert examiners, with questions ranging from the globally conceptual to the specific factual. All grading in the program is pass-fail.

How has the program fared? One student's reactions are revealing. He reports first that the case-based learning is relatively successful in fostering a deeper understanding of the relationship between basic and clinical sciences in medicine. "Only after gaining acquaintance with the Krebs cycle, insulin, and electrolytes," he comments, "could we understand what diabetic ketoacidosis is and how to help the unconscious patient presented in the case. Only after learning about cell structure and function would we understand how Georgie Markov could die from a tiny dose of diphtheria toxin placed on the tip of an assassin's umbrella" (Silver, 1994, p. 124). But case-based learning also creates "holes" in the curriculum, critical areas of knowledge that none of the presenting cases dealt with. The student continues, "Although our case on diabetic ketoacidosis forced us to learn some of the metabolic pathways and principles of their hormonal regulation, we were never guided to read about amino acid synthesis. And while patients in many of our cases received a wide variety of drugs, we never had a systematic introduction to the subject of pharmacology" (p. 125). To prepare for part 1 of the National Board of Medical Examiners examination, students organized a special class covering missing topics, which supplemented the case-based curriculum.

Group learning also produced some mixed but generally beneficial results. Silver (1994) reports that the group process was often filled with anxiety and conflict, while at the same time yielding some unexpected learning results:

> Tutorial often served as a painful reminder that you do not understand something until you can teach it to someone else. All too often, what we thought we knew, we knew in only a superficial way. Teaching one another and learning from one another, we were forced to grapple with the material in a highly critical manner. We learned that a quick reading on adrenal function in a physiology textbook does not an endocrinologist make. Only after we had worked through adrenal function in a group, asking tough questions, helping others who did not comprehend, organizing the material on a blackboard, had we taken the first step toward real knowledge [p. 127].

He goes on to report a very important peripheral lesson from this work—that medicine is filled with uncertainty. "Perhaps no achievement of the New Pathway curriculum was more impressive," he writes (p. 127).

Formal evaluation of the program has produced slightly positive results in favor of the new option, although researchers are cautious due to flaws in the evaluation design (Block and Moore, 1994). For our purposes, though, two other observations about this program are significant. First, design of the program forced faculty to reorient their thinking from courses to learning objectives and then to organize learning experiences that would meet those objectives. This proved to be an important conceptual shift for the program as a whole and served as one principle for the selection of cases. Second, problem-based learning may achieve success as a method only if a broad spectrum of faculty agrees to implement it (Kaufman, 1985). The reform at Harvard produced a strong institutional response that underwrote the extensive development effort that was needed. While problem-based learning did not replace other methods entirely, it did serve as the backbone of the curriculum around which other methods and pedagogies were deployed. This may be key to its effectiveness, much as the emphasis on case method across law school courses reinforces a single analytic paradigm. At the same time, however, the shortcomings of problem-based learning have produced some compensatory responses such as student-initiated didactic learning that assisted in preparation for the external medical exams.

These cases of innovation in professional education contain some common themes. For example, learning in groups where students assume control over significant aspects of the process appears increasingly widespread. Likewise, projects or simulations organized around problems of practice occupy a larger space in the curriculum and serve as the context for theoretical or foundational knowledge. Finally, each of the reforms represents a reaction to perceived shortcomings of the extant program and its model. In this sense, the reforms emphasize elements that are unique to particular fields. Medicine, for example, has to grapple harder with the explosion of new knowledge than theology does, although even there new scholarship continues to expand the perspectives available to future clergy and theologians. To tease out implications for educational leadership might involve attention both to cross-cutting themes in these and other professions and to distinctive aspects of the leadership enterprise in education. We invite you to draw your own implications while we conclude with ours.

Implications for the Preparation of School Leaders

A recent study of the modern presidency from Franklin D. Roosevelt to Bill Clinton (Greenstein, 2000) identified six qualities as crucial to leadership effectiveness:

- Mastery of the bully pulpit (FDR, John Kennedy, and Ronald Reagan get high marks here)

- Organizational capacity (Dwight Eisenhower, with his military experience, ranks high; Kennedy's Bay of Pigs fiasco is a textbook case of organizational incapacity)
- Political skill (Lyndon Johnson was masterful in his early years; Jimmy Carter was woeful)
- Policy vision (Eisenhower, Nixon, and Reagan had very clear goals and programs; Johnson fell into the quagmire of Vietnam)
- Cognitive qualities (Carter's engineering mentality led to obsession with details, while Nixon saw the big picture in his dealing with China and the Soviet Union)
- Emotional intelligence (Eisenhower, Ford, and Bush were largely free of distracting emotional highs and lows; LBJ's volcanic temper and Nixon's anger and suspiciousness limited both men; LBJ, Carter, Nixon, and Clinton, all with first-class intellects, were the opposite of FDR, whom Oliver Wendell Holmes characterized as a second-class mind but a first-class temperament)

Trait-based views of leadership have long been out of favor, replaced by situational conceptions. Ranking presidents on qualities may be no more than an entertaining parlor game, but such lists raise an issue. If human qualities are important to leadership—if leadership style is a serious matter—then can leadership be learned through formal programs in the same way as brain surgery or architectural design? Some of the listed qualities may be developed or enhanced through formal education, but with others it is less clear. One view regards the most important elements of leadership as a function of life experience and inborn qualities, with formal training playing a decidedly minor role. Other views, however, suggest that ordinary individuals can learn to lead and that formal training can play a significant part in the process. In considering the best ways to prepare school leaders, we should not overlook the human qualities that undoubtedly play a part in effectiveness and should consider how learning experiences might cultivate such qualities or at least raise awareness about their importance. With this as preamble, we suggest three ways of using this tour of professional education to improve leadership development in education.

Heuristic Uses of Professional Models

First, the distinctions embodied in the models may be employed as a heuristic device to evaluate the merits of program designs. Professional work of all kinds may be conceptualized in terms of skills, theoretical and principled knowledge, analytic processes of various kinds, and deliberation in action. The advantage of selecting one mode is the success that may be achieved in the terms identified by the model. The clearest case of this advantage is the legal studies curriculum, which features a well-defined pedagogy that is practiced by all instructors. There is little doubt that law school produces graduates who are adept at using the legal paradigm for critical analysis. They have opportunity to practice the method over three years, in the company of many professors and in relation to the major substantive areas of the law. The disadvantage of such single-mindedness, however, is obvious. Law school graduates receive little experience with the actual work of lawyering, under real conditions, nor do they acquire a broad, foundational view of the field. These matters the law schools resolutely allocate to other experiences such as preparation for the bar exam or learning on the job.

Conversely, preparation programs that attempt to include some attention to skill acquisition, theories underlying practice, analytic paradigms of various kinds, and deliberation in action face the difficulty of setting ambitious goals with limited resources. They run the risk of doing nothing well in the attempt to do too much. Likewise, program guidance that consists of lengthy lists of objectives, standards, competencies, and the like may encourage coverage-based approaches to curriculum that fail to encourage deep, flexible learning. This has been the bane of medical education, which kept adding new knowledge to the regimen of lectures and textbook assignments.

To address these classic problems of curriculum development, two moves are frequently invoked. One might be termed "killing two birds with one stone"; the other follows the aphorism that it is better to teach a man to fish than to supply him with a catch of fish. As a design principle, the first move seeks experiences and activities that serve more than one learning function. A good example of this is the selection of problem-based exercises in Harvard's new medical curriculum. The sum of cases encountered by students must accomplish two purposes: to encourage self-directed learning in groups and to acquaint students with the bodies of knowledge regarded as foundational to initial medical practice. Work on selected problems cannot leave out pharmacology, for example, because this field is evidently basic to medical practice today. Likewise, the legal curriculum must include cases that introduce students to important topics in the law such as torts and contracts, while giving them practice in the critical analysis of cases.

The second move is to construct a program that inculcates both skills and dispositions associated with continued learning. An explicit aim of the new Harvard medical curriculum is to teach students how to learn so that they can—and will—continue to be students of medicine, continuously expanding their repertoires, keeping up with the progress of scientific medicine, honing their skills and their knowledge. This move counters the wrongheaded procedure of enumerating every conceivable competency that a practitioner might require and then representing it all in a curriculum. Instead, the aim of preservice education is to form the "well-launched novice," who will continue to grow and develop. Professional education in this regard shares an aim with liberal education: to prepare the individual for a lifetime of learning.

Whether these aims are adopted, the four models provide a set of alternatives that may be used both at the design stage of program development and thereafter, in an appraisal of a program. In effect, they encourage us to ask such questions as "What skills will be acquired?" "What is the role of theoretical or principled knowledge in the program?" "What analytic procedures will be taught and learned?" and "How will knowledge and skill be transferred and applied in a variety of contexts and situations of use?"

Representative Reforms

A second use of insights from cross-professional practice is to identify consensus trends that represent "best practices" and then design leadership programs accordingly. We cull the following recommendations from the models, examples, and reforms described earlier.

1. *Provide an expansive role for adult learners in leadership development.* One common element in the reforms we cited is a more active role for students in directing their own professional learning. This is a relatively new theme in professional education, reflected in the cluster concept, the student tutorial in medical education, the use of design projects in engineering education, and other programs. Rather than casting students as passive recipients of well-formed bodies of knowledge, contemporary approaches introduce open-ended, action learning projects and experiences that are more reflective of real-world, on-the-job experience. Then the trick is to provide adequate scaffolding, debriefing, and feedback around student efforts.

2. *Educate students in carefully formed groups, and use group learning.* A second element in many reforms relies on action projects, skill use, and the application of knowledge in group tasks. In addition to the substantive aims of such simulations and exercises, students also must grapple with interpersonal issues, take on various roles, learn how to modulate their own tendencies in response to others, and work in teams. Bifocal debriefing attends both to group process and to outcomes. Evaluations attend to individual learning and to group learning. In addition to group projects, programs in many fields are inducting students in cohorts, using this pattern to form a stable community of learning. Reforms in educational administration (for example, see McCarthy, 1999; Milstein and Associates, 1993) already have picked up this theme, but the real question may be how or whether programs make planful uses of cohorts for learning. It would be useful to know more about this feature of program design. And it would be helpful if expertise about

group dynamics, organizational and interpersonal communication, conflict resolution, and related matters were available among educators and program designers (see, for example, Kaagan, 1999, on the use of experiential learning exercises to facilitate learning for leadership).

3. *Utilize the problem as a central building block of the curriculum.* Case methods of various kinds have long been a staple of professional education. But there are strong arguments today for expanding the use of problem-based learning (PBL). Certainly, this was the cornerstone of the reform at the Harvard Medical School, and situated problems of practice could become a more prominent feature of education for leadership. Here, too, precedents exist in the educational administration field, most notably the stellar work of Edwin Bridges (1992; Bridges and Hallinger, 1995). As an organizing motif, PBL has a number of advantages. Problems may be selected and arrayed to represent knowledge in the field. Intellectual resources of various kinds (such as theories and principles) may be assembled for use on problems. Students may be given practice with various skills in the conduct of simulations related to the exercises. Students take a lead role in the work, with instructors serving as coaches, evaluators, and sources of feedback. Processes and outcomes provide opportunities for learning. And the PBL format fits well with the deliberate action frame. However, as Harvard learned, the difficulty is to represent the major bodies of knowledge in a PBL curriculum with tight time constraints.

4. *Integrate foundational knowledge and analytic procedures with field experiences.* With the exception of the legal studies, most professional education today involves substantial field-based experience under real conditions, where novices can explore the application of theory, practice skills, and employ analytic paradigms on real problems of practice. The major challenge, however, is not simply to provide experiences but to carefully structure professional learning from such experiences. This recommendation raises a host of practical questions about how to bring analytic resources to bear on practice. The use of retired school principals as mentors for

novices may be one promising development (already under way in Seattle), but new institutional arrangements may be needed as well.

5. *Shift program orientations from courses to learning objectives; build integrating mechanisms across learning experiences*. The course with its associated metric of "student credit hours" represents the DNA of most universities and is very difficult to replace in much the same way that the Carnegie unit has come to exercise decisive influence on the high school curriculum. Nevertheless, an important part of the emerging story in medical education and in executive education is the move away from such programmatic definitions to building blocks that are more directly related to learning itself. The Harvard faculty had to reconceptualize the curriculum in terms of learning objectives in order to replace didactic courses with problem-based learning and group tutorials. The faculty had to increase their interdependence within the program around a common pedagogy and set of curriculum materials. The advantage, though, came in the reinforcement supplied across courses by a common method. This has been the historical advantage enjoyed by law schools and business schools that use the case method across courses.

6. *Utilize external examinations to supplement and complement programmatic learning in professional study*. Staged professional examinations in fields such as medicine, architecture, and engineering have a number of advantages. They allow sequencing of knowledge and skill from basic to advanced, and they provide formal representations of the knowledge base of practice around which to organize student learning. However, in these fields, such examinations do not drive the professional studies curriculum; professional study responds to its own imperatives. Nevertheless, as was evident in the medical school case, students had to supplement their PBL work with formal study to prepare for part 1 of the medical licensure exams. And in the engineering case, apprenticeship arrangements were not the only requirement for advanced certification. Engineers also had to take an advanced exam. It may be, then, that external examinations that supplement rather than

determine the professional studies curriculum can aid in providing well-rounded education. In the law, as noted earlier, the bar exam does not drive the legal studies curriculum, and students must typically prepare for the bar outside the scope of legal education. The education field might consider such uses of external examinations, not to mandate particular professional study, but to complement it.

7. *Plan for and take account of peripheral or incidental learning in professional education.* A final recommendation takes note of what students are learning through their experience with the curriculum. Sometimes such learning is associated with the concept of "hidden curriculum." Unplanned learning can be quite powerful and must therefore be carefully monitored. In our medical example, the student provided an excellent example. The exercises taught students about the uncertainty inherent in medicine, notwithstanding its strong scientific base. Many important peripheral lessons are communicated informally through experience with professional study. What do students learn about cooperation? About distributed leadership? About trusting or distrusting self and others? About learning to learn? These questions may not tap the formal curriculum of study, but they are directly pertinent to learning for leadership. Therefore, it is incumbent on program designers to consider such issues and to seek feedback from students to learn about the effects of a program's hidden curriculum.

Novel Reforms

Our final exercise is to select particular innovations that appear promising for the education field and adapt them for use in education. Of the reforms described, trends in executive education are particularly provocative. Concepts such as customization, cascading, and distributed leadership point to a fundamental reorganization of learning for leadership. The major shift is to conceive of leadership development as a primary strategic resource for accomplishing organizational goals rather than as a generic process that prepares individuals for standard administrative roles. The implications of this shift are potentially far-reaching. It would require the creation of partnerships between school districts and other service organizations, such as universities, consultant groups, or intermediate agencies, to develop and continuously refine programs tailored to local conditions and strategic plans. Such programs might supplement rather than replace traditional programs, increasing investment in leaders' ongoing learning in the context of actual work teams in districts that were attempting to foster specific changes. The content of the curriculum would concentrate on actual problems and challenges that particular districts or district consortia face, and the aim would be not only to enhance individual leader knowledge and skill but also to advance organizational goals.

As we indicated, one prototype for innovation along these lines is New York City's Community District 2, where superintendent Anthony Alvarado presided over "the intentional blurring of the boundaries between management of the system and the activities of staff development" (Elmore and Burney, 1999, p. 281). Although this reform concentrated on teacher learning and relied on recruitment in and out as well as training, the basic stance fits well with the trends in executive education.

A Final Word

This review of trends in professional education has uncovered several aspects of reform notable for their absence. First, relatively little attention has been given to innovations in the assessment of learning. Harvard's medical school has introduced some new performance assessments (such as the triple jump) associated with PBL, but little else is prominent. Second, commentators note the absence of carefully conducted evaluations of professional education. Program designs cannot benefit from empirical evidence that warrants any particular practices, pedagogies, or other elements. A major task ahead is to ground professional education more strongly in evaluation studies that test the claims of reformers. Evidence related to PBL, for example, reveals some modest learning gains over traditional programs, but the results are not dramatic. Argument, not evidence, underlies most reforms in professional education—a state of affairs that does not go unchallenged in K–12 education. Last, the new technologies have not yet made much appearance in professional education and do not appear to be a driving force for change. Yet at least some observers believe that technology holds revolutionary potential. At present, though, we await such developments.

References

Armstrong, E., and others. "Curriculum Design." In D. C. Tosteson, S. J. Adelstein, and S. T. Carver (eds.), *New Pathways to Medical Education: Learning to Learn at Harvard Medical School.* Cambridge, Mass.: Harvard University Press, 1994.

Block, S., and Moore, G. "Project Evaluation." In D. C. Tosteson, S. J. Adelstein, and S. T. Carver (eds.), *New Pathways to Medical Education: Learning to Learn at Harvard Medical School.* Cambridge, Mass.: Harvard University Press, 1994.

Bolman, L. G., and Deal, T. E. "Looking for Leadership: Another Search Party's Report." *Educational Administration Quarterly*, 1994, 30, 77–96.

Bridges, E. M. *Problem-Based Learning for Administrators.* Eugene, Ore.: ERIC Clearinghouse on Educational Management, 1992.

Bridges, E. M., and Hallinger, P. *Implementing Problem-Based Learning in Leadership Development.* Eugene, Ore.: ERIC Clearinghouse on Educational Management, 1995.

Brillinger, M., and Pocock, S. "Learning Needs of Clergy Who Have Not Participated in Continuing Education Events for Clergy." *Canadian Journal of University Continuing Education*, 1993, 19(2), 25–35.

Cardoza, M. [Untitled]. In B. A. Boley, *Crossfire in Professional Education: Students, the Professions, and Society.* New York: Franklin, 1977.

Carmichael, L. "Working Within the Authority Pyramid: The Principal as Learner." *Education and Urban Society*, 1985, 17, 311–323.

Clune, W. "Institutional Choice as a Theoretical Framework for Research on Educational Policy." *Educational Evaluation and Policy Analysis*, 1987, 9, 117–132.

Conger, J., and Xin, K. "Executive Education in the 21st Century." *Journal of Management Education*, 2000, 24, 73–101.

Costa, A. L., and Garmston, R. *Cognitive Coaching: A Foundation for Renaissance Schools.* Norwood, Mass.: Christopher-Gorden, 1994.

Elmore, R., and Burney, D. "Investing in Teacher Learning: Staff Development and Instructional Improvement." In L. Darling-Hammond and G. Sykes (eds.), *Teaching as the Learning Profession: Handbook of Policy and Practice*. San Francisco: Jossey-Bass, 1999.

Greenstein, F. I. *The Presidential Difference: Leadership Style from FDR to Clinton.* New York: Free Press, 2000.

Guttman, R. "Educating Architects: Pedagogy and the Pendulum." *Public Interest*, 1985, *80*, 67–91.

Harrisberger, L. "Curricula and Teaching Methods in Engineering Education." In S. Goodlad (ed.), *Education for the Professions: Quis custodiat . . . ?* Guildford, England: NFER-Nelson, 1985.

Joyce, B., and Showers, B. *Student Achievement Through Staff Development: Fundamentals of School Renewal*. New York: Longman, 1988.

Kaagan, S. S. *Leadership Games. Experiential Learning for Organizational Development.* Thousand Oaks, Calif.: Sage, 1999.

Kaufman, A. (ed.). *Implementing Problem-Based Medical Education: Lessons from Successful Innovations.* New York: Springer-Verlag, 1985.

Kennedy, M. "Inexact Sciences: Professional Education and the Development of Expertise." In E. Z. Rothkopf (ed.), *Review of Research in Education*, Vol. 14. Washington, D.C.: American Educational Research Association, 1988.

March, J. "American Public School Administration: A Short Analysis." *School Review*, 1978, *86*, 217–249.

McCarthy, M. "The Evolution of Educational Leadership Programs." In J. Murphy and K. Senshore-Louis (eds.), *Handbook of Research on Educational Administration*. (2nd ed.) San Francisco: Jossey-Bass, 1999.

McNeal, R. *Revolution in Leadership: Training Apostles for Tomorrow's Church.* Nashville, Tenn.: Abingdon Press, 1988.

Milstein, M., and Associates. *Changing the Way We Prepare Educational Leaders: The Danforth Experience*. Newbury Park, Calif.: Corwin Press, 1993.

Naman, T., & McCall, C. "Pastoring the Church into the 21st Century." Paper presented at the annual meeting of the American Educational Research Association, Montreal, 1999.

National Association of Elementary School Principals. *Elementary and Middle Schools Proficiencies for Principals*. (3rd ed.) Alexandria, Va.: National Association of Elementary School Principals, 1997.

Phillips, D. C. "The Good, the Bad, the Ugly: The Many Faces of Constructivism." *Educational Researcher*, 1995, *24*, 5–12.

Schlossman, S., and Sedlak, M. "The Age of Autonomy in American Management Education." *Selections*, 1985, *1*(3), 16–26.

Schön, D. A. *The Reflective Practitioner: How Professionals Think in Action.* New York: Basic Books, 1983.

Schön, D. A. *Educating the Reflective Practitioner*. San Francisco: Jossey-Bass, 1987.

Schwab, J. J. *Science, Curriculum, and Liberal Education: Selected Essays* (ed. I. Westbury and N. J. Wilkof). Chicago: University of Chicago Press, 1978.

Sfard, A. "On Two Metaphors for Learning and the Dangers of Choosing Just One." *Educational Researcher*, 1998, *27*, 4–13.

Silver, M. "The Student Experience." In D. C. Tosteson, S. J. Adelstein, and S. T. Carver (eds.), *New Pathways to Medical Education: Learning to Learn at Harvard Medical School.* Cambridge, Mass.: Harvard University Press, 1994.

Stevens, R. B. *Law School: Legal Education in America from the 1850s to the 1980s.* Chapel Hill: University of North Carolina Press, 1983.

Sykes, G., and Bird, T. "Teacher Education and the Case Idea." In G. Grant (ed.), *Review of Research in Education,* Vol. 18. Washington, D.C.: American Educational Research Association, 1992.

Sykes, G., and Elmore, R. "Making Schools Manageable: Policy and Administration for Tomorrow's Schools." In J. Hannaway and R. Crowson (eds.), *The Politics of Reforming School Administration.* Bristol, Pa.: Falmer Press, 1989.

Thomson, S. (ed.). *Principals for Our Changing Schools. The Knowledge and Skill Base.* Fairfax, Va.: National Policy Board for Educational Administration, 1993.

Tosteson, D. C. "Toward a New Medicine." In D. C. Tosteson, S. J. Adelstein, and S. T. Carver (eds.), *New Pathways to Medical Education: Learning to Learn at Harvard Medical School.* Cambridge, Mass.: Harvard University Press, 1994.

Notes

1. The business field cannot be reckoned a "profession" according to the features outlined here, but it has adopted many of the elements of the professional model, including a central role for the university-based professional school. Because business schools are centrally engaged in the preparation of managers, executives, and leaders at various levels of the commercial enterprise, we included this field in our review.

2. Writing about the use of cases in teacher education, Sykes and Bird (1992) identified four "kinds of conversation and reasoning," each informing a particular "community of practice." They referred to these modes as *foundational* (cases as instances of the-

ory), as *pragmatic action and deliberation* (cases as problematic situations), as *narrative knowing* (cases as literature), and as *casuistry: reasoning independent of theory* (cases as a body of knowledge). These distinctions overlap with Kennedy's but are not identical. Her first model, technical skill, is not represented in the Sykes-Bird set, which introduces narrative and the literary qualities of cases as another option. On this latter point, two anecdotes are suggestive. Robert Coles, research psychiatrist at Harvard University, relies heavily on literary classics to teach ethics courses in many of Harvard's professional schools, including medicine and law. Likewise, when James March, the renowned organizational theorist, taught a course on leadership at Stanford University, his major texts were *Don Quixote* and *War and Peace*, not the pop manuals proliferating in airport bookstores. Other leadership courses rely on biographies and autobiographies of great leaders. Program designers, then, have multiple frames available to work with.

3. Kennedy (1988, p. 155) defines a problem as "a multidimensional situation that contains an unresolved question: should company X purchase company Y, for instance. Students may attack the problem by analyzing cash flow, net balance sheets, impact on stock prices, impact on bond ratings, or impact on the organization and its human resources. A project is analogous to conventional term papers in that students determine their own goals and strategies. They may be required to design a building or bridge of their own choosing, for instance. Like problems, projects are multifaceted, and can simulate the full complexity of practice. They have the advantage of making students choose their own goals."

4. These particular headings are derived from the divinity degree program at a Lutheran seminary. They are merely indicative of the kinds of topics and issues that make up study for the clergy.

Appendix A

I.   LEADERSHIP PROFICIENCIES

1.   Leadership Behavior

A. Demonstrate vision and provide leadership that appropriately involves the school community in the creation of shared beliefs and values.

B. Demonstrate moral and ethical judgment.

C. Demonstrate creativity and innovative thinking.

D. Involve the school community in identifying and accomplishing the school's mission.

E. Recognize the individual needs and contributions of all staff and students.

F. Apply effective interpersonal skills.

G. Facilitate leadership of others.

H. Conduct needs assessments and use data to make decisions and to plan for school improvement.

I. Identify, pursue, and creatively coordinate the use of available human, material, and financial resources to achieve the school's mission and goals.

J. Explore, assess, and implement educational concepts that enhance teaching and learning.

K. Understand the dynamics of change and the change process:
   - Be knowledgeable about change
   - Be able to assess the organization's readiness for change
   - Understand the dynamics of resistance to change and how it can be reduced

L. Advance the profession through participation as a member of local, state, and national professional groups.

M. Initiate and effectively coordinate collaborative endeavors with local and state agencies.

N. Participate in professional development to enhance personal leadership skills.

2. Communication Skills
   A. Articulate beliefs persuasively, effectively explain decisions, check for understanding, and behave in ways that reflect these beliefs and decisions.
   B. Write and speak clearly and concisely so the message is understood by the intended audience.
   C. Convey opinions succinctly and distinguish between facts and opinions when communicating priorities.
   D. Understand the impact that his or her nonverbal communication has on others.
   E. Use appropriate communication modes, including current technologies, to communicate the school's philosophy, needs, mission, and accomplishments.
   F. Accurately interpret others' written communications.
   G. Make effective use of the media.
   H. Use active listening skills.
   I. Express disagreement without being disagreeable.
   J. Demonstrate skill in giving and receiving feedback.
   K. Model the behavior expected of others.
   L. Exhibit multicultural awareness, gender sensitivity, and racial and ethnic appreciation.

3. Group Processes
   A. Understand group dynamics and apply effective group process skills.
   B. Establish a framework for collaborative action and involve the school community in developing and supporting shared beliefs, values, mission, and goals for school.
   C. Use appropriate team-building skills.
   D. Implement appropriate decision-making and conflict resolution techniques.
   E. Identify, in collaboration with the school community, the decision-making procedures the school will follow.
   F. Work to build consensus both as a leader and as a member of a group.

G. Recognize when direction and intervention are necessary.

4. CURRICULUM AND INSTRUCTION
   A. Maintain a visible presence in the classroom.
   B. Work with staff and community representatives to identify a curriculum framework and common core of learning that support the mission and goals of the school.
   C. Demonstrate to all stakeholders knowledge of the school's curriculum framework and common core of learning.
   D. Convene staff to review and modify the curriculum framework and common core of learning on a regular basis.
   E. Seek financial resources sufficient to meet the needs generated by the common core of learning.
   F. Facilitate the allocation of financial and instructional resources within the school.
   G. Ensure that a diverse, gender-sensitive, and developmentally appropriate program is provided for each child.
   H. Encourage students and staff to participate in co-curricular activities, such as community service, that enhance and complement what is learned in the classroom.
   I. Engage staff in the study of effective teaching practices.
   J. Provide varied support strategies, such as mentors, research, and support teams.
   K. Seek information and advice from a variety of sources.
   L. Encourage staff to create professional networks both within and outside the school.

5. ASSESSMENT
   A. Ensure that the assessment process is both positive and constructive.
   B. Develop, plan, and offer resources for growth and improvement.
   C. Use due process procedures and legal assistance in dealing with non-compliance, disciplinary, and dismissal issues.
   D. Involve others in analyzing assessment data to help design instructional programs that ensure the mission and goals of the school are being met.

E. Maintain high expectations for students, staff, parents, and self.

F. Work with staff to create an effective professional development plan.

G. Expect staff participation in professional development activities.

H. Cooperate with staff to develop a comprehensive counseling, advisory, and support program for students.

I. Ensure instruction is appropriate to the developmental level of the child.

J. Ensure teaching strategies and learning styles are appropriately matched.

K. Ensure a variety of strategies is used to help students succeed.

L. Stress the importance of purposeful planning.

M. Engage parents in discussions on ways to improve student learning.

N. Ensure that staff members communicate regularly with parents regarding student progress.

II. ADMINISTRATIVE/MANAGEMENT PROFICIENCIES

1. ORGANIZATIONAL MANAGEMENT

   A. Possess a clear view of the past, present, and future of the school.

   B. Use collaborative planning to help identify objectives that accomplish the school's mission and goals.

   C. Select, assign, and organize staff in a way that assures the greatest potential for clarifying and accomplishing the school's mission.

   D. Consider research findings in making program decisions.

   E. Analyze problems effectively and reach logical conclusions.

   F. Develop and implement administrative procedures consistent with local policies, state and federal rules and regulations, and contractual agreements.

   G. Ensure that students are offered programs that are relevant to their unique needs.

H. Attract volunteers and provide them with effective training and meaningful assignments.

I. Work with staff and community to create and maintain a safe and orderly learning environment.

J. Coordinate service of community agencies so that appropriate resources are directed to all children.

K. Develop and implement equitable and effective schedules.

L. Employ time management principles.

M. Identify staff strengths in order to appropriately delegate tasks.

N. Develop and facilitate a process for the review of curriculum and instructional issues raised by individuals or groups outside the school.

O. Create and implement policies that assure appropriate and confidential collection and use of school and student data.

P. Keep abreast of developments in education law.

Q. Manage the operation and maintenance of the physical plant.

R. Develop plans for applying technologies to instruction and management.

S. Promote the placement of teaching practicum students, student teachers, and teacher and administrative interns in the school.

2. FISCAL MANAGEMENT

A. Understand the school district budget and its implications for the school.

B. Involve members of the school community in developing budget priorities based on the mission and goals of the school.

C. Prepare the school budget in accordance with school district budgeting procedures.

D. Employ and monitor acceptable accounting procedures in the maintenance of all fiscal records.

E. Use cost control procedures and institute cost-effective practices in the management of all school funds.

   F. Exercise creativity in finding new resources to support school programs.

3. POLITICAL MANAGEMENT
   A. Develop strategies to attract appropriate financial support for public education.
   B. Involve community leaders in the development and support of the school's program.
   C. Use effective strategies to deal with the political issues and forces that affect the school's operation.
   D. Understand the dynamics of school district decision making.
   E. Work effectively with diverse elements of the school community.
   F. Position the school as a community resource.
   G. Participate in local, state, and federal legislative activities.

Source: National Association of Elementary School Principals, 1997.

Appendix B
KNOWLEDGE CATEGORIES—EXAMPLE 2

I.   FUNCTIONAL DOMAINS

1. LEADERSHIP — providing purpose and direction for individuals and groups; shaping school culture and values; facilitating the development of a shared strategic vision for the school; formulating goals and planning change efforts with staff and setting priorities for one's school in the context of community and district priorities and student and staff needs.

2. INFORMATION COLLECTION — gathering data, facts, and impressions from a variety of sources about students, parents, staff members, administrators, and community members; seeking knowledge about policies, rules, laws, precedents, or practices; managing the data flow; classifying and organizing information for use in decision making and monitoring.

3. PROBLEM ANALYSIS — identifying the important elements of a problem situation by analyzing relevant information; framing problems; identifying possible causes; seeking additional needed information; framing and reframing possible solutions; exhibiting conceptual flexibility; assisting others to form reasoned opinions about problems and issues.

4. JUDGMENT — reaching logical conclusions and making high quality, timely decisions based on the best available information; exhibiting tactical adaptability; giving priority to significant issues.

5. ORGANIZATIONAL OVERSIGHT — planning and scheduling one's own and other's work so that resources are used appropriately, and short- and long-term priorities and goals are met; scheduling flows of activities; establishing procedures to regulate activities; monitoring projects to meet deadlines; empowering the process in appropriate places.

6. Implementation — making things happen; putting programs and change efforts into action; facilitating coordination and collaboration of tasks; establishing project checkpoints and monitoring progress; providing "midcourse" corrections when actual outcomes start to diverge from intended outcomes or when new conditions require adaptation; supporting those responsible for carrying out projects and plans.

7. Delegation — assigning projects, tasks, and responsibilities together with clear authority to accomplish them in a timely and acceptable manner; utilizing subordinates effectively; following up on delegated activities.

II. PROGRAMMATIC DOMAINS

1. Instruction and the Learning Environment — creating a school culture for learning; envisioning and enabling with others instructional and auxiliary programs for the improvement of teaching and learning; recognizing the developmental needs of students; ensuring appropriate instructional methods; designing positive learning experiences; accommodating differences in cognition and achievement; mobilizing the participation of appropriate people or groups to develop these programs and to establish a positive learning environment.

2. Curriculum Design — understanding major curriculum design models; interpreting school district curricula; initiating needs analyses; planning and implementing with staff a framework for instruction; aligning curriculum with anticipated outcomes; monitoring social and technological developments as they affect curriculum; adjusting content as needs and conditions change.

3. Student Guidance and Development — understanding and accommodating student growth and development; providing for student guidance, counseling, and auxiliary

services; utilizing and coordinating community organizations; responding to family needs; enlisting the participation of appropriate people and groups to design and conduct these programs and to connect schooling with plans for adult life; planning for a comprehensive program of student activities.

4. STAFF DEVELOPMENT — working with faculty and staff to identify professional needs; planning, organizing, and facilitating programs that improve faculty and staff effectiveness and are consistent with instructional goals and needs; supervising individuals and groups; providing feedback on performance; arranging for remedial assistance; engaging faculty and others to plan and participate in recruitment and development activities; and initiating self-development.

5. MEASUREMENT AND EVALUATION — determining what diagnostic information is needed about students, staff, and the school environment; examining the extent to which outcomes meet or exceed previously defined standards, goals, or priorities for individuals or groups; drawing inferences for program revisions; interpreting measurements or evaluations for others; relating programs to desired outcomes; developing equivalent measures of competence; designing accountability mechanisms.

6. RESOURCE ALLOCATION — procuring, apportioning, monitoring, accounting for, and evaluating fiscal, human, material, and time resources to reach outcomes that reflect the needs and goals of the school site; planning and developing the budget process with appropriate staff.

III. INTERPERSONAL DOMAINS

1. MOTIVATING OTHERS — creating conditions that enhance the staff's desire and willingness to focus energy on achieving educational excellence; planning and encouraging participation; facilitating teamwork and collegiality; treating staff as professionals; providing intellectual stimulation; supporting

innovation; recognizing and rewarding effective performance; providing feedback, coaching, and guidance; providing needed resources; serving as a role model.

2. Interpersonal Sensitivity — perceiving the needs and concerns of others; dealing tactfully with others; working with others in emotionally stressful situations or in conflict; managing conflict; obtaining feedback; recognizing multicultural differences; relating to people of varying backgrounds.

3. Oral and Nonverbal Expression — making oral presentations that are clear and easy to understand; clarifying and restating questions; responding, reviewing, and summarizing for groups; utilizing appropriate communicative aids; being aware of cultural and gender-based norms; adapting for audiences.

4. Written Expression — expressing ideas clearly in writing; writing appropriately for different audiences such as students, teachers, and parents; preparing brief memoranda, letters, reports, and other job-specific documents.

IV. CONTEXTUAL DOMAINS

1. Philosophical and Cultural Values — acting with a reasoned understanding of the role of education in a democratic society and in accordance with accepted ethical standards; recognizing philosophical influences in education; reflecting an understanding of American culture, including current social and economic issues related to education.

2. Legal and Regulatory Applications — acting in accordance with federal and state constitutional provisions, statutory standards, and regulatory applications; working within local rules, procedures, and directives; recognizing standards of care involving civil and criminal liability for negligence and intentional torts; and administering contracts and financial accounts.

3. Policy and Political Influences — understanding schools as political systems; identifying relationships between public policy and education; recognizing policy issues; examining and affecting policies individually and through professional and public groups; relating policy initiatives to the welfare of students; addressing ethical issues.

4. Public Relations — developing common perceptions about school issues; interacting with internal and external publics; understanding and responding skillfully to the electronic and printed news media; initiating and reporting news through appropriate channels; managing school reputations; enlisting public participation and support; recognizing and providing for various markets.

Source: Thomson, 1993.

Part Three

An International Perspective

Chapter Seven

Mission Possible?

An International Analysis of Training for Principals

Brian J. Caldwell
Gerard T. Calnin
Wendy P. Cahill

This chapter provides an international comparative survey of the training of principals. It describes best practices; emerging ideas, theories, and issues; standards in representative nations; and other information regarding international practices. The context is an apparent crisis in the role. Expressed bluntly, few people want the job, vacancies are growing fast, and the preparation for those who take the job is generally considered to be inadequate.

Reports from nation after nation refer to the shrinking pool of applicants. The most negative is from New Zealand, where only 9 percent of assistant and deputy principals apparently want the job. Darrell Ward, president of the New Zealand Education Institute (the elementary teachers' union), which commissioned the study that yielded this finding, went to the heart of the problem. "These people are the closest to the principal in terms of working relationships in a school, and I think it's safe to say that they're seeing the workload issues, they're seeing the stress, and they're saying, 'It's not for me.'"

The conditions Ward described appear endemic in much of the English-speaking world. Any report of best practices in training, current or proposed, must take account of the "workload issues." At first sight, these derive from higher standards that are expected of schools; decentralization of authority, responsibility, and accountability; changes in the technology of learning and teaching; and limited resources. A deeper analysis reveals that these and similar trends are associated with—indeed, are a consequence of—fundamental changes in society, especially in Australia, Britain, Canada, New Zealand, and the United States. Some commentators argue that we are experiencing the most sweeping societal transformation in the history of humankind. A successful training program for principals must equip a person who wants the job with the knowledge, skills, and attitudes to operate under these conditions.

Our preparation for the report that formed the basis of this chapter began in 1999 with the assumption that exemplary programs existed. It soon became apparent that this was not the case, at least on the scale that provided exemplars for a national effort. There have been favorable reports of small-scale projects at the district or state level. Some programs have been successful on a wider scale, at the state, regional, and national levels, but they are not part of a coherent collection of strategies that systematically and successfully address the need for principal training. Other programs with a broad mandate may have been highly successful in the past, even on a large scale, but are no longer so.

Soon after our work began, an effort to design a program on a national scale moved beyond the preliminary planning stage with the creation of the National College for School Leadership in Britain, and the NCSL has moved closer to the status of an exemplar.

Note that we use the term *principal* throughout this chapter except where reference is made to practice in Britain, where the term *headteacher* is used.

Factors That Shape Interest in the Principalship

Considerable change in the role of the principal has occurred and continues to occur. Although change was endemic in the profession for the last quarter of the twentieth century, the recent acceleration of change and its pervasiveness for schools are causing concerns about the way we prepare candidates for principalships and the shortage of suitable applicants for the available positions. The literature suggests that the ubiquity of change, complexity of the role, level of remuneration, status of the profession, legal constraints, and impact on family life are all reasons for the dearth of candidates seeking leadership roles in schools.

Cooley and Shen (1999) demonstrated that ten key factors influence prospective administrators in deciding whether to seek a position as a school leader. Results from their study suggest that "organizational relationships, more than other factors, affect a teacher's willingness to seek an administrative position in a particular district" (p. 79). Relationships among the governing body or board, administration, and teachers were the most important consideration, followed by salary and community support. Other factors included the impact on home and community life, stress levels associated with the position, poor working conditions, and the unattractive nature of the work in a society that is placing more and more demands on teachers, schools, and principals.

Daresh and Male (2000) explored the changes that affected principals in both the United Kingdom and the United States in their first year of their new jobs. This research supports the view that the role is complex and in particular that new leaders are ill-prepared for the degree of responsibility thrust on them. It found that they had difficulty learning to reduce conflicts and problems in a wide range of constituent groups. The candidates reported that they were not prepared for the life-changing event of assuming the role and felt unprepared for major decisions that require reflection and assistance, with a strong emphasis on personal values and ethics. The personal lives of new leaders were altered significantly, with most reporting feelings of alienation, isolation, and frustration in their work. Britain and the United States follow quite distinct models for preparing prospective leaders, but Daresh and Male (2000) conclude that neither method has prepared aspiring leaders adequately, adding a further dimension to the problem of the position. They conclude: "British headteachers do not feel as if they were prepared totally for their posts simply because they had years of experience in roles similar to but not the same as head-teachers. And American principals report that academic pre-service training does not prepare them completely for their jobs. The issue, therefore, is not one of suggesting that one is prepared either by previous practice or by courses. It is an issue of finding appropriate balance" (p. 99).

Davis (1996) identified a number of impediments to the role of the modern principal but gives weight to the problem of values in a postmodern and pluralistic society where absolutes are replaced by relativism and legislation has sought to mandate much in the public and private lives of citizens. Davis sees potential problems for principals when they face a values vacuum and overzealous litigation:

> We are approaching a time of increasing uncertainty, when the absence of shared values will complicate life for school principals and for school systems. In default of a clear understanding of what is right and what is wrong, people will make assessments on the basis of what they *feel* is right and wrong. No condition could give more opportunity for debate and disagreement. . . . There is no doubt that the first part of the next century will see litigious proceedings become commonly accepted responses to schools' management of such areas as student misbehavior, curriculum choice and attendance at class [pp. 10–11].

James and Whiting (cited in Gunter, 1999) report research into the decision to become a headteacher at a time of a shortage in recruits. They argue that "the notion that there is a large pool of potential heads out there who have the capacity to assume leadership and who will, of course, choose to do so in sufficient numbers is unsustainable" (p. 261). They go on to show that the decision not to become a headteacher involves contextual reasons, from job satisfaction through to family commitments, combined with a view that headship was not professionally or personally attractive. The formal utilitarian aspect of the training and the projected life of a headteacher remains unattractive and is not helped by the ridiculing of educational values and of those who "resist" business management.

Consider some of the changing dimensions to the job of a headteacher in Britain over the past ten years:

- Competitive tendering for cleaning and canteen facilities
- The hiring, firing, promotion, and dismissal of staff
- The selection, recruitment, retention, discipline, and departure of pupils
- The bidding for resources from external funding agencies
- The installation and operation of information systems to measure and report on performance
- The school inspections by a privatized team according to the OFSTED [Office for Standards in Education] framework
- The need to bring in trainers and consultants to support staff training and development

Other changes include a national curriculum; national testing; teacher appraisal (evaluation); site-based financial decision making, including responsibility for hiring and firing staff; and per-pupil funding and parental choice linked to accountability at the school level for results and value for money (Creissen and Ellison, 1998). These tasks are typical of senior executives' work in other fields. It is therefore understandable that "school principals are increasingly regarded as the equivalents of senior managers in medium-sized business enterprise[s]. . . . The message which the government wishes to emphasize is that of schools as businesses in a market-led economy for education" (Thody, 1998).

Centralization and decentralization are apparently competing trends in education introduced from the late 1980s onward. Reflecting centralization of the British system, a national curriculum now applies to all public schools, national standards are set by the central government, and all schools are subject to frequent inspections on nationally set requirements. To decentralize, schools have become individually self-managed. If centralized control is the intention of the government, as it appears to be, then nationalization of the training of school principals is yet another part of the control mechanism.

Olson (2000a) reported that some reasons for a shortage of appropriate qualified candidates for U.S. school leadership were related to the quality of training programs. A leader in the National Association of Elementary Principals (NAEP) believes that the traditional leadership training programs "have not been able to move from the theoretical to the practical issues that principals face in a manner that's been, in our minds, as effective as they need to be" and believes that better alternatives are emerging. Sibyll Carnochan, director of policy and research for the Broad Foundation, argues that "new training programs should blend coursework and on-the-job experience; provide ongoing support for novices; and combine a deep knowledge about instruction with management training" (Olson, 2000a).

Elsewhere, Olson (2000b) suggests other reasons for concern about the quality of leadership in schools:

> Most noticeably, the push for standards-based reform—and the pressure on schools to deliver in terms of academic performance—have raised the demands and pressures on principals and brought an unprecedented level of public scrutiny to their job performance. In some cases, principals' salaries and contracts are now dependent on gains in student achievement. . . . But the focus on leadership also reflects a belated recognition that standards and procedures alone can't energize a dispirited teaching staff or bring parents and community leaders together to turn around a failing school. . . . At the same time, the student population is becoming more diverse, increasing the demands placed on school. . . . Nor have the management functions traditionally associated with school leadership gone away—if anything, they've become more demanding. Princi-

pals are expected to exert more control over budgets and hiring and to work more collaboratively with their communities.

A Review of Principal Training Programs

We shall now review developments in a number of nations, with particular reference to Britain, Australia, the United States, Hong Kong, and Sweden.

Britain

In Great Britain, increasing responsibility and accountability at the school level through site-based management in the form of local management of schools (LMS), grant-maintained status (GMS), and the city technology college (CTC) initiative "led to pressure from a wide range of sources, including the government and the teaching profession, for a more coherent approach to leadership and management development for both middle managers and head-teachers" (Creissen and Ellison, 1998).

National Professional Qualification for Headteachers. The trend in training programs for aspirant principals has been toward a centralized, compulsory, competency-based scheme based on the National Standards for Headteachers. In 1997, launched by the Teacher Training Agency, the National Professional Qualification for Headteachers (NPQH) was introduced to address the professional development needs of aspiring and practicing headteachers. The qualification is aimed at providing aspiring headteachers with the skills and abilities to take up the leadership of a school. This program has moved away from conventional models of training that traditionally served the profession through diverse and pluralistic multiple providers and an emphasis on voluntary participation. The move toward a centrally determined and accredited training program is seen as a break with the past that reflects the failure of traditional programs to meet the needs of the modern principal.

The National Standards for Headteachers (Teacher Training Agency, 1998) contain five sections that prescribe criteria a candidate needs to meet and training that will facilitate attainment. The five sections are as follows:

1. Core purpose of headship
2. Key outcomes of headship
3. Professional knowledge and understanding
4. Skills and attributes
5. Key areas of headship, namely:
   a. Strategic direction and development of the school
   b. Teaching and learning
   c. Leading and managing staff
   d. Efficient and effective deployment of staff and resources
   e. Accountability

Training centers and providers were established in ten NPQH training and development centers in England and Wales and regional assessment centers. Alternative training is provided through a partnership of the Open University and the National Association of Headteachers. Training is focused on activities that are both practical and relevant to school improvement and provided by accredited trainers. It is useful to note at this point that the scale of the project is very large indeed, as there are about twenty-five thousand public schools and about three thousand private schools in Britain.

The NPQH has six stages and is based on the separation of assessment from training (Gunter, 1999):

Stage 1: *Application and selection*. Eligibility is determined by the local education authority (or an assessment center if the person was in a grant-maintained or independent school; the grant-maintained classification was abolished in 1998).

Stage 2: *Needs assessment.* Candidates undergo a needs assessment at an assessment center and produce an action plan for their training.

Stage 3: *Training and assessment.* Candidates undertake compulsory training related to key areas a and e in section 5 and produce four assessment tasks.

Stage 4: *Remaining standards assessment for candidates not following the training.* All candidates need to complete the assessment tasks for key areas b, c, and d in section 5, a total of six tasks. Training modules are available for candidates who identify these areas in their action plan.

Stage 5: *Final assessment.* Candidates return to the assessment center, having demonstrated that they have met the national standards through the ten assessment tasks. The decision to award is based on a day at the center in which, through "group and individual exercises," the candidates demonstrate that they are ready for headship. Emphasis is on the core requirement for headship: candidates must "demonstrate their overall readiness for headship by showing that they are capable of exercising the professional judgment and leadership qualities of a headteacher" (Teacher Training Agency, 1998).

Stage 6: *Award of the qualification.* The award of the NPQH signals readiness for headship, which means that "governing bodies can be confident that anyone who has successfully completed this program of training can perform effectively in [the] post. The NPQH will also give aspiring headteachers the confidence to know they are ready for the top job" (Teacher Training Agency, 1998).

Anthea Millett, former chief executive of the Teacher Training Agency, responsible for headship training programs, claimed that "the program is unique in bringing together development of personal leadership effectiveness with school improvement strategies" and says that the program is right to "aim at raising the game of all headteachers, and that trials so far suggest this has been a very successful outcome." She added: "Research and inspection evidence makes clear the extent to which the quality of leadership is crucial to school improvement. In highly effective schools, as well as schools which have reversed a trend of poor performance and declining achievement, it is the headteacher who sets the pace, leading and motivating the pupils and staff to perform to their highest potential" (Millett, 1998).

Not all commentators subscribe to this sanguine view. Gunter (1999) reviewed some of the literature that evaluated the current NPQH program and expressed concern that the type of training offered by the NPQH program fails to provide candidates with sufficient differentiation in terms of their needs and those of their schools, in areas ranging from gender issues to spiritual leadership, which might be essential in religious or denominational schools. A further concern involved the "deficit model" of sorting out potential but weak candidates or effective but failing headteachers, a task with little appeal for education professionals. Also, the emphasis in the training program was more on achieving competence than on drawing on what has been learned about the importance of mentoring.

Another criticism was that much of the training program appears to be geared toward management processes rather than issues associated with leadership and assumed a causal connection between what the headteacher does and the eventual outcome. The emphasis on organization, management, and production of measurable facts suggests a process devoid of issues related to values, power, and relationships. Gunter argued that "we have been moved radically, perhaps tragically, from what traditionally has been known as the preparation of headteachers to the training of headteachers, and in doing so all the debates that have gone on nationally and internationally about pedagogy and purpose are being marginalized" (p. 259). The adoption of business competencies and strategies has, in part, served to alienate those candidates who hold firm to the centrality of their educational role in their professional identity.

A further perceived problem with the NPQH training program was that it assumed a rational or linear view of change and change management. The teaching of or training in competencies presupposes that these skills in areas of technical expertise will effectively equip the principal to initiate and implement change in a turbulent school environment. Other writers (for example, Fullan, 1993; Stacey, 1992) argued that the pace of change, the degree to which it is externally imposed or arises internally, and the complexity of large organizations such as schools mean that the management of change is far more complex, that there is no clear relationship between input and outcomes, and that change management in the future will be far less linear or rational. In this environment, change management will involve a complex interplay of skills, motivation, and capacity to provide meaning and animate others. Change, then, is more about a journey, making and refining plans to achieve a particular set of objectives, rather than setting a predetermined pathway. Leaders will be required to be flexible, responsive, and adaptive to increasing turbulence in the school milieu. Ouston (1998) argued that "incremental approaches to organizational change are more likely to be successful in a complex environment: decisions made rationally are those which are most likely to *contribute* to achieving long-term objectives" (p. 128). It would be difficult to see how the skills of flexibility, adaptability, motivating, and providing meaning for others could easily be achieved in a rational, universal, competency-based model of principal training.

In concluding her remarks on problems associated with the NPQH model of training, Gunter posited that "the promotion of agency is creating a picture of headship which will put a lot of very creative people off, as it denies the broader connection with the social and the moral" (1999, p. 262).

Leadership Program for Serving Heads: The Hay/McBer Program. Another initiative in Britain is the National Program for

Serving Heads (NPSH), which commenced in November 1998. The NPSH was developed for the Teacher Training Agency by private consulting organization Hay/McBer, in partnership with the National Association of Headteachers (the professional body that serves elementary school principals) and the Open University. As described by the Department for Education and Employment (2000), the program

- Draws on national standards for headteachers and research evidence on the characteristics of highly effective headteachers
- Begins with a thorough and confidential analysis of personal and school performance, providing a sharp focus for subsequent training and development
- Features a four-day residential workshop followed by further professional development and support
- Directly links personal target setting by the headteacher and school target setting for raising pupils' achievements
- Combines challenge and support in a neutral and confidential setting where heads can share expertise with colleagues from other types of schools and different parts of the country

The program is conducted in four stages, with preworkshop preparation requiring participants and staff members to complete a questionnaire on leadership style (providing 360-degree feedback); a four-day residential workshop; postworkshop support, including electronic networking and the use of a development guide; and a follow-up day that calls for preparation by the participants and members of their school communities. The program is delivered through seven national training providers, most of which are consortia whose members include at least one university. The University of London Institute of Education, through its Leadership Center, is the only university acting in its own right. It is an expensive program, costing £2,000 per participant, with an optional

£250 to be matched with a business partner through the Partners in Leadership scheme. Participants may seek support from their local education authorities, or they may self-fund. The program has consistently received very positive ratings by participants.

This is clearly just one component of a more comprehensive suite of programs but is selected for recommendation as an exemplar for two reasons: its evident success on a national scale and as a successful adaptation from another country. The Hay/McBer organization successfully tendered for its role in the scheme on the basis of its success with an almost identical program in Victoria, Australia, brief details of which are given in another section of this chapter. Anthea Millett, former CEO of the Teacher Training Agency, visited Victoria to gather firsthand information on the scheme as implemented in that state. She was aware of the similarities in the reform agendas of Britain and Victoria but noted three points of difference. In Britain, the target population is all serving heads, numbering about twenty-five thousand in public schools, to participate at the rate of three to four thousand a year, whereas for Victoria the program is intended for experienced heads only. In Britain, the program is implemented through seven national providers, with staff trained by Hay/McBer, whereas Hay/McBer conducts the Victorian program with its own staff. Third, the Partnership in Leadership scheme has no counterpart in Victoria.

The framework and other aspects of the program are derived from the work of David McClelland, founder of the McBer practice in the Hay Group and formerly a professor at Harvard. It is based on the view that four variables—individual characteristics, job requirements, leadership styles, and school climate—come together and affect performance. Early evidence cited by Hay/McBer in both Victoria and Britain suggests an association of this kind.

It is noteworthy that Hay/McBer secured a contract with the Department for Education and Employment in 1999 to research teacher effectiveness as part of a scheme for threshold assessment and performance management of teachers. The outcomes were scheduled for announcement in May. It is understandable that the commissioning of this project drew mixed reactions from university researchers who might normally expect to be engaged for such work.

National College for School Leadership. The program in Britain may be viewed as exemplary, despite reservations and critiques, for it is national in scope and has been implemented. However, it is the next stage that will surely attract considerable international attention. In mid-1999, the government released its prospectus for a National College for School Leadership (NCSL) (Department for Education and Employment, 1999). It is noteworthy that Prime Minister Tony Blair made the announcement and appears to have made the project his own in many ways. He cowrote the foreword to the prospectus with David Blunkett, secretary of state for education, employment, and training.

The main purpose of the following short account is to establish the significance of the initiative on the world stage, for the United Kingdom has a population of more than fifty million, with about twenty-five thousand public schools and around three thousand private schools whose leaders will be involved in the NCSL program in one way or another.

The intention was signaled by Blair and Blunkett (Department for Education and Employment, 1999, p. 2):

> Leadership and vision are crucial to raising standards and aspirations across the nation's schools. We cannot leave them to chance. That is why we intend to establish a National College for School Leadership, as a key part of our modernization of the teaching profession.
>
> The National College for School Leadership is among the most radical and innovative proposals in our Teachers Green Paper [Department for Education and Employment, 1998]. Rooted in outstanding practice, it will offer heads, deputies and other school leaders for the first time the professional support and recognition they deserve as they strive to transform our schools. . . .
>
> Up to now, leadership development has lacked coherence, direction and status. For the first time, the college will provide a

single national focus for leadership development and research, offering school leaders the quality support other professions take for granted.

A national competition was conducted to select a site for the college. Those that submitted tenders were required to assemble a consortium of public and private interests in educational and noneducational domains, demonstrating a capacity to provide the kind of site required; build local support and commitment; and make a contribution to resourcing the enterprise. The University of Nottingham was chosen. A director (Heather Du Quesney, currently director of education for the London borough of Lambeth) took up her appointment in September 2000. The college is responsible for the NPQH and, more broadly, for designing and delivering a range of programs at its site in Nottingham and around the country. Building capacity for on-line learning is clearly a priority, as is ongoing research about school leadership. A feature is the international linkage, and this alone is exemplary, with scores of people from many nations invited to contribute their ideas so far. Particular features of the program are likely to include problem-based learning, mentoring, international travel and exchange, and use of the "master class" approach. The government has committed £10 million to building the NCSL headquarters in Nottingham and £100 million per year for three years for mounting its programs.

At the time of writing, the NCSL was gaining momentum in each of the areas in its mandate, with plans for delivery now including scores of local and regional learning networks. Leadership in middle management has been added, increasing the number of potential clients at any one time to more than a quarter of a million people.

Australia

We would like to have included reports of exemplary practice in our own nation, but no coherent and comprehensive strategy is in place at this time. Elements of such a strategy do exist and are briefly described here. The situation in Australia is similar to that in the United States in that the constitutions of both nations make education a state responsibility. The national government has an influence on policy and practice through the provision of grants to states and to other bodies, with particular conditions attached regarding use and accountability. Our review of Australia's training programs is divided into three sections. The first describes noteworthy practices in Victoria. The second summarizes efforts to develop a competency-based approach. The third provides an overall assessment, highlighting the fragmentation of effort around the country.

Noteworthy Practices in Victoria. In Victoria, the change in the role of principal has been greater than in other states. However, all states have programs for principal development.

An example of best practices in the 1980s was the program of the Institute of Educational Administration (IEA) in Victoria. Its centerpiece was a four-week intensive residential experience modeled on that of management colleges in the business sector. Its building in Geelong was purpose-designed around forty-five people assigned to syndicates of fifteen people each. Some leading international experts in educational administration served as consultants for two of the four weeks. Other consultants assisted in particular fields of administration, including developments of local (state) interest. A problem-based or case study approach was preferred in syndicate work, and the program was noted for its coherence.

The IEA also conducted short programs and developed resources for use or purchase by others. About two thousand people participated in its extended residential programs over nearly fifteen years prior to its closure in early 1993. Although the IEA's impact was likely a very powerful one for participants and the institutions they served, the number of participants was but a small fraction of the population of school leaders during the time of its operation. This was a function of program design. Aside from the issue of impact, the IEA was dependent to a large extent on state grants and came under pressure as the financial circumstances in Victoria deteriorated in the late 1980s and early 1990s. A change in government in 1992 saw closure and sale of the property.

A similar program may be a worthwhile element of a comprehensive strategy, especially if it is offered in several locations, is of somewhat shorter duration, and is supported with advanced on-line learning and powerful interactive multimedia resources of the kind now available. A combination of revenue from the sale of on-line services, public and private funds, and a major client contribution would ensure financial viability.

The administration that closed the IEA had a commitment to principal development that was manifested in several noteworthy ways. Its focus was the package of reforms from 1993 known as Schools of the Future. This brought together a state curriculum and standards framework, local selection of teaching staff who remained under contract with the state education department, the decentralization of more than 90 percent of the state's education budget to schools for local decision making, the introduction of statewide assessment tests in key learning areas at two points in elementary schooling and one point in secondary schooling (there is also the program for the Victorian Certificate of Education at the end of secondary schooling), and a system of annual and triennial reviews with external validation. An integrating mechanism is the school charter, a document outlining school priorities over a three-year period and reflecting agreement between the school and its community on the one hand and the school and the education department on the other.

Several large-scale training efforts were mounted. Brian Caldwell and the late Max Sawatzki contracted to provide five-day residential training programs for more than one thousand principals from 1994 to 1997 on the theme "Creating a School of the Future." The program was conducted in three parts, the first a three-day residence, the second a work-based project, and the third a two-day residence. Major themes fell into the broad areas of strategic leadership and management; self-management in the personal sense, with opportunities for gaining 360-degree feedback and personal career planning; performance management and quality assurance; and team-building. Mean ratings were invariably in the high 4s on a 5-point scale.

Other major efforts centered around various curriculum initiatives, starting with literacy. The Early Literacy Research Project (ELRP), led by Peter Hill and Carmel Crévola, yielded valuable findings that undergirded programs for principals and teachers in most schools. Impact on learning outcomes has been demonstrated. Related projects have been implemented in several U.S. cities. A similar effort is under way for school improvement in the middle years, based on findings in the Middle Years Research and Development Project (MYRAD), led by Peter Hill. Hill and Crévola have proposed a general design for improving learning outcomes that includes standards and targets; monitoring and assessment; classroom teaching programs; professional learning teams; school and class organization; intervention and special assistance; and home, school, and community partnerships—all underpinned and centered on beliefs and understandings (Hill and Crévola, 1999). Training programs based on the notion of school design show promise as an integrating mechanism for a major component of principal development.

Two other initiatives in Victoria are noteworthy: the creation of the Australian Principals Center (APC) and the Hay/McBer program that was the forerunner of the Leadership Program for Serving Heads in Britain, described earlier. The APC was created as a limited company in 1995 with directors from the Education Department of Victoria, the Victorian Association of State Secondary Principals, the Victorian Primary Principals Association, and the University of Melbourne through its Faculty of Education (which provides the site of the enterprise at its Hawthorn campus). The board of the APC has been chaired from the outset by Peter Hill. The organization has a small core staff and offers a range of programs, including several under contract to the education department. It has pioneered a program of peer recognition with various grades of fellowship. Like the former Institute of Educational Administration, it is dependent on the state government for much of its funding. An attempt to develop the APC into a national organization has not succeeded, with other states preferring to establish their own centers or institutes. It links well with other organizations in Victoria interested in teacher and principal development. Its future may be resolved in the next year or so in the context of plans by the new state government to establish an institute of teaching. It is interesting to note that the longest-serving chief executive officer of the APC, Bruce Davis, is currently the senior consultant to the Education Department in Hong Kong in the design of a comprehensive program for principal development (which we discuss later in this chapter).

The final development in Victoria reported here is the Hay/McBer program described earlier in connection with the Leadership Program for Serving Heads in Britain. It is likely that success in Victoria led to its adoption in Britain. The Hay/McBer Leadership Development Program (LDP) in Victoria was in turn based on programs conducted for major corporate clients including ICI, IBM, PepsiCo, and Mobil. It was introduced in Victoria as part of a package of programs to support the Schools of the Future initiative. The program was piloted and refined in 1994, and more than four hundred experienced principals and eighty senior managers in the education department have taken part. The Hay Group provided us with the findings of an independent review suggesting that it was an efficient and effective professional development program with a positive impact on the performance of principals and the climate of the school. More recently, Hay/McBer has been invited to develop a program in Victoria for aspiring principals. It is interesting that a trigger for this work was the decline in number and quality of teachers seeking the principalship. Hay/McBer was also chosen to conduct research and prepare a school leadership competency model for principals and others who hold positions of responsibility in schools.

Likely future developments in Victoria concern the Victorian Institute of Teaching, established in 2001 as a professional body that will accredit programs for preparation and professional development of teachers and have oversight of a standards-based system of teacher accreditation. The legislation contains provision for various "colleges" to deal with these matters for particular classes of teachers. One such class is the "principal class," and it is expected that a college of principals will be created. The future of the Australian Principals' Centre in relation to this entity was not clear at the time of writing.

A Competency-Based Approach. A competency framework for standards of principals' work is currently in use in two states, Queensland and, in a modified form, Western Australia. The competency framework identifies seven key areas of responsibility, including areas such as curriculum management and people management. Each of these key areas is subdivided into six or eight competencies—for example, the development of "an effective performance management process for all staff." The standard of performance in each competency is to be judged by indicators such as these: "Performance management process is in place which is clearly understood by all staff and is consistent with the regulatory framework" or "Staff are encouraged to reflect on their performance and identify strengths and areas for development." The competency-based model developed in these states is therefore one that describes observable behaviors based on a close scrutiny and analysis of the role of principal (Louden and Wildy, 1999).

Louden and Wildy (1999) have three concerns about the competency approach. First, "standards frameworks attempt to divide complex professional performances into hierarchical lists of dispositions, knowledge, or duties" with seven key responsibility areas. Under each are three to eight competencies and then a further subdivision into indicators, with a total of 134 items on the lowest level of the hierarchy. Despite caveats suggesting that these items are not to be viewed in isolation, "the consequence of long hierar-

chical lists is to fragment professional performance. Careful warn-
ings not to see the lists as fragmentary do not overcome the problem of fragmentation. Within a single incident, principals may
demonstrate a whole range of competencies, which appear as separate items on separate lists" (p. 102).

Louden and Wildy's second objection is that such standards and
competencies "separate the performance from the context within
which it occurs." The context in which a specific competency is
required will affect the skills and knowledge brought to bear on the
situation. "For example, quite different knowledge and skills would
be required to demonstrate the competency [standard] 'provides and
receives regular and constructive feedback' in the context of well-
established collegial relationship than the knowledge and skills
required in giving feedback in the context of an alleged moral
impropriety by a teacher. . . . A performance that appears to be an
obvious and separate competency when stated in a general form
may require a range of different knowledge and skills in different
contexts" (1999, p. 103).

The third concern about the competency model, with its lists
of duties or dispositions, is the degree of precision required to prove
the operation of such competencies. It is difficult to determine
absolute degrees of competence — one has the skill or not — within
a professional role that requires a more detailed and nuanced understanding of particular abilities or dispositions and of the complex
environment in which they are performed. The impact of the list of
competencies, therefore, is to dichotomize the skill rather than esti-
mating where a person's skill level sits on a continuum of development or progression.

In Victoria, the introduction of Schools of the Future was
supported by the range of leadership programs described earlier. A
performance management system based on the specification of
competencies was also introduced. It has two components: accreditation, which certifies the demonstration of key skills and competencies and evidence of their application to the job; and assessment,
which certifies the achievement of agreed outcomes. Geoff Spring,

former director of schools and secretary for education, reported on the role of mentors or coaches and the intended outcome: "The widely accepted model of mentoring and coaching is being implemented with a pool of experienced principals receiving training to act as coaches and mentors for their colleagues. The performance management system is the centerpiece for ensuring quality management practices and links improving student learning to performance management" (1996, p. 28).

Though not a program designed for aspiring principals, Performance Standards for School Principals is an attempt in Western Australia to explore an alternative to the competency-based models by using a probabilistic standards framework to support the judgments made by principals. The project is a collaborative research and development project undertaken by Edith Cowen University and the Department of Education of Western Australia.

Rather than describing in detail the work of a principal, the purpose of the project was to specify and illustrate the range of performance within the principal's work. After initial research into selecting trial dimensions of principals' work (for example, managing staff) and establishing a continuum of performance, the second phase provided an account of the content of principals' work, the duties to be undertaken, and the skills and dispositions required to perform the duties at a high level of performance. The third phase was designed to develop progress maps of performance on each of the dimensions in the standards framework (Louden and Wildy, 1999).

The project attempted to deal with several weaknesses identified in competency-based standards, such as the hierarchical lists, the decontextualizing of performance, and the false dichotomies between those who reach a prescribed standard and those who fail. In contrast, "the probabilistic standards framework used in this research project locates performance on a set of continua, not on either side of a dichotomy; it offers an estimate of performance, rather than a final determination; it uses assessment items as expendable exemplars rather than as essential elements of principals' work; and it describes what can normally be expected of people at a given level of performance rather than whether an individual has attained mastery of a skill" (Louden and Wildy, 1999, p. 118).

The research project demonstrated that it is possible to construct a probabilistic standards framework describing principals' performance. Dimensions representing duties, interpersonal skills, and moral dispositions have been developed inductively, based on principals' ratings of a series of case studies of principals' work. Louden and Wildy (1999) are optimistic that the project has the potential to offer an alternative and more rewarding response to the professional development of principals and suggest that rather than listing duties and responsibilities as competencies, "they abstract from commonly shared experiences and familiar dilemmas those interpersonal skills and moral dispositions which appear to differentiate the quality of principals' performance. For these reasons, the rich reality of the case studies appears to engage principals at a deeper level than lists of duties and dispositions" (p. 118).

Research such as that associated with Performance Standards for School Principals may well provide insight into alternative training programs for aspiring principals.

A Fragmented Effort. Much on the Australian scene is commendable, dating from the exemplar of the Institute of Educational Administration that functioned for a decade and a half until the early 1990s. Currently, however, the effort is fragmented. Neither across the nation as a whole nor within a single system is there a coherent and comprehensive approach to the preparation and professional development of principals. In Victoria, where reform has been relatively coherent, even if controversial in some respects, the many commendable initiatives do not come together in the way envisaged, for example, with the National College for School Leadership in Britain. This may have been intended with the Australian Principals Centre, essentially a Victoria-based organization, but it has not been achieved. Leadership development for learning and teaching in literacy, numeracy, and the middle years is designed and delivered in other agencies, as is the Hay/McBer program. Units of the education department, variously named in recent years, have served as the coordinating mechanism to the extent that state funding and the needs of leaders in government or public schools are involved. However, cooperation with professional associations and organizations serving nonpublic schools is high.

A major national effort in Australia along the lines of that under way in Britain is constrained by constitutional arrangements that make education a state responsibility. Professional associations of principals are organized along the same lines. These same constraints are likely in other nations, including the United States, that are a union or federation of states. However, the national bodies representing principals at different levels and in different sectors have reached a general agreement, and representations have been made to the national government to support a national institute.

United States

In the United States, many successful programs, such as the Harvard Principals' Center, have built a national and international reputation. Regional "principals' institutes" have been common in recent decades. What follows is an account of programs with national scope or mentioned in recent international literature.

Several groups in the United States have responded to the concern for effective leadership in schools by introducing alternative training programs. One such program is the Interstate School Leaders Licensure Consortium (ISLLC), which has brought together many of the major parties with a stake in educational leadership — the states, relevant professional associations, and universities. Under the auspices of the Council of Chief State School Officers and in cooperation with the National Policy Board for Educational Administration, the ISLLC has set out to develop ways of redefining school leadership in light of the changes in school education and the sociopolitical forces that affect the role of the school principal.

These emerging ideas about leadership are predicated on a new set of values and principles about teaching and learning and on the obsolescence of the bureaucratic model of school administration. Murphy and Shipman (2000) identify this shift, in which hierarchical structures are being replaced by more "decentralized and professionally controlled systems" that in turn alter role relationships and responsibilities: "Traditional patterns of relationships are altered, authority flows are less hierarchical, role definitions are both more general and more flexible, leadership is connected to competence for needed tasks rather than to formal position, and independence and isolation are replaced by cooperative work. Furthermore, . . . the operant goal is no longer maintenance of the organizational infrastructure but rather the development of human resources."

In redefining the role of the principal, the ISLLC has sought to prepare and develop a set of competency-based content standards to use in training. These were shaped by a guiding set of beliefs and principles and have over two hundred indicators that help define them, clustered under three headers for each standard: knowledge, dispositions, and performances. The content standards that emerged from the development process say the following:

A school administrator is an educational leader who promotes the success of all students by

- Facilitating the development, articulation, implementation, and stewardship of a vision of learning that is shared and supported by the school community
- Advocating, nurturing, and sustaining a school culture and instructional program conducive to student learning and staff professional growth
- Ensuring management of the organization, operations, and resources for a safe, efficient, and effective learning environment
- Collaborating with families and community members, responding to diverse community interests and needs, and mobilizing community resources

- Acting with integrity, fairness, and in an ethical manner
- Understanding, responding to, and influencing the larger political, social, economic, legal, and cultural context

The ISLLC standards and indicators seek to strengthen school leadership in a number of ways: improving the quality of training programs, ensuring greater program accountability, creating a framework for better assessment of candidates for licensure and relicensure, and establishing a framework and foundation for certification programs. Although no data have been systematically collected to date, a number of groups have employed the standards for preparation and accreditation programs across America.

In other districts, the challenge of nurturing high-quality principals has been addressed through specially designed leadership training programs. The International Labour Organization (2000) recently reported on two such programs:

> To counter the growing shortage of quality candidates prepared to move from teaching to principal positions, the city of Philadelphia launched the Leadership in Education Apprentice Design (LEAD) program. Emphasis is placed on instruction in six-week internships under exemplary principals, an applied research requirement and a performance-based assessment of the candidates' leadership skills. Assistant principals are invited to join the assessment center, and new principals may take part in monthly seminars. Complementing this program, a coalition of more than 30 private enterprises has joined together to set up an Academy for Leadership and Learning to improve local leadership training.
>
> In New York State, a more modest program of half-day seminars organized by the School Administrator's Association, "Look Before You Leap," is aimed at promising teacher candidates for principal positions, and proposals have been made to provide financial incentives to school districts who hire interns in administrative jobs.

Two comments are relevant. First, the standards approach of the ISLLC, with more than two hundred indicators, may be challenged along the lines of Louden and Wildy's 1999 critique of developments in Australia, as discussed earlier. Second, the Philadelphia program has particular features that are emerging in other places: internships with exemplary principals and problem- or performance-based projects and assessments.

The National Center on Education and Economy (NCEE) in Washington, D.C., has a particular interest in establishing a national program for the development of school leaders. This chapter is in fact based on a report submitted to the NCEE in mid-2000 when that organization was seeking exemplars in other nations to guide the effort.

Hong Kong

Hong Kong, while having a dynamic East-West culture, is now a special administrative region of the People's Republic of China. It has about twelve hundred schools in its public education system, which is large by U.S. district standards, and has a mix of mostly urban and some small rural schools. While most of these schools are almost fully funded publicly, only about 8 percent are publicly owned, administered by the Education Department. Almost all the remaining 92 percent of schools are in the so-called aided sector, set up and managed by a trust, foundation, or church.

Hong Kong's relevance arises from a similarity between a substantial package of reforms there and those in the other nations we studied. An education commission representing major stakeholders has been in place in Hong Kong for a number of years and has issued seven major reports. The most recent (Education Commission, 2000) brings together a number of proposals to reform the curriculum, improve assessment mechanisms, remove obstacles to learning (especially in the middle years), and reform the university admission system, with a resource strategy that takes account of the costs of reform. A high level of school-based management is intended for all schools. The driving force for change is similar to that in other nations: recognition of the importance of lifelong learning and the need for an education system that responds to the needs of all students in every setting. The compendium of reform proposals is currently the focus of community consultation.

Hong Kong education leaders recognized in 1999 that the coming changes "will require principals to take on new leadership roles in quality development and quality assurance. They also highlight the need for a more focused and systematic leadership training and development program to enhance the quality of school leadership" (Education Department, 1999). A consultation paper of the Task Group on Training and Development of School Leaders proposed that all newly appointed principals participate in such a program from 2000 to 2001. Five core modules were proposed (learning and teaching, human resource development, financial management, strategic management, and school administration). The seven elective modules were school visits outside Hong Kong, international perspectives on educational development, professional responsibility and the law, future economic development and its impact on education, education in the age of information and technology, equality issues in education, and education development in the mainland. It was proposed that participants be attached to schools with good practices and that there be an eight-month school project experience, facilitated by a principal, academic, or senior manager from the public or private sector. It was proposed that participants be assessed in modules by the training provider, with the facilitator assessing the experiential project. The proposal is noteworthy for its connection to systemic reform at the same time that it provides exposure to developments elsewhere in society, nationally and internationally, and for its connection to a mentor or facilitator.

More detailed planning began in late 1999, with an interesting appointment as senior consultant: Bruce Davis, who had previously served three years as chief executive officer of the Australian Principals Center in Melbourne. Before that, he was secretary for education in Tasmania, Australia, for many years, winning the respect and confidence of school principals. He has been a career public servant but was initially trained as an architect. Davis consulted widely in developing a detailed specification of knowledge and skills for successful school leadership in a time of reform. He acknowledged that different sets of knowledge bases and skills come to the fore at different stages of career development and that there are differences among requirements for potential, new, and experienced principals. The complex role of school principal was organized in three domains: the principal as leader of the school, the principal as leader of teaching and learning, and the principal as leader of the wider educational community.

The merit of the approach lies in its coherence, its links to a comprehensive school reform movement, its recognition of a context beyond the immediate school system that extends internationally and to other sectors of public and private endeavor, and the connection between training or development and one's career.

Some qualifications on this assessment of progress in Hong Kong are relevant at this point. One is the potential for reductionism and fragmentation in an approach based on a detailed specification of role. This criticism applies as well to some programs elsewhere (see Louden and Wildy, 1999, on developments in Australia). Another is the capacity of "the system" to achieve implementation. Hong Kong is exemplary in the way that it puts almost all proposals out for community consultation, but stakeholders are many and powerful. The Education Department is relatively small, as noted at the outset; this contrasts with the situation in Britain, where a relatively powerful central government is clearly bent on implementing the programs and intentions of the National College for School Leadership.

It is intended that universities will be the main providers of modules, with three — the Chinese University of Hong Kong, the Hong Kong Institute of Education, and the University of Hong Kong — as primary sources. Although substantial public funding will support the endeavor, it is likely that participants will contribute substantially, for the program is viewed as individual career advancement. It is noteworthy that many Hong Kong principals are already engaged in professional development in mainland China through a highly regarded program offered at East China Normal University in Shanghai. The director of education in Hong Kong assisted in the launch of that program.

At the time of writing, the final form of the program in Hong Kong had not yet been established.

Sweden

Programs for preparation and professional development of principals in Sweden were viewed as exemplary a decade or so ago. We gained new insights through meetings with study groups of secondary school principals from Sweden whose visits to Melbourne were organized on a regular basis by their professional association. Local arrangements in Australia were made by the Victorian Association of State Secondary Principals, working with particular schools, school systems, and the University of Melbourne. These tours are part of a systematic approach that has emerged in Britain in the program of the National College for School Leadership.

Principals in Sweden are appointed by local government and undertake a two-year induction program. It is significant that Sweden does not pretrain principals per se. The local board of education appoints its leaders after a suitable recruitment program. They want to be able to make a choice based more on the "integrity" of the person than on the simple possession of a training certificate.

Recruitment programs operate at the local level, and local government boards of education are encouraged to identify people with the qualities required for leaders of their schools. One approach for the would-be leader is to undertake a ten-meeting study circuit offered to all educators as a way to enhance their educational background. This adds luster to anyone's professional profile, but it is not set up specifically for potential principals, nor is it focused entirely on leadership.

When principals are appointed in Sweden, the first step in their formal induction program brings them together with four others under the guidance of a tutor who is a very experienced school leader. The tutor is freed from normal responsibilities for a month to assist the new principals on the job. Ten percent of a new principal's working time is devoted to exercises set by the induction program organizers. The entire induction is closely mentored yet is sufficiently flexible to provide for individual differences. It aims at developing individual strengths.

After the two-year induction program, the still-new principal undertakes a three-year "deepening" program. In addition to studying school-focused leadership, the school leader must study leadership in two other organizations: a business or factory and another public service organization such as a welfare agency. This deepening is coordinated through the School Leader Education Project (SLEP), which has overall responsibility for school leader training in Sweden.

Two features of this approach are noteworthy. The first is the matching with an experienced school leader, and the second is the extended time in the "deepening" program. The latter conveys a sense of "formation," a concept explored later in this chapter.

Overview of Practice in Other Nations

In a recent report titled *Lifelong Learning in the Twenty-First Century: The Changing Roles of Educational Personnel*, the International Labour Organization (2000) includes accounts of programs in other nations with a similar dearth of qualified school leaders. The following extended excerpt is a helpful summary:

> Most European countries now offer some form of training for new school heads. Up to the mid-1990s, such training was neither widespread nor compulsory. Increasingly, however, training of school heads is required, and combines theoretical and practical training of up to several weeks or months, as in France, which has a system alternating course work and placements in companies, ministry offices and schools. The Czech Republic program to upgrade competencies since 1996 has, among other features, a compulsory training period on average of two years for prospective heads. Based on successful completion of a qualifying exam, applicants undergo

management, pedagogical and psychological training at a mixture of educational sites.

The general lack of systematic initial training and recruitment criteria for principals, which has prevailed in many low-income African countries, appears to be shifting towards a conscious effort to organize such training, and even to render it mandatory for newly appointed principals. Efforts such as Lesotho's in-service program for primary-school managers and administrators, the Nigerian National Institute of Educational Administration and Planning's in-service training of principals and inspectors, and Swaziland's national training program for school principals (expected for all newly appointed principals) emphasize mastery of many of the intricacies of modern principals' work: educational planning; financial and personnel management; organizational development; and instructional leadership.

In Asia, Malaysia has pioneered leadership and management skills development through the "Excellent Schools" and "Excellent Heads" programs designed to stimulate creativity and excellence in school leaders. Initial and continual training of planners, administrators, supervisors and principals in other countries is furnished through more traditional, national-level institutions such as the Academy of Educational Planning and Management of Pakistan, Jordan's Learning Difficulties Center of Princess Sarvat College, and the United Arab Emirates' school administration development program in cooperation with UAE University.

Latin American and Caribbean countries are not exceptions to trends elsewhere. Decentralized school management in Belize has prompted educational leadership and administration programs for prospective principals, backed up by support from supervisors and regular workshops. A combination of national-level training courses of several months' duration and longer courses overseas may also be employed, as in Trinidad and Tobago.

This account illustrates that the issue of principal training and development is of international importance. One approach worth closer attention is that in the Czech Republic, not only because it is an extended two-year program for all prospective principals but also for its use of a qualifying examination and a range of approaches at different sites. It is noteworthy that the Czech Republic is in the top ten of more than forty nations in rankings of student achievement in the Third International Mathematics and Science Study.

International Initiatives

International links and partnerships of one kind or another are starting to emerge on a large scale and ought to feature in the design of new programs. The trend reflects the globalization of education but also indicates that reform proposals have much in common across the world and that leaders can learn from leaders in other settings.

Several universities and professional associations have organized partnerships in recent years, including the three-nation International Principals Institute (Australia, Britain, and the United States) that the University of Southern California conducted for five years in the 1990s; travel programs organized for secondary principals in Sweden; and similar ventures organized in England at the University of Hull (by Brent Davies, who was instrumental in establishing the program at the University of Southern California) and by the National College for School Leadership.

Universities are starting to form international strategic alliances for delivery of their programs; one is emerging for the training and professional development of school leaders. This will involve Britain's University of Hull, University of Nottingham, and University of London through its Institute of Education, and Canada's University of Toronto through the Ontario Institute for Studies in Education, Claremont Graduate University in California, and the University of Melbourne in Australia. London, Melbourne, and Nottingham are members of the Universitas 21 global alliance, which currently has nineteen partners on four continents. It is intended that this will be tightly connected to the program of the National College for School Leadership at Nottingham.

The Principalship in Nonpublic Schools

This project is focused on the principalship in public schools, but this section is concerned with nonpublic schools, a setting that is generally perceived as more stable and in which the principalship is still a sought-after position with high status. We have used Australia as a case study. More than 30 percent of students attend nonpublic schools, or "nongovernment schools," as they are termed here. Most of these are systems of Catholic education. There are also small systems of non-Catholic schools and a number of independent nonsystematic schools, most owned by a body connected to a church. Many of these independent schools have a long history and high social prestige. Nongovernment schools in Australia receive some funding from the public purse at a level determined by placement on an index that reflects socioeconomic circumstances and the capacity to raise funds. Systematic Catholic schools receive most of their revenue from government. Some well-established independent schools receive relatively small amounts from the government and therefore have high fees.

It is readily apparent that the role of principal in the nonpublic sector is as complex as in the public sector. It is more so in the number of stakeholders who must be dealt with and its scale of financial and building operations. It is less complex where the school community is more homogeneous and the socioeconomic level of the school population is higher. It is also apparent that few coherent and comprehensive training programs are available for preparation or ongoing professional development. University programs are seen as helpful, and in-house programs provided from time to time by employing authorities are regarded as worthwhile, as are specialist programs on particular topics by professional bodies.

The Formation of Leaders

The concept of "formation" is helpful in describing how capacities for the principalship are acquired and sustained, with a role for university-based diploma and degree programs as well as specialist professional development opportunities. But the emphasis is on systematic "formation," with opportunity for mentoring along the way. The view that there are stages in development that align with career progression supports the approach adopted so far in the Hong Kong design and the Swedish induction program. It is given most eloquent expression in recent literature by Gronn (1999), based on studies of principals in the nonpublic sector, and Ribbins (2000).

Gronn's purpose was "to provide a helpful new framework for understanding leadership as a longitudinal and developmental career" (1999, p. vii). His "career model" of leadership identifies four stages of a leader's career—formation, accession, incumbency, and divestiture—and these are set in three macrocontexts: historical, cultural, and societal. These macrocontexts account for the differences in practices across nations, the reasons that approaches effective in one era may not be effective in another, and the ways that biographies of leaders who succeed in different eras and in different settings may suggest different conclusions about the development of leaders.

Formation can be understood at two levels, according to Gronn. For society and key sectors of it, formation is "the totality of the institutionalized arrangements which, either by intention or effect, serve to replenish or reproduce cohorts of leaders." For individuals, formation "means those preparatory socialization processes and experiences which served to later position them in their previous incarnation as leadership aspirants in a state of social and psychological readiness to assume responsibility and authority" (1999, p. 32). Accession is "the stage of grooming or anticipation in which candidates for leadership roles rehearse or test their potential capacity to lead by comparison with existing leaders and the field of potential rivals for advancement" (pp. 35–36). Incumbency or leadership proper, as Gronn describes it, is the stage where "leaders have developed and honed their public personas, they have learned to project their authoritativeness, and they now seek to give further expression to their quest for mastery and self-realization by gaining experience through circulating amongst various elite postings and leadership roles" (p. 39). Divestiture is simply the process of "letting go," which may "come about voluntarily or involuntarily" (p. 39).

It is readily apparent, in this view of leaders' development, that formal programs of training may be entirely inadequate, especially those that do not take account of context and do not provide for or recognize in an aspirant the rich range of experiences and particular constellation of personal qualities that come from an extended process of formation.

Ribbins (2000) has taken the same approach, reflecting his collaboration with Gronn in recent years. While acknowledging the potential of the National Professional Qualification for Headteachers in Britain, he reports a number of concerns about its efficacy, described earlier in this chapter. He sees that other nations may seek to learn from the British experience thus far: "England and Wales are widely regarded as having taken an important lead in the evolution of a distinct, and possibly transferable, strategic approach to the initial preparation and professional development of headteachers" (p. 81). He includes Hong Kong and, surprisingly, Cyprus among these nations. He notes intentions described earlier in this chapter to make training compulsory for school principals in Hong Kong. The program design in Hong Kong makes the connection between program orientation and stage of career.

Ribbins (2000, p. 87) advocates the "career model" proposed by Gronn and argues for an approach to development that

- Is centrally concerned with improving the quality of schooling and the achievement of pupils
- Is systematic, comprehensive, and of high quality
- Makes available continuing professional development opportunities for every career phase
- Has concern for practical skills but also for a more philosophical approach
- Involves a range of providers, with the universities engaged fully at a variety of levels

- Provides core training but supports development opportunities that mean more
- Is based on the best available evidence and fosters the research that generates it

Designing an Exemplary Training and Development Program

We found a range of approaches that might be classified as "best practices" or "exemplars," but no nation appears to have put them together into a single coherent and comprehensive program. Among nations with comparable proposals for reform, only Britain is on the verge of creating a national system that meets the needs of about twenty-five headteachers of public schools and probably four times that number of aspiring headteachers and many more again in middle management whose needs may be served by the National College for School Leadership. This will be a remarkable achievement. Among particular programs, leaving aside adaptations of training, only the Hay/McBer program that was developed in Victoria based on successful business approaches has been adapted for full scale-up in another nation, namely, Britain.

Each nation will clearly have to wrestle with its own constraining forces. In Australia and the United States, these constraints are constitutional to the extent that education is a state responsibility. What follows is a brief account of what might be included in the design of an exemplary training and development program, with the caveat that specific design in a particular setting is beyond the scope of this chapter.

1. It is apparent that no single organization can design and deliver a program of the kind needed from a single site or with its own staff. While the National College for School Leadership in Britain may have overall responsibility and will deliver much of the program, it is clear that a network of providers will still be required.

2. It is unlikely that a small collection of programs will meet the needs of a state or nation in preparing people for the principal-

ship or sustaining current principals. The concept of "formation" emerged from Cahill's reflection on programs for leaders in non-public schools, and this has been advocated by Gronn (1999) and Ribbins (2000) as an alternative way of viewing the issue. This is connected, in turn, to the concept of lifelong learning. Induction and "deepening" programs in Sweden have promise in this regard, as do the design elements in Hong Kong that match program focus to stage of career (potential, new, experienced).

3. While the logic is sound, many reservations surround competency-based approaches that have dozens or even hundreds of indicators of desirable behavior that ought then to be the focus of training and development. A simpler structure may account for the success of the Hay/McBer program, which is based on the links between four key concepts (school climate, leadership style, job requirements, and personal characteristics) and school performance.

4. Almost all innovative programs reviewed in this chapter are connecting participants to practice in a variety of ways, including the use of mentors and coaches who are experienced school principals, attachment to exemplary schools for a period of time, and school-based projects for assessment of progress or achievement.

5. Although specific programs of preparation will be based on functional areas of leadership and management—for example, budgeting and staffing—it is clear that these cannot form the entire program and that to require all candidates to go through such courses would be dysfunctional. Participation in such programs should be determined by a needs assessment. Much learning can occur on the job or through the field-based placement and mentoring programs described in this chapter.

6. A promising approach is to base programs on domains where particular issues arise from time to time. Caldwell (2000) proposed nine "domains of innovation": curriculum, pedagogy, school design, professionalism, funding, leadership, management, governance, and boundary spanning. He drew on Drucker's concept of abandonment

(1999) to suggest that issue- or problem-based learning and development ought to take participants into "domains of abandonment."

7. Issues and problems will vary from setting to setting and from time to time. There is a good match between this approach to training and development and practices such as field placement and mentoring and coaching. The approach also lends itself to regularly constructing and reconstructing networks or cohorts of learners who have a common interest in the issue or problem. On-line learning will play an important role.

8. A "virtual college," such as that proposed within the National College for School Leadership in Britain, is essential if scale-up is to meet the needs of all. Recent stunning advances in technology have been taken up in other fields such as medicine, and it is critically important that such technology be applied to the training and development of educators, including aspiring and currently serving principals.

9. Most of the worthwhile practices identified in this chapter involve international links or partnerships. These include the design of the National College for School Leadership, the study programs of principals from Sweden, the global leadership-learning alliance of universities that will be linked to the National College for School Leadership, on-line learning, and the concept of the "virtual college."

Despite the promise of practices like those summarized here, there remains an underlying concern that the role of the principal as it is emerging worldwide is essentially unfeasible and that this, more than limitations in training and development, is the fundamental reason for the shortage in number and quality of applicants. This seems to be the case in nonpublic schools as well as public schools, even those in highly favorable circumstances. Some may argue that our whole approach to schooling, still based on models developed in the last century or even the century before, is no longer relevant and that problems such as those addressed in this project will remain until a fundamental reengineering of schooling occurs. This reengineering may come to have overarching priority, but in the meantime, training and development along the lines proposed here may make a significant contribution to the quality of schooling and the satisfaction of those who lead the effort.

References

Caldwell, B. J. "Leadership and Innovation in the Transformation of Schools." Keynote address at the Vision 2020 Conference of the Technology Colleges Trust, London, May 4, 2000.

Cooley, V., and Shen, J. "Who Will Lead? The Top 10 Factors That Influence Teachers Moving into Administration." *NASSP Bulletin,* 1999, 83(606), 75–80.

Creissen, T., and Ellison, L. "Reinventing School Leadership: Back to the Future in the UK?" *International Journal of Educational Management,* 1998, 12(1). [http://www.emerald-library.com/brev/06012ad1.htm]. Mar. 25, 2000.

Daresh, J., and Male, T. "Crossing the Border into Leadership: Experiences of Newly Appointed British Headteachers and American Principals." *Educational Management and Administration,* 2000, 28, 89–101.

Davis, B. "Leadership in the Next Millennium." *Practising Administrator,* 1996, 18, 6–11.

Department for Education and Employment (UK). *Teachers Meeting the Challenge of Change.* London: Department for Education and Employment, 1998.

Department for Education and Employment (UK). *National College for School Leadership: A Prospectus.* London: Department for Education and Employment, 1999.

Department for Education and Employment (UK). *Leadership Program for Serving Headteachers.* London: Department for Education and Employment, 2000.

Drucker, P. F. *Leadership Challenges for the 21st Century.* Oxford: Butterworth Heinemann, 1999.

Education Department (Hong Kong). *Leadership Training Program for Principals.* Hong Kong: Task Force on Training and Development of School Principals, 1999.

Education Commission (Hong Kong). *Review of Education System: Reform Proposals.* Hong Kong: Education Commission, 2000.

Fullan, M. G. *Change Forces: Probing the Depths of Educational Reform.* Bristol, Pa.: Falmer Press, 1993.

Gronn, P. *The Making of Educational Leaders.* London: Cassell, 1999.

Gunter, H. "Contracting Headteachers as Leaders: An Analysis of the NPQH." *Cambridge Journal of Education*, 1999, 29(2).

Hill, P. W., and Crévola, C. A. "The Role of Standards in Educational Reform for the 21st Century." In D. D. Marsh (ed.), *ASCD Yearbook 1999: Preparing Our Schools for the 21st Century*. Alexandria, Va.: Association for Supervision and Curriculum Development, 1999.

International Labour Organization. *Lifelong Learning in the Twenty-First Century: The Changing Roles of Educational Personnel*. Report for discussion at a joint meeting in Geneva, Apr. 10–14, 2000. [http://www.ilo.org/public/english/dialogue/sector/techmeet/jmep2000/jmepr2.htm#_Toc 478302505]. Mar. 29, 2000.

Louden, W., and Wildy, H. "Short Shrift to Long Lists: An Alternative Approach to the Development of Performance Standards for School Principals." *Journal of Educational Administration*, 1999, 37, 99–120.

Millett, A. "New Leadership Program Takes Shape." 1998. [http://195.44.11.137/coi/coipress.nsf]. Mar. 25, 2000.

Murphy, J., and Shipman, N. "The Interstate School Leaders Licensure Consortium: A Standards-Based Approach to Strengthening Educational Leadership." 2000. [http://www.aasa.org/issues/leadership/murphy.htm]. Mar. 29, 2000.

Olson, L. "New Thinking on What Makes a Leader." *Education Week*, Jan. 19, 2000a. [http://www.edweek.org/ew/ewstory.cfm?slug=19lead.h19]. Mar. 30, 2000.

Olson, L. "Policy Focus Converges on Leadership." *Education Week*, Jan. 12, 2000b. [http://www.edweek.org/ew/ewstory.cfm?slug=17lead.h19]. Mar. 30, 2000.

Ouston, J. "Management in Turbulent Times." In A. Gold and J. Evans (eds.), *Reflecting on School Management*. New York: Routledge Falmer, 1998.

Ribbins, P. "Understanding Leadership: Developing Headteachers." In T. Bush and others (eds.), *Educational Management: Redefining Theory, Policy and Practice*. London: Chapman, 2000.

Spring, G. "System Support for Self-Managing Schools: Victoria's Schools of the Future." *Practising Administrator*, 1996, 18, 14–17, 28–30.

Stacey, R. D. *Managing the Unknowable: Strategic Boundaries Between Order and Chaos in Organizations*. San Francisco: Jossey-Bass, 1992.

Teacher Training Agency (UK). *National Standards for Headteachers*. London: Teacher Training Agency, 1998.

Thody, A. "Training School Principals, Educating School Governors." *International Journal of Educational Management*, 1998, 12(5). [http://www.emerald-library.co./brev/06012ed1.html]. Mar. 25, 2000.

Part Four

A Current Situation Report: Preparing School Principals in the United States

Chapter Eight

The Work of Principals and Their Preparation

Addressing Critical Needs for the Twenty-First Century

Carolyn Kelley, Kent D. Peterson

> There are more vacancies for principals and a greater dearth of qualified candidates than I've seen in the last 40 years.
>
> —*Seymour Fleigel, Center for Educational Innovation (1999)*

Fleigel's comment reflects a broad concern about the quality and quantity of candidates for principalships now being echoed across the United States. The concern is critical because of the central role that the principal plays in orchestrating school reform and improvement. Ultimately, realization of the promise of education reform rests on our ability to enhance the professional development of principals through significantly improved preparation programs and carefully linked ongoing professional development.

American schools remain central to the fabric of society and productivity. Every citizen has the right to develop skills and knowledge that will enhance his or her quality of life—this is a core tenet of the social purpose of education. For almost two decades, since the publication of the *Nation at Risk* report (National Commission on

Excellence in Education, 1983), policymakers, communities, and educators have been concerned with creating and maintaining the highest-quality schools to serve both individual and social goals.

However, the quality and improvement of American public schools is threatened by a crisis in school leadership. For some time, critics of principal preparation programs have expressed concern about the inadequacies of systems of recruitment, screening, selection, and training of principal candidates. In the next three to five years, a large proportion of today's principals are expected to retire, and the number of quality candidates for those positions appears to be dwindling.

To address this coming shortfall of candidates, the nation needs to examine carefully the systems that support the development of future school leaders. In this chapter, we examine the principalship; the knowledge, skills, and abilities needed by principals; and some recent efforts to enhance the preparation of principals. While many preparation programs do not possess the curricular coherence, pedagogy, and structure to provide the skills, knowledge, and attitudes necessary to lead America's eighty thousand public schools, we examine model programs that have attempted that task, and we examine features of these programs that do provide the building blocks required to enhance the professional preparation and development of future principals.

Current Principal Characteristics

The nation's schools currently have about 105,000 principals, about 80,000 of them working in public schools. A significant proportion is over fifty years of age. In 1993–94, 15 percent of public school principals were fifty-five or older, and another 75 percent of them were between forty and fifty-five. The proportion of public school principals under age forty declined between 1987–88 and 1993–94 from 19 to 10 percent of the total public school principal population (National Center for Education Statistics, 1997). Given the nature of state retirement systems and current norms, it is highly probable that a significant proportion of the current population of school principals will retire in the next several years.

The rising age of principals may be partly related to the hiring of greater numbers of women into the principalship. Female principals tend to enter the principalship later in their careers (Andrews and Basom, 1990; Miklos, 1988). They tend to have more teaching experience prior to becoming administrators, are as likely to have a master's degree in elementary education as in educational administration, and are more likely to have experience as curriculum specialists or coordinators prior to entering the principalship. While virtually all principals have a background in teaching, about a third of female principals also have prior experience as a curriculum specialist or coordinator; a slightly higher percentage of male principals continues to have a background in athletic coaching. Perhaps as a result, female principals tend to spend more of their time in the classroom and on instruction-related activities. Male principals continue to outnumber female principals, but the proportion of women in the role has been rising, due to changes in hiring patterns favoring female candidates. The proportion of female principals increased from 25 percent of the total in 1987–88 to 34 percent in 1993–94 (National Center for Education Statistics, 1997).

Most minority principals continue to be concentrated in central cities (35 percent of public school central-city principals were minority members) and large districts (29 percent of public school principals in districts with more than ten thousand students were minority members). Overall, the ratio of minority principals is rising slowly, up from 13 percent in 1987–88 to 16 percent in 1993–94 (National Center for Education Statistics, 1997).

A recent survey of superintendents supported self-reported evidence that there is a shortage of qualified candidates for the principalship. About half of districts responding indicated that an inadequate number of qualified candidates were applying for positions open in their districts (Educational Research Service, 1998). Shortages may be even greater in specific regions and districts. The Schools and Staffing Survey data indicate that 39 percent of principals participated in a program for aspiring principals. New principals were more likely than experienced principals to take part (National Center for Education Statistics, 1997); most of these programs appear to be located in urban rather than suburban or rural school districts (Educational Research Service, 1998). Anecdotal evidence suggests that the demand for principals is even greater in specific regions and districts. For example, in Texas, some 34 percent of all elementary principals reported they planned to retire in the next three years and almost two-thirds within eight years (Sandi Borden, Texas Elementary Principals and Supervisors Association, personal communication, Jan. 2000). In one Maryland district, the numbers are even more daunting, with upwards of 70 percent considering retirement in three years (Albert Bertani, chief officer for professional development, Prince George's County Public Schools, personal communication, Jan. 2000).

Compensation and the nature of the principal role appear to be the major factors that discourage candidates from seeking principal positions (Educational Research Service, 1998). The average salary for public school principals is often similar to that of teachers at the high end of the salary scale. Since most teachers operate on a nine-month contract and most principals on a twelve-month contract, the daily salary rate is often lower for principals than for teachers. If teachers accept additional compensated roles in the district, they may make the same amount or even more than the principal. In 1993–94, the average public school principal was paid about $55,000; private school principals earned about $32,000 (National Center for Education Statistics, 1997). The average teacher salary was about $35,000 in that year (American Federation of Teachers, 2000). More recent data show similar differences (see American Federation of Teachers, 2000, tabs. II-6 and V-2).

The averages mask the variation across districts. An analysis of teacher and principal salaries in Wisconsin in 1999 showed that in many districts, the salary differential was negligible. In contrast, some districts such as Chicago have made a concerted effort to raise principal salaries relative to teacher salaries in order to attract stronger candidates. Without a significant salary differential, teachers may decide not to become principals because they will not be sufficiently compensated for the longer workdays, greater pressure and stress, and reduced job security.

Studies of the shortage of principals reiterate the effect of these factors on discouraging potential applicants from seeking a principalship. In the 1998 Educational Research Service study, superintendents with a shortage of qualified candidates identified the following as important factors discouraging principal applicants:

- Compensation is insufficient compared to responsibilities (60 percent)

- Job is too stressful (32 percent)

- Too much time is required (27 percent)

- It is difficult to satisfy parents/community (14 percent)

- Societal problems make it difficult to focus on instruction (13 percent)

- Fewer experienced teachers are interested (12 percent)

- Testing/accountability pressures are high (7 percent)

- Job is viewed as less satisfying than previously (6 percent)

Importance of the Role

Schools need more than leadership. They need a carefully conceived curriculum, quality instructional strategies, assessment strategies that guide planning, and school improvement efforts that continuously improve processes. But research and practical knowledge also point to the key importance of strong principal leadership that can effectively manage complex systems and lead instructional improvement.

Over the past decade, research on school principals has reiterated their importance in promoting school effectiveness, restructuring, school improvement, and the implementation of reform (Elmore and Burney, 1997; Ford and Bennett, 1994; Fullan, 1997;

Hallinger and Heck, 1996; Kelley, 1998; Levine and Lezotte, 1995; Louis and Marks, 1998; Murphy and Louis, 1994; Newmann and Associates, 1996). Principals are also central players in the implementation of comprehensive reform programs such as Accelerated Schools and the Comer Model (Peterson, 1995; Yale Child Study Center, 2000). Good principals engage their schools in the core processes of establishing, maintaining, evaluating, and improving their structures and cultures. Schools need a principal to keep the organization going effectively and improving continuously. At times, reform groups have thought that schools could be managed and led by committees of empowered teachers; seldom have these approaches worked. In fact, one seldom finds an instructionally effective school without an effective principal.

The importance of principals to school success makes it essential to examine the role more carefully in order to consider ways to improve the preparation and professional development of these leaders.

Educational Leadership

The recent interest in school leadership follows many years of relative inattention. During the 1990s, educational rhetoric and reform efforts focused primarily on empowering teachers and other stakeholders, with particular attention to elevating the role of the teacher and on restructuring schools, especially school governance. Interestingly, there were calls to replace the principalship with administrative committees of dedicated teachers. Policymakers and state reformers paid relatively little attention to school leadership.

Both research on school reform and practical knowledge of what it takes to run a successful school have pointed to the importance of administrators to school success. Research on the role of principals in effective schools, school improvement, restructuring, instructional improvement, and standards-based reform all support a need for well-prepared leaders. Recent research on implementing reforms demonstrates the central role of principals and other leaders to successful change. Principals are key to initiating, implementing, and sustaining high-quality schools.

Research on the Work of School Principals

Critics call for changes in preparation programs to better match the realities of the work of school principals. Muse and Thomas (1991) summarize this view: "Regardless of the year appointed, [principals] have been trained and certified as administrators through programs largely irrelevant to and grossly inadequate for the work responsibilities found in the school principalship" (p. 32). Any effort to redesign and implement more meaningful preparation programs for school principals must be carried out with a clear picture of the nature of a principal's work.

Work Realities

The daily work world of school principals is little understood and yet extremely complex and demanding. The nature of a principal's work suggests the need for schools and districts to consider ways to substantially reframe or restructure it to enable principals to accomplish the tasks expected of them. One approach might restructure the work to enable principals to engage more fully in instructional improvement. In most districts, this role redesign has not been accomplished. The discussion here focuses on worklife realities, many of which are inadequately addressed in most preparation programs. What are these realities?

The daily work of managers in any organization is shaped by the nature of the core technology, the structure of the organization, and the demands from customers, clients, and colleagues, as well as social mores and the culture of the organization (Deal and Peterson, 1994). Thus what schools are and what people expect and desire of them shape the daily work realities of principals.

For principals, like other managers, brevity, variety, and fragmentation characterize their daily work (Mintzberg, 1973; Peterson, 1982, 1989). About half of the day is spent dealing with problems, demands, or activities that have not been scheduled and are often unique. More than 80 percent of the day is spent in verbal interaction, much of it face to face. Problems, demands, and new requests for decisions or direction flow to the principal continuously, with many of the problems unique and unexpected, occurring in seemingly random patterns. Routine notions of time management developed by corporate trainers often do not apply as irate parents, injured children, intransigent students, safety issues, and mundane breakdowns are pressed into the principal's office for attention. What is this work like?

First, much of a principal's day is spent on interactions lasting less than a minute, with little time for longer reflection on issues. Principals are expected to address problems and questions quickly, often with little time for careful consideration of alternative solutions (Peterson, 1982).

Second, the tasks vary considerably, depending on many features. These include the nature of the persons involved (social variability), the nature of the problem (problem complexity), the thinking or emotional processes involved (cognitive and affective diversity), and the knowledge base needed (expansive nature of expertise). Presented problems often vary as well, making them more difficult to analyze and address. Complex social and legal issues exacerbate many seemingly simple problems.

Third, the day of principals is characterized by extreme fragmentation, interruptions caused by needs, demands, and problems that come to the principal's office for resolution because no other organizational role is assigned to address them. In most schools, principals are the primary managers of issues and concerns that arise from every source—parents and community members, teachers, and students. District reports and paperwork can sometimes be delegated to skilled staff, but often schools are understaffed and so the task of completing paperwork also falls on the principal.

Thus the day is filled with a flood of problems, issues, ideas, and people; the unexpected becomes the norm, and little time remains to reflect, plan, or strategize on deeper systemic or organizational opportunities (Peterson, 1982, 1989).

Principals, in short, are problem solvers, expected and needed to address and buffer the technical core of the organization (the classroom) from the immediate and pressing demands of students, parents, and other short-term sources of perturbation in the system. But principals are also leaders in the school. If the school is to be successful in helping students learn and in addressing problems of teaching and learning, principals must be able to develop a mission focused on student learning, to conduct analyses of student performance, to design and implement new systems and approaches to improve learning, and to reinforce and enhance the professional culture in the school (Deal and Peterson, 1994; Hallinger and Murphy, 1987).

Principals, like other managers of individual units of organizations, are responsible for a wide variety of basic tasks. They must set goals and develop plans; build budgets and hire personnel; lead the organization of work (in this case, curriculum and instruction); select structures and coordinate time use; evaluate staff and assess student learning at the school level; organize improvement efforts and develop processes for working with clients, customers, and community; and understand and reinforce positive organizational cultures. In sum, they must both maintain the routine functioning of the schools and provide vision and motivation; they must both manage and lead (Deal and Peterson, 1994).

New Responsibilities and New Roles

In recent years, new responsibilities have been added to an already complex and demanding position. Some sources include decentralization of decision making to the school site, increased use of collaborative decision making, expanded accountability for principals and schools, the increasingly diverse nature of communities, and greater concern for listening to stakeholders.

With *decentralization*, principals in many districts are taking on budgetary and decision-making responsibilities that were once the domain of central offices or superintendents. In Chicago, for example, principals have local school councils (acting like miniature school boards) who hire and fire them and oversee the budget and school improvement plans. In Seattle, principals act as chief executive officers of their schools, with broad powers over resource allocation and reallocation, staffing, and instructional technology. San Diego operates a high-stakes environment in which principals' tenure depends on their ability to act as effective instructional leaders, developing and improving instructional programs and student outcomes (Kelley, 2000).

Principals in many schools engage in *collaborative planning and decision making* with staff and parents. In Chicago, this is a useful and important democratizing reform, but it increases the political and governing responsibilities and tasks of principals.

The roles of principals in states with *increased accountability* reforms have been changed qualitatively by curriculum standards reforms, more focus on higher-order thinking, high-stakes testing, and accountability for student learning. They are pressed to be more responsible for student learning and its improvement but must also lead planning efforts that involve developing a clear mission and goals for the school, analyzing student performance data, identifying areas that need improvement, developing sustainable programmatic reforms, and facilitating implementation of those reforms. The new high-stakes tests and the detailed reporting of student scores require a more advanced notion of instructional leadership that involves complex analysis of data, application of new instructional technologies, and other responsibilities.

Principals are also expected to work effectively in increasingly *diverse, fragmented, and pluralistic communities with vocal stakeholders.* They must respond positively and democratically to the vocal stakeholders, who have a legitimate and intense personal interest in schools. "Listening to the customer" (Peters and Waterman, 1982) takes on special meaning in schools where everyone—from states to central offices, from booster clubs to property owners, from teachers to parents—wants to be involved in decision making and governance.

No doubt districts and boards need to consider ways to redesign and support the work of principals. But for those going into the

position, preparation programs need to address existing realities—
by providing skills, knowledge, and experiences that will prepare
future principals until changes are made in the role. Leaders of
other organizations face many of these conditions as well. But principals face a special set of problems not found in organizations with
clearer goals, more routine technologies, and fewer social
expectations.

Special Problems for Principals

As managers of educational organizations for young people, principals face some special problems. Principals, unlike leaders in other
organizations, work in settings where the following conditions
prevail:

- Local constituencies view schools more as symbols of the
  community than as places of learning, where looking and acting like "school" may be more important than achieving
  learning outcomes (Meyer and Rowan, 1978).

- Use of traditional, often outdated, techniques (eight-period
  days; students working alone on projects; paper-and-pencil
  tests) are often valued by clients more than improving student
  learning with new, less traditional approaches.

- Staff norms of autonomy are extremely high, and collaboration on schoolwide projects is often uncommon.

- Existing organizational cultures reinforce conceptions of purpose and pedagogy that are reified and outmoded.

- Organizational goals are constantly shifting, depending on
  educational fashion, fancy, funding, and politics.

- Many important goals, such as citizenship or lifelong learning,
  are hard to measure and viewed as achievable in some distant
  future.

- Informal, competing goals (such as having winning sports
  teams) may absorb time, effort, and problem-solving attention
  that could be devoted to improving student learning.

- The core technology needed involves motivating captive participants (called students) to work and produce.

These conditions make leadership more challenging in schools than in many other organizations. They make the work of principals more complex, variable, and difficult both to do and to learn how to do.

Skills and Knowledge for Principals

The foregoing description of the roles and responsibilities of the principal suggests that the job is both complex and demanding. Next, we identify key knowledge, skills, and dispositions that seem important for effectiveness in the role. Various authors have put forward different attributes needed for success in the principalship. Keller (1998, p. 2) suggested that a good principal has the following attributes:

- Recognizes teaching and learning as the main business of a school
- Communicates the school's mission clearly and consistently to staff members, parents, and students
- Fosters standards for teaching and learning that are high and attainable
- Provides clear goals and monitors the progress of students toward meeting them
- Spends time in classrooms and listens to teachers
- Promotes an atmosphere of trust and sharing
- Builds good staff and makes professional development a top concern
- Does not tolerate bad teachers

Others have suggested that to be effective, principals must be able to both manage and lead. In other words, they must be strong administrators, attending to the structural features of the organization, and strong leaders, working to shape the school culture and context to promote student learning (Deal and Peterson, 1994).

The complexity of the principal's role and the innumerable decisions that must be made have led some analysts to focus on the importance of strong problem-identification and problem-solving orientations for school leaders (Hallinger, Leithwood, and Murphy, 1993). Effective principals clearly communicate a vision through their work, which means finding ways to make meaning out of the endless stream of activity in a principal's workday. Some have argued that in order to use these problem-solving activities as a vehicle for communicating values and direction, principals require a clear and highly developed values orientation that can focus and drive decision-making processes (Raun and Leithwood, 1993).

Other critical skills include a working knowledge of educational research findings, methods, and approaches; strong communication skills; and human resource management skills (recruitment, selection, evaluation, professional development, motivation, and so on). Research on some of these knowledge and skill areas is extensive. In the next section, we review some of this literature.

Models of Leadership

A number of models of leadership have been proposed over the years. In an analysis of a decade of articles on leadership in schools, Leithwood and Duke (1999) identified and defined six types of leadership: instructional, transformational, moral, participative, managerial, and contingent. These approaches are defined as follows:

- *Instructional leadership* "typically focuses on the behaviors of teachers as they engage in activities directly affecting the growth of students" (p. 47).
- *Transformational leadership* focuses on "the commitments and capacities of organizational members" and frequently refers to "charismatic, visionary, cultural, and empowering concepts of leadership" (p. 48).

- *Moral leadership* focuses on "the values and ethics of the leader" (p. 50). A major concern in this body of research is the ways in which values and ethics are used in decision making and how conflicts in values are resolved.
- *Participative leadership* examines "the decision-making processes of the group" (p. 51), particularly with respect to shared or group decisions.
- *Managerial leadership* "focuses on the functions, tasks, or behaviors of the leader" (p. 52).
- *Contingent leadership* examines the ways in which "leaders respond to the unique organizational circumstances or problems that they face" (p. 54).

In various ways, each of these approaches to leadership is designed to enhance school culture or performance. For example, instructional leadership focuses on student growth and learning outcomes; transformational leadership, on increasing the capacity for high performance; and moral leadership, on enhancing the ethical and moral purposes in schools (Leithwood and Duke, 1999). An extensive research literature has built up around these leadership styles. We focus here on two forms that have been identified as potentially promising for improving student achievement, transformational and instructional leadership.

Transformational leadership is perhaps the model most fully developed in the literature. Leithwood (1994) has identified six major dimensions: articulating a vision, fostering group goals, conveying high-performance expectations, providing intellectual stimulation, offering individualized support, and modeling best practices and values. To date, modest evidence supports the positive effects of transformational leadership on organizational effectiveness (Leithwood, Steinbach, and Raun, 1993).

Instructional leadership, identified in the early 1980s as a central feature by the effective schools research, was developed and specified in several studies and analyses. The Bossert model (Bossert, Dwyer, Rowan, and Lee, 1982) identified two major components to which Hallinger and Murphy (1987) added a third. The three components are defining the school mission, managing the instructional program, and promoting the school climate. Specific leadership practices were delineated under each of these components, and their function in schools were studied. A number of studies have supported the model and showed how these three components and the specific practices contribute to student achievement and other educational outcomes (see Leithwood, Jantzi, and Steinbach, 1999, for a review).

A complementary approach to leadership can be found in the work of Deal and Peterson (1994), which focuses on principals as both managers and leaders. As managers, principals ensure that the basic roles, rules, responsibilities, structures, and processes of the school are functioning effectively. As leaders, they help foster an engaging, meaningful vision and mission for the school, shape the culture, and provide motivation, high expectations, support, and encouragement. Again, good principals must be able to both manage the school and lead it.

To be effective *managers*, principals must know the administrative, legal, and policy rules and procedures and be able to apply them. To be effective *leaders*, principals must know about and have skills to address the tasks and roles of transformational and instructional leadership. They must also have a well-developed moral and ethical core of values that translate into everyday behavior. In both managerial and leadership roles, principals need strong problem-finding and problem-solving skills that they can draw on to address both routine and unique challenges.

Cognitive Issues and Leadership

Another significant knowledge and skill area researchers identified in the 1980s and early 1990s was cognitive aspects of the principalship (Hart and Pounder, 1999). These scholars delved into the nature of problem finding and problem solving among administrators. Professors generated studies of problem solving, suggestions for changes in preparation programs to foster improved skill at it, and several new techniques for increasing problem-solving skills. These included problem-based learning, design studios, and apprenticeships (see, for example, Bridges and Hallinger, 1993; Hart, 1993; Prestine, 1993). Attention to problem solving may be important in the design of preparation programs.

Problem-Solving

Like many managers in other industries, principals must be able and willing to solve a wide variety of problems, both those that are brought to them and those they select. Problem identification and problem solving are central features of their work. An important skill of principals is the ability to take care of the many problems and demands of their jobs, at the same time leading their schools, nurturing teacher leadership, and moving the instructional program forward.

Problems are often complex, ambiguous, unsequenced, hard to analyze, and highly emotional, with few routine solutions. As a contrasting example, consider medicine, which also confronts a large range of problems. In medicine, many problems are routine, some problem-solving processes can be fairly routinized, and even complex problems may have a fixed set of solutions from which to draw. In educational administration, the range of problems that present themselves is also large, but procedures for solving them tend to be less routinized, and unique problems present themselves much more frequently. Few routinized solutions exist for a large proportion of many problems (Leithwood, Jantzi, and Steinbach, 1999).

Standards for Practice

In an attempt to improve the preparation of school leaders, a number of groups have developed standards for practice that define what good principals should know and be able to do. Some have been long and detailed, such as the list of proficiencies published by the National Association of Elementary School Principals (NAESP);

others have been short and broadly defined, like the standard of the National Policy Board for Educational Administration (NPBEA) and the Interstate School Leaders Licensure Consortium (ISLLC).

These models provide another look at the knowledge and skills principals need and provide a potential list of knowledge bases, skills, and abilities that a comprehensive model of preparation might address. Although there are similarities across the standards, each takes a slightly different approach to defining what is important. Because they represent an important indication of what the *profession* considers important, we shall summarize them here.

The NPBEA Standards

One of the earliest sets of standards was developed by the National Policy Board for Educational Administration in an attempt to provide more structure and quality for educational administration preparation programs (Hart and Pounder, 1999). They include the following standards:

1. *Strategic leadership*—the knowledge, skills, and attributes needed to identify contexts, develop with others vision and purpose, use information, frame problems, exercise leadership processes to achieve common goals, and act ethically for educational communities.

2. *Instructional leadership*—the knowledge, skills, and attributes needed to design with others appropriate curricula and instructional programs, develop learner-centered school cultures, assess outcomes, provide student personnel services, and plan with faculty professional development activities aimed at improving instruction.

3. *Organizational leadership*—the knowledge, skills, and attributes needed to understand and improve the organization, implement operational plans, manage financial resources, and apply decentralized management processes and procedures.

4. *Political and community leadership*—the knowledge, skills, and attributes needed to act in accordance with legal provisions and

statutory requirements, apply regulatory standards, develop and apply appropriate policies, be conscious of ethical implications of policy initiatives and political actions, relate public policy initiatives to student welfare, understand schools as political systems, involve citizens and service agencies, and develop effective staff communications and public relations programs.

5. *Internship*—the process and product that result from application in a workplace environment of the strategic, instructional, organizational, and contextual leadership guidelines. When coupled with integrating experiences through related clinics or cohort seminars, the outcome should be a powerful synthesis of knowledge and skills useful to practicing school leaders.

NAESP Proficiencies for Principals

A second set of standards (termed "proficiencies") was developed in the mid-1980s and refined through the 1990s by the National Association of Elementary School Principals. This set took a bimodal approach and delineated a detailed set of leadership proficiencies and administrative and management proficiencies. The NAESP created a professional development inventory and professional development activities related to the standards so that aspiring, new, or experienced principals could assess their level of competence and create a professional development plan to strengthen their skills.

The NAESP proficiencies are as follows:

1. Leadership proficiencies
    Leadership behavior
    Communication skills
    Group processes
    Curriculum and instruction
    Assessment

2. Administrative and management proficiencies

    Organizational management

    Fiscal management

    Political management

For each area, specific skills are delineated. For example, under leadership behavior, the National Association of Elementary School Principals (1997, pp. 6–7) states:

In the exercise of leadership, the proficient principal

- Demonstrates vision and provides leadership that appropriately involves the school community in the creation of shared beliefs and values
- Demonstrates moral and ethical judgment
- Demonstrates creativity and innovative thinking
- Involves the school community in identifying and accomplishing the school's mission
- Recognizes the individual needs and contributions of all staff and students
- Applies effective interpersonal skills
- Facilitates the leadership of others
- Conducts needs assessments and uses data to make decisions and to plan for school improvement
- Identifies, pursues, and creatively coordinates the use of available human, material, and financial resources to achieve the school's mission and goals
- Explores, assesses, and implements educational concepts that enhance teaching and learning
- Understands the dynamics of change and the change process
- Advances the profession through participation as a member of local, state, and national professional groups

- Initiates and effectively coordinates collaborative endeavors with local and state agencies

- Participates in professional development to enhance personal leadership skills

Basic analysis of the construct validity and reliability of the NAESP Professional Development Inventory has generally supported the use of the instrument (Coleman and Adams, 1999).

The Connecticut Standards

Leithwood and Duke (1997) developed another useful set of standards for the state of Connecticut. It was to be used to develop assessment and evaluation rubrics for principals and to encourage more aligned and structured preparation programs. These standards begin with an integrated view of education, schools, and teachers, using a set of assumptions about what constitutes an "educated person," the nature of the learning process, and the teacher. The Connecticut model then goes on to delineate specific standards for principals based on these assumptions. The standards address the following areas:

1. Purposes and culture of productive schools

    School goals

    School culture

2. Structural and organizational characteristics of productive schools

    Policies and procedures

    Organization and resources

    Teaching faculty

    Programs and instruction

    School-community relations

3. Keys to school order and stability

> Communications and coordination
>
> Time management
>
> Budget and resource management
>
> School governance
>
> Student discipline

Like the other standards, these included a subset of skills and knowledge for each of the standards.

Council of Chief State School Officers Standards for School Leaders

The most widely used standards for principals were developed by a team of practitioners, academics, and policymakers in 1996. The Interstate School Leadership Licensure Consortium (ISLLC) consists of a number of states interested in pursuing the use of the ISLLC standards for teacher licensure. The Educational Testing Service has developed an assessment tool for states to use or adapt that assesses candidates' knowledge and skills as they relate to the ISLLC standards.

The purpose of the ISLLC standards was to provide a clear, organized set of curriculum content and performance standards that could be used to drive the preparation, professional development, and licensure of principals. The ISLLC core includes the following standards (Council of Chief State School Officers, 1996):

> Standard 1: A school administrator is an educational leader who promotes the success of all students *by facilitating the development, articulation, implementation, and stewardship of a vision of learning that is shared and supported by the school community.*
>
> Standard 2: A school administrator is an educational leader who promotes the success of all students *by advocating, nurturing, and*

sustaining a school culture and instructional program conducive to student learning and staff professional growth.

Standard 3: A school administrator is an educational leader who promotes the success of all students *by ensuring management of the organization, operations, and resources for a safe, efficient, and effective learning environment.*

Standard 4: A school administrator is an educational leader who promotes the success of all students *by collaborating with families and community members, responding to diverse community interests and needs, and mobilizing community resources.*

Standard 5: A school administrator is an educational leader who promotes the success of all students *by acting with integrity, fairness, and in an ethical manner.*

Standard 6: A school administrator is an educational leader who promotes the success of all students *by understanding, responding to, and influencing the larger political, social, economic, legal, and cultural context.*

In addition to these standards, the National Council for the Accreditation of Teacher Education (NCATE) has developed standards for preparation programs, and the American Association of School Administrators has developed standards for superintendents. These efforts to develop standards of practice are laudable in that they represent an attempt by the key stakeholder groups — policymakers, preparation programs, and professional associations — to identify a knowledge base for the profession. The standards are being used to shape licensure policy as well as the content and scope of preservice and in-service administrator preparation programs.

In examining the standards, several major areas of emphasis stand out: (1) defining the mission of the school, (2) ensuring that the school is well managed, (3) shaping a positive school culture, (4) managing and leading the instructional program, and (5) building positive relations with parents and community. To their credit, these points closely parallel the research on principals' work, instructional leadership, and effective schools.

Perhaps more important than the broad categories are the specific skills and knowledge defined under each one, the relative emphasis placed on each category (how much of each factor), and the ways the skills and knowledge are learned and can be applied in complex, real-life situations. These features are not systematically detailed in the standards model.

The standards should also be recognized for what they are: an attempt to identify a basic level of knowledge for the profession. The ISLLC, for example, developed a set of licensure standards. As a result, the ISLLC standards reflect a basic understanding of the literature on effective schools and a generic approach to administrator knowledge and skills. They differ from the work of the National Board for Professional Teaching Standards in that they are *not* an attempt to identify the "expert" knowledge of highly effective administrators. They are also divorced from any particular model of administrative practice.

Schools vary considerably on many dimensions, and effective leadership is enacted in a particular context. Skills and knowledge should be developed so that principals can lead effectively in their particular context. Specifically, schools differ in their leadership demands, depending on such factors as level (elementary, middle, and high schools); the socioeconomic, racial, and ethnic characteristics of students and community; school size; the professional culture of the school; and the governance model driving the system. Principals at both the preservice and in-service stages should develop leadership that can be enacted effectively in the context of their particular schools. The standards, therefore, would likely prove inadequate as a template for preparation of administrators for highly decentralized, focused, or specialized management systems like the ones in Seattle, San Diego, or Chicago.

Further, while the standards provide a broad overview of the knowledge, skills, and abilities needed by principals, they do not provide a clear model of daily administrative practice, specific guidance on how administrators best obtain these skills, or information on how these skills interact with one another in the practice of leadership. Leadership is not simply engaging in a smorgasbord of actions. Rather, it involves a carefully selected complex system of thoughts, actions, and processes that occur in a temporal order that solves problems, builds culture, nurtures leadership in others, communicates values and purpose, and institutes meaningful changes.

Thus leadership preparation is not simply a matter of developing a set of discrete skills and building isolated bits of knowledge. Instead it means embedding skills and knowledge in a complex, analytical "mental map" that can be applied to complex, varied, and uncertain situations. Leaders facing complex situations need complex mental maps to address those situations. The more complex the work situations, the more complex the mapping needs to be.

Leadership preparation programs therefore need to do much more than simply address lists of skills. They need to provide learning experiences that develop complex mental maps and models for action in specific contexts.

The Nature of Educational Preparation

Criticism of preparation programs, certification, and licensure is not new. In the late 1980s, considerable attention focused on the problems of preparation programs.

Sirotnik and Mueller (1993) provide an excellent example of a prototypical administrator preparation program. It involves part-time students taking courses at night or on weekends, taught by adjunct faculty. Reading and academic work is often atheoretical, textbook-based, and minimal. Sequencing and scheduling of courses is determined by students according to the scheduling demands of a busy professional rather than by issues of curriculum content and educational purpose. Field experiences are short, poorly organized, disconnected from the curriculum, and planned according to the availability of small blocks of time for working teachers. Curriculum, instruction, and assessment are seldom planned, coordinated, or linked in a coherent manner.

For years, preparation of educational administrators has been criticized in ways that are in fact descriptions of typical programs. Here are some of the critiques' findings (Peterson and Finn, 1985; Sirotnik and Mueller, 1993; Bredeson, 1996):

- Little, if any, recruitment to identify potential leaders and increase diversity in those selected
- Eased entry to graduate programs with few significant selection criteria (if any) and usually no interviews
- Admission policies that allow students to begin the program at any time during the year and continue taking courses in whatever sequence fits their work schedules or preferences
- Convenience scheduling of courses around students' full-time work schedules, with classes offered in the evenings or, more recently, on weekends
- Graduate programs that are a patchwork quilt of courses, sometimes taken at different institutions and transferred in for the final application for certification
- Program content and curricular alignment based more on textbook sequencing or faculty interest than on careful curricular design
- Pedagogic techniques that are frequently lectures and, more recently, case- or activity-based
- In-class performance expectations that are unclear, inappropriately low, or nonexistent
- Program structures and learning activities offering little in the way of meaningful experiential or mentoring opportunities, as they are often arranged by the student or occur in their school during off hours, with little reflection on or analysis of the experience

- Few, if any, programmatic links with local districts that would tie students to existing district realities
- Learning sequences and content that are rarely based on career stages or the development of expert knowledge

Efforts by various programs, associations, and foundations did attempt in the 1990s to ameliorate some of these deficiencies through investment in the development of model programs. (In the following case examples, some of the better programs include those developed during this early reform period.) Nonetheless, with the hundreds of certification programs in the country, many have improved little, and many remain weakly structured, inadequately designed, and poorly implemented. Critics of educational administration programs have suggested that the reform discussion of the late 1980s and early 1990s simply led to add-on features (for example, more case discussions) that did not significantly change the quality or efficacy of these programs (Murphy and Forsyth, 1999).

Program Inertia: Why Quality Suffers

Why haven't more programs improved on their own? Several structural and organizational reasons exist, in spite of association and group pressure and interest in change.

First, overall *accountability* for quality remains with state agencies that approve programs for administrator preparation in their states. Often almost any program with a collection of "appropriate" syllabi can gain approval. Some states have taken a more active role in trying to improve preparation programs for principals and other administrators. These actions include closing programs, requiring significant restructuring, or developing performance-based licensure systems (National Association of State Directors of Teacher Education and Certification, 2000). For example, in North Carolina, programs were required to reapply for the right to offer administrator preparation classes. Some programs were closed. In Ohio, several educational administration doctoral programs were closed and offered the chance to reapply for status. But in most states, educational administration programs have proliferated, with private universities expanding into states where they have no campuses with part-time programs.

The *norms and values* of many universities are focused more on research and grant getting than on instruction. Faculty norms, especially in major research universities, encourage time and attention to scholarship and publication. Incentives and merit are often tied to research and not to teaching or to the development of meaningful connections with the field.

Financial incentives are considerable for universities to support marginal programs with adjunct faculty. These programs have been for many colleges and universities the proverbial "cash cow," with adjunct faculty paid a few thousand dollars to teach twenty to thirty paying students in their own schools. It has always been easy to hire adjunct faculty and build an entire program around low-paid, part-time practicing administrators. Although these people are often superb in bringing real-life experiences to the classroom, they are seldom expected to devote time to current research or to program development, alignment, and refinement.

Improving preparation programs takes *time and money*, two resources in short supply in many programs. Many educational administration programs have huge doctoral advising loads compared to the arts and sciences, taking time away from program improvement. Furthermore, few departments have the budgets necessary to design, develop, or purchase instructional materials, let alone invest in the development of new course materials using current information technologies.

So even though the barriers to enhancing principal preparation programs are significant, the research literature suggests a number of program foci that could better prepare principals for the challenge of leadership. These will be considered in the next section.

Considerations in Program Design

We found several additional features beyond simple lists to be important when considering program design. These include career stages, district and state context, problem finding and problem solving, and the nature of expert leadership.

Career Stages and Leadership Development

The development of effective school leaders cannot occur in any single program or time period. Rather it must be part of a long and complex process that builds and accumulates skills and knowledge over time and in different ways. Leadership development is part of the broader career and personnel process that includes recruitment to the profession, early preparation and licensure, recruitment and selection to a district and placement in a school, ongoing evaluation and supervision and coaching, and continuous careerlong professional development. At each stage of the career, a different set of possibilities exists for leaders to gain knowledge, skills, and values that match the needs of the school and district.

We have insufficient room in this chapter to describe all the points along the career that offer opportunities for states or districts to enhance leadership development, so we will focus here on preservice preparation programs; Chapter Nine focuses on in-service professional development efforts. Considerable attention is being paid to both these arenas in recent years, but little systematic research or evaluation has enlightened the field about these efforts.

District and State Context

Corporate leadership training has regularly viewed local organizational context as a central feature of effective leadership development. This is also the case in education, though it is less frequently addressed. Programs should consider linking leadership development, both in preparation and in in-service settings, to the district and increasingly the state context of curriculum reform and accountability.

Problem Finding and Problem Solving

During the 1980s and early 1990s, a number of programs designed opportunities to develop cognitive skills in problem finding and problem solving (Bredeson, 1996; Hart and Pounder, 1999). Given the continuous problem-finding and problem-solving tasks of principals, especially in the area of instructional improvement, this is a key feature of their work. It should thus be an explicit feature of preparation and in-service programs.

Expert Knowledge

The need to address problem solving in developing leaders is considered by several writers. Most organizations do not expect new hires to be experts. But over time, additional training, experience, and mentoring should work to make neophytes into experts. Such training should be carefully built into ongoing programs.

What does expert behavior look like? Ohde and Murphy (1993, pp. 75–76) suggest that the features of expert behavior integrated into some of the model preparation programs include the following:

1. An expert within a specific domain will have amassed a large yet well-organized knowledge base.

2. This extensive body of knowledge allows experts to classify problems according to principles, laws, or major rules, rather than by surface features.

3. The knowledge base is highly organized, allowing experts to identify patterns and configurations quickly and accurately. This ability reduces cognitive load and permits the expert to attend to other variables within the problem.

4. The problem-solving strategies of experts are proceduralized. Experts can invoke these skills automatically, whereas novices often struggle with the problem-solving process.

5. The acquisition of this complex knowledge base takes a long time. Expertise within a domain is linked to years of practice, experience, or study.

The Landscape of Licensure

The National Commission on Teaching and America's Future (1996) identified licensure, certification, and accreditation as critical foundations on which teacher quality rests. *Licensure* refers to the initial permit to practice and is typically granted by the state. *Certification* refers to recognition by the profession of high levels of professional practice. *Accreditation* refers to the review of an educational unit to acknowledge and ensure that the unit is meeting specific standards of quality (Hart and Pounder, 1999).

The landscape of licensure requirements for principals is evolving slowly. As of 2000, twenty-three states required administrators to take at least one of five different examinations for licensure. The exams include the National Teachers Examination, the California Test of Basic Skills, Program for Licensing Assessments for Colorado Educators, individual state exams, and one or more examinations from the PRAXIS series of the Educational Testing Service. More recently, the ETS assessment linked to the ISLLC standards has been adopted in a large number of states. In 1998, twenty-five states were using or planning to use that assessment in some form (Crawford, 1998).

Appendix A presents the licensure requirements for a sample of eight states. Typical requirements include teaching certification and experience, a master's degree, and administrator training in an approved program, with continuing professional development needed to retain the license. The modal requirement is three years of teaching experience for principal licensure; the range is from one to seven years. In most states, the initial license is issued for five or fewer years, with renewal granted for additional coursework or participation in other professional development activities. As of 2000, three states—Louisiana, New Jersey, and Texas—remained the only ones that issue lifetime administrator licenses (Crawford, 1998; National Association of State Directors of Teacher Education and Certification, 2000).

Promising Programs: Case Examples

The following are case examples of particularly promising programs. Though most programs have not conducted rigorous evaluations of their effectiveness, these seem to have developed some successful approaches to preparation. These descriptions of programs and their features are not meant to be exhaustive, but they should provide some insights into the most current thinking about leadership preparation. (A description of the methodology used to collect case data and the interview protocol used can be found in Appendix B.)

University of Washington: Danforth Educational Leadership Program

The University of Washington's Danforth Educational Leadership Program is a cohort-based program focusing the development of moral leadership and organizational change, implementation, and evaluation. The program uses intensive twelve-month internship placements with carefully screened and trained mentors to provide an experiential base for the development of moral and ethical leadership. Classroom instruction is provided by faculty and practicing administrators in modular units of varying length rather than in traditional course-length units. The instructional staff, mentors, and internship supervisors maintain a close collaboration to give students continuity in educational experience. The program also communicates the value and process of evaluation through an intensive formative evaluation from students and other program participants.

As is reflected in its name, the University of Washington - program was developed through seed money from the Danforth Foundation. The program itself began in 1988–89 as a small experimental program for administrator training. In 1992, the traditional program was closed, and Danforth became the only administrator preparation program offered by the University of Washington.

Selection. Students are selected through an evaluation of academic credentials and leadership potential. Candidates must submit recommendations focusing on leadership ability that are completed by the candidate's principal, a teacher of the principal's choice, and a second teacher identified by the candidate. Candidates must also participate in an interview focusing on their values and clarity in use of those values in leadership decisions and in a one-hour essay exercise centered on how they would lead given the current context of today's schools. Participants are required either to possess a master's degree prior to entry or to obtain one through additional coursework.

Program Structure, Pedagogy, and Curricular Focus. Each year, from about forty applicants, a cohort of no more than twenty students is selected to participate in the yearlong program, which features a summer institute, internships, and classroom instruction.

An intensive ten-day summer institute uses interaction, reflection, cases, simulations, and discussions to build the cohort and begin the transition into leadership. The summer institute provides an opportunity to socialize students to challenge one another in productive ways and to clarify their values and beliefs about education. The institute also gives program staff an opportunity to get to know the students' strengths, weaknesses, and personalities, which facilitates placement in productive internship experiences.

Internships involve placement of candidates with carefully screened mentor administrators. Mentors are nominated by district administrators and must provide peer recommendations and put together a portfolio describing the school, its program, its staff, and its community situation. A university team visits the site to develop a miniportrait of the site dynamics and leadership behaviors of the principal. Selected administrators sign a letter of commitment, including a detailed description of the nature of their role and the extent of their involvement. Mentors are not compensated but have an opportunity to interact with faculty and maintain access to current research and faculty participants.

About half the students participate in full-time internships (about fourteen hundred hours); the other half are placed in internships for at least four half-days per week throughout the academic year (about seven hundred hours). Districts are asked to provide students with half-time leave from their positions to participate in the program. (The state requires a 320-hour internship for educational administration certification and provides some monetary compensation for districts to defer this cost.) Students are expected to participate in three different internships during the year; only one of the three can be a placement in the student's own district. At least one of the placements must be at a different level from the one at which the student intends to administer; and at least one must be from a different setting (urban or rural, for example).

Field experiences are supervised by faculty and the program coordinator, with the expectation that supervisors will meet with students and mentors in the field at least five times during the year. Faculty are given a course reduction of two quarter-length courses for every four students they supervise.

Classroom instruction is integrated with the internship experience and organized into modules. Students meet every Thursday and on selected weekends (Friday or Saturday) throughout the year for this classroom component. The modules vary in length, depending on content, and are taught with collaborative teams of faculty and practicing administrators selected for their content expertise.

"The most fundamental assumption of [the program] is that human inquiry and action are never value-free, suggesting that explicit treatment of values, beliefs, and human interests should be a routine and rigorous part of organizational life. Also suggested is a position that eschews value-relativism; we argue that one set of values is *not* just as good as any other. . . . The set of values promoted in the Danforth Program is rooted in the ideals of human caring and social justice" (Sirotnik and Mueller, 1993, pp. 62–63).

Program Effects. Evaluation is a core value of the program and is communicated through student and faculty participation in ongoing evaluation and feedback. The evaluations suggest that key factors in producing individual change were the cohort structure, seminar format, significant relationships, integrated theory and internship experiences, involvement in program change, role models provided by faculty and mentor principals, and program intensity. Key individual changes include gaining an understanding of multiple perspectives, strengthening personal values and beliefs, improved ability to discuss substantive issues, and important changes in habits of thought and interaction (Sirotnik and Mueller, 1993).

The evaluation data show that approximately 75 percent of program graduates move directly into administrative positions, compared to only 25 percent in the traditional program (Milstein and Associates, 1993).

Program Cost and Other Challenges. The program requires a significant commitment from the university in that it is significantly more costly than the traditional program structure. Key costs include a program coordinator, faculty release time for internship supervision, and the opportunity cost of choosing not to run an income-generating certification program. The program also requires a willingness on the part of the university to sidestep traditional educational delivery mechanisms (the program is a 36-credit program, which students can take in variable credit units); significant commitment from faculty to maintain the level of collaboration, supervision, and curriculum revision demanded; commitment from districts to provide release time for participating students; and the time and talents of mentors, compensated primarily through intrinsic rewards of participation.

East Tennessee State University

The East Tennessee State University (ETSU) administrative endorsement program was also developed in the 1980s and was one of the original Danforth program sites. Ongoing commitment to the Danforth program is shown by the fact that the former executive director of the Danforth Foundation is a faculty member in the program.

Program Structure. The ETSU administrator training program is designed to accommodate the work schedules of full-time teachers. Students enter the two-year program in January. The cohort group meets once a week from 4:00 to 10:00 P.M. (twice a week during the six-week summer term). Students are expected to participate in five separate placements in a 540-hour internship, which extends for the duration of the program. Placements include elementary, middle, high school, special education, and community services. Internship placements are identified by students, and the internship experience is woven into the curriculum throughout the program. For example, when coursework focuses on school finance and law, students may be asked to participate in the development of school budgets and may become involved in legal issues emerging in the school or district. The internship mentors are not screened, since the purpose is not to provide models of ideal leadership but rather to expose students to issues and examples that can be analyzed and discussed in the classroom context. The internship itself can be carried out in the context of a full-time teaching schedule, since students are largely required to participate in interviews, observations, and projects that can be conducted outside regular teaching hours.

Students complete their program requirements in December and are then available for hire at the peak hiring time of the year, spring semester.

Curriculum. The curriculum is based on the ISLLC standards and matrix, with particular attention given to the ethical and moral dimensions of leadership. The following is a list of required courses:

Interpersonal Relations (6 credits)

Emerging Perspectives Influencing the School (6 credits)

Professional Needs of Individuals and Groups (6 credits)

Developing Learners Through Instructional Leadership (6 credits)

Implementation Strategies (6 credits)

Shaping the Quality and Character of the Institution (6 credits)

No dominant pedagogical approach is used, but field experiences and use of technology are required in eleven courses.

Core and Supplementary Faculty. The faculty all hold doctorates and have experience as educational administrators. Classes are planned and taught by "tag teams." Adjuncts are rarely used, but when they are, they are paired with faculty and are current practitioners. Most adjunct faculty are graduates of the ETSU program and are selected for their familiarity with the innovative teaching strategies used by ETSU.

Recruitment and Selection. Only twenty students are admitted into each cohort; the program currently admits only one new cohort per year. Just over half of applicants are admitted; demand is thought to be related to the program's strong reputation in the region. Students are screened through both written application and an interview; criteria include academics, experience, and leadership potential. The program's commitment to strong moral and ethical leadership is indicated by the fact that it recently turned down a student with an outstanding academic record because she did not appear to share the program's values. In addition, the capstone to the master's degree is a portfolio, which has an ethical component.

Relation to State Policies. The program has recently aligned itself with the ISLLC standards in response to state action to adopt those standards and an ISLLC-based exam for administrator licensure. The state also requires a minimum grade point average and teaching experience. Two forms of certification are available from the state: internship-based and non-internship-based; ETSU requires the internship version for its participants. Administrators are also required to hold a master's degree.

California State University-Fresno

The California State University (CSU)-Fresno's principal preparation program is a third example developed with seed money from the Danforth Foundation. The program began in 1991 and involves a strong collaboration with area superintendents. It uses the Professional Development Inventory (PDI) of the NAESP as part of its initial student assessment. Scores on the PDI help shape the students' initial professional growth plan (similar to an individual educational plan), which is advanced throughout their work. A portfolio is used to build evidence that they have addressed any deficiencies identified in the assessments. Students have exit interviews at the end of each semester with faculty and district supervisors. These evaluations serve as preliminary evaluations for the next semester. At the same time, students are taking coursework linked to their field experiences.

Program Structure. Students enroll in a sequenced set of courses. The program is divided into two tiers of 24 credits each, and each tier takes about two years to complete. The first tier provides the training required by the state to become an entry-level administrator; students meet one night a week for two classes. The second tier is for beginning practicing administrators and provides the advanced credential for continuing administrators. Classes meet on weekends, and students take one course per semester.

Pedagogy. The program is experience-based. Students apply knowledge and skills developed through coherent fieldwork coordinated with coursework. Some faculty use case studies or simulations as well. Technology is available for the second-tier program in the form of teleconferencing for students who cannot travel to Fresno.

Curriculum. The program has developed a matrix that conceptualizes knowledge development and identifies course content and sequencing.

The first-tier program is focused on developing strong instructional leaders. Students participate in a 120-hour internship as a master teacher; many work as resource teachers for two to three years. During their first semester, they take two courses, one in advanced educational psychology and the other in administrative theory and management; second-semester coursework includes curriculum management and educational leadership; the third semester focuses on site-based leadership, and students do a simultaneous research project. Graduates typically advance to vice principal positions for three to four years and then to principal.

The second-tier program, designed for beginning administrators, focuses on developing transformational leaders. In addition to an internship, students take practice-based courses, including organizational development, school law, and public relations (first semester) and school finance, personnel, and systems analysis and design (second semester). Courses are scheduled to coincide with principals' responsibilities. Since these are practicing, licensed administrators, they carry out all the functions of their roles. So the program has scheduled the school finance course in early spring, when students are planning their budgets, and the personnel course in late spring, when they are starting the hiring process.

The first summer of the second-tier program is a two-unit induction course in which students take assessments and develop their growth plans. In the fall semester, students take three two-unit courses in transformational leadership, law and policy, and school-community relations. In the spring, students take three two-unit courses: school finance, personnel, and an elective. In addition, students participate in eight units of professional development activities throughout the academic year. Students take eight one-unit seminars from a menu of offerings. In the second summer, they take part in a two-unit assessment seminar in which they produce a portfolio highlighting their knowledge and skills.

Students in both tiers are assessed when they first enter the program and again at the end of each semester. Three measures are used. The first is a test on the content of the sixteen courses that they will take (based in part on state performance indicators). Students are given data on the means and standard deviations of the entire group so that they can compare themselves to others. Second, they go through the PDI, the NAESP performance-based assessment that is designed to assess knowledge and performance in relation to planning, organizing, problem solving, creativity, decisiveness, systems analysis, vision, communications, instructional analysis and supervision, instructional leadership, group leadership and team building, climate development, and moral responsibility. Third, they are required to submit their district's most recent job performance evaluation. These elements all contribute to the professional development plan that each student will complete as part of the advanced credential. The plan is updated on the basis of assessments and evaluations relating to fieldwork or internship.

Core and Supplementary Faculty. For the first-tier program, the courses are all taught by faculty, with the exception of site-based leadership, which is taught by an alumnus Ph.D. and current principal. Three former well-respected superintendents conduct a significant share of the fieldwork supervision. Faculty members supervise other field experiences.

The second-tier program relies largely on adjunct faculty experts to teach the content areas. For example, a school lawyer teaches law, a school finance person teaches finance, and a district human resource director teaches personnel management. A faculty member teaches the organizational development and systems courses.

Recruitment and Selection. The program has a strong working relationship with area districts. A group of local superintendents meets four times a year with program staff to provide feedback on the program. Many of these districts screen and select candidates, although district selection is not a requirement for program participation. Although the two-tier program is demanding in terms of student time and commitment, the two-tier structure is a requirement of California state law. Many students are attracted to the CSU-Fresno program because of the relatively low price (competitors in the area are more expensive private schools). The program also attracts students for its perceived quality and strong placement record. Each of the area districts' high schools has a vice principal who is a graduate of the program. The quality of these graduates is an excellent recruitment tool.

To enter the program, students must have a master's degree. Selection is based on academic credentials and experience. The program typically seeks outstanding teachers who have a knack for providing leadership, although they may not be aware of their leadership skills.

Relation to State Policies. The state of California requires everyone pursuing the principalship to go through a two-stage process. Candidates participate in a provisional training program (24 credits) to work in an administrative capacity; once in an administrative position, they need another 24 credits to achieve advanced certification.

The California accountability context provides an interesting backdrop to the administrator preparation environment. The state has enacted regulations requiring school accountability, peer review, and competency exams to graduate from high school and has banned social promotion. As part of the accountability program, low-performing schools have three years to improve performance on the Stanford Nine Achievement test. If schools don't improve, principals face losing their jobs. This has affected the demand for quality preparation programs. Principals and districts are looking carefully at their professional needs, identifying weak areas, and coming to the universities for help in addressing those areas. This has provided another important incentive to educators to focus on professional development plans.

Program Effectiveness. CSU research shows significant growth in the perceived competencies between beginning and ending participants. Student self-assessment scores are consistent with district supervisors' assessments. In addition, Donald Coleman, a member of the faculty, has conducted research on the validity and reliability of the PDI assessment, and on the validity of the ISLLC standards (Coleman and Adams, 1999; Coleman, Copeland, and Adams, 2000). Coleman and his colleagues have found the PDI to be both valid and reliable, and based on a limited sample, they have found that the ISLLC standards need modification to improve their validity.

Program Cost and Other Challenges. The program is funded primarily through state funds. Local districts pay for the PDI assessment ($450 per student) and donate the time for program feedback and some supervision of interns.

University of Louisville: IDEAS

The University of Louisville (UL) now runs two different program models. Officials are conducting an internal evaluation to determine whether to continue with both models or to eliminate the traditional one. The two share some characteristics and overlap in some places but have major differences as well. The first model is traditional in that students take classes to become certified and develop a portfolio to meet the state ISLLC-based requirements for certification.

The second program is called IDEAS (Identifying Educational Administrators for Schools). It was developed in collaboration with the Jefferson County school district and initially involved a cohort of prospective administrators from Jefferson County schools. Now two cohorts run simultaneously: one from Jefferson County and one from the Ohio Valley Education Cooperative, a cooperative of outlying districts.

In addition, Jefferson County and the University of Louisville run a yearlong program called Principals for Tomorrow for administrators who are certified but have not taken administrative positions. Principals for Tomorrow provides additional professional development opportunities to enhance the knowledge and skills of these licensed administrators. This review focuses on the preservice training program.

Program Structure. The entire administrator training program is one-and-a-half years in length (18 units). IDEAS is a nine-credit unit with traditional coursework and modules of field experience. The internship is part time; students are recommended and sponsored by a principal with whom they work eight to ten hours per week shadowing or collaborating. IDEAS integrates coursework and internship for 9 of the 18 credits needed for certification. The remaining courses are taken with students in the traditional administrator training program.

IDEAS cohorts begin in late May, using two National Association of Secondary School Principals (NASSP) Individual Professional Development (IDP) programs to shape a professional development path for each student based on needs. The cohorts meet twice a month and have an embedded internship during the school year. They are expected to have a minimum of sixty hours of school-site leadership. The bimonthly meetings of courses are rotated among district sites. When the course is taught at a school site, the principal at that school serves as a guest speaker.

Each participant has a sponsor-mentor who is a principal. Sponsors are responsible for providing access to internship experiences, reviewing the student's portfolio (with two faculty members) for ISLLC standards, and participating in the summer NASSP program as coaches and to provide feedback.

Pedagogy. The program is predominantly field-based, with some lectures but field experiences in all classes. Students have two mentors — one in the school and one out of it. Students intern at their schools. Program leaders are also experimenting with using Web-based technology to enhance classes between face-to-face meetings. For example, to review and discuss University Council for Educational Administration (UCEA) case studies, discussions are on-line. Technology is also used for things like PowerPoint presentations.

Three of the classes are largely traditional in delivery but are somewhat interdisciplinary, taking advantage of school-year variations to teach a variety of issues.

Curriculum. The curriculum is based on the ISLLC standards but has a significant focus on instructional leadership, including best practices, diversity, knowledge of instruction, and evaluation training. Prior to the ISLLC, the UL program used standards developed by the Educational Policy Standards Board (EPSB); some students are still grandfathered into these standards.

Core and Supplementary Faculty. The department is small and recently hired additional people. Five of the six professors are former practitioners; two are higher education professors and former higher education administrators. The off-campus classes are team-taught, and much learning is practice-based; the mentors provide an important additional learning resource.

Recruitment and Selection. Students in the IDEAS program are recommended for participation by the district and the sponsoring principal. If after formal admission procedures at UL there are too many candidates, the executive director for administration and recruitment for the Jefferson County schools chooses among them. The program has a growing number of women and elementary school principals, but it is having trouble attracting middle school and high school principals.

Students are attracted to the IDEAS program in large part because it is an honor to be selected by the district to participate. It suggests that the district is interested in promoting them to administrative positions upon completion of the program. IDEAS is also the only public program in the area, and the district defers a small amount of the cost for many applicants; therefore, some applicants may select it on cost considerations.

The formal educational experience of applicants is declining. Until recently, Kentucky allowed certification only for individuals who already had master's degrees, so applicants tended to have more teaching experience. These students came in with a significant length of service and usually a master's degree in a curricular area. The newer students have much less experience (some are first- and second-year teachers), and most have only a bachelor of science degree. There is no admission requirement for teaching experience, but Kentucky does require three years of teaching experience for certification.

Relation to State Policies. Kentucky state requirements mandate that students take credits at a program certified by the state teacher standards board. Graduates must pass the Kentucky specialty certification test, which is multiple-choice and focuses on school law and the Kentucky Education Reform Act. In addition, students must pass the Student Leadership Licensure Assessment (SLLA), ETS's ISLLC exam.

Program Effects. The University of Louisville surveyed 170 local administrators, 70 percent of whom are program graduates. The respondents indicated that the cohort model is probably better than conventional approaches, but the logistics make it hard for everyone who wants or needs training to use that method. They also indicated the following:

- The internship is highly valued. Respondents wanted more of them, early in their program.
- Women were more positive about the portfolio than men.
- The cohorts were viewed as very valuable for support and networking during the job search.

The Jefferson County school district has also evaluated program effectiveness based on feedback from participants and district evaluation of program graduates' effectiveness (the district has placed eighty to ninety principals). The evidence suggests that the program is very effective.

Program Costs and Other Challenges. Districts pay for many cohort activities, and some districts provide release time for the program. They also donate mentoring services and commit significant time from district leadership for evaluation and feedback. The districts also heavily market the program internally.

Wichita State University

The Wichita State University administrator preparation program was developed following a major revision in the doctoral program. It has a field-based research emphasis that parallels the research emphasis of the doctoral program. Based on feedback from graduates, the most valuable experience of the certification program was field placement. So the program was turned around. Now, rather than have fieldwork supplement coursework, the program is structured around fieldwork and continuous practical research, and coursework supplements the fieldwork.

Program Structure. The cohort-based program is designed not just to accommodate the lives of practicing teachers but also to use their access to schools as a core building block. Classes are held from 5:00 to 6:30 P.M. From 6:30 to 8:00 P.M., students work with their field study teams. In addition, the team has two field days during the semester to collect and analyze data. One professor guides the team on its problem or topic, and members conduct the study as a full participatory team (even the professor participates). At the end of the semester, the teams present their research. Students stay with their teams (of six to eight students) throughout the two-year program.

The internship represents fifteen of the thirty-three hours of required coursework, spread over the two-year period. This equals twelve hours per week of internship experience. Of the twelve hours, students are expected to gain six hours of experience per week during the day, with the remaining six hours conducted before or after school hours. Students are also expected to spend a full week in internship placement before and after the school year, participating in planning activities.

Pedagogy. Students learn content primarily through participation in individual and group research studies. Coursework accounts for half the total credit hours required for the master's degree. The courses themselves are heavily field-based, so that (for example) a law course is made up of twelve to fifteen contact hours rather than forty. The remaining time is dedicated to developing and carrying out a research project related to the coursework.

Curriculum. Coursework is provided in interwoven units: law with personnel; interpersonal communication with supervision; finance with leadership. The integration of curriculum works well with some subjects and less well with others. Students are assessed on research projects and coursework (papers and exams), and individual competencies are reviewed in a leadership performance assessment (Furtwengler and Furtwengler, 1998). Graduation is based on team reports and performance evaluations. Students are also scored on papers, research, and exams. The program includes a comprehensive written exam done in teams of two to four people.

If the group meets the required standard, its members all pass; if it does not, they are given further assistance.

Core and Supplementary Faculty. The faculty are all full-time university faculty members. The department carefully selects them to fit with the philosophy of the program, which is heavily based on collaboration. New faculty need to learn to work in a highly collaborative environment, a unique feature of this program. Faculty members team-teach all courses in groups of three, and the courses are integrated on the basis of content.

Recruitment and Selection. The program is in high demand, due to its strong reputation in the region. It has a waiting list from year to year; candidates are typically hired for principalships before completing the program. The standards for admission are high, involving academic criteria, personal statements, and recommendations. Some students have been counseled out of the program for underperforming.

Relation to State Policies. The state is moving toward the ISLLC standards, but they won't be fully implemented until 2004–05. The Wichita program is aligned with the ISLLC standards. When designing the program, originators discussed the features of leadership they felt to be important and found a high correlation between these criteria and the ISLLC standards.

Program Effects. The program is about to undertake an extensive review by external evaluators; they anticipate strong positive results. An informal gauge of success is the growth of study groups in schools where graduates work. On their own initiative, many graduates have established discussion groups on problems or current research.

Program Costs and Other Challenges. With only thirty students admitted each year, the program is costly to run. However, the department has enjoyed support from the university for this small-cohort approach. In 1990, the regents indicated a desire to end the practice of using professional certification programs as cash cows or diploma mills and moved to raise the quality and rigor of their offerings.

A bigger challenge for the program has been the need to fight the university culture of faculty individualization and competition. The faculty had to overcome bureaucratic barriers to collaboration. To obtain approval for team teaching, for example, the department negotiated a deal with the dean that all courses would be divided such that every professor would end up with the same workload. Faculty in other departments sometimes view the program with suspicion.

San Antonio: Region 20 Educational Service Center

The Region 20 Educational Service Center in San Antonio, Texas, provides an alternative certification for principal licensure, as well as an aspiring-leader program and a project for first-year principals. Our review will focus on the alternative certification program.

In Texas, an organization can be a licensing agency at a traditional university or apply through a school district to be an alternative certification program. The Region 20 Service Center currently works with fifty-one school districts in the San Antonio area to provide certification for educational administrators.

Program Structure. The program is structured in cohort groups of twenty to twenty-two participants called a "cohort of leadership associates," or COLA. During the program, candidates take training classes and some take university classes at the university of their choice, and they all participate in an extensive paid internship. After two years, they can take the exit exam (state test), or if they do not feel ready, they can extend one or more years in the program. Applicants need 130 hours of pretraining up front. In the end, they have close to four hundred hours of training over and above the internship. If participants have not taken courses beyond their master's degree, they must take at least two university courses, depending on their districts' priorities. Despite the alternative nature of this program, its philosophy is that good practitioners stay linked to universities.

Pedagogy. The program uses the NASSP selecting and developing assessment as a checkpoint and five-year growth plan for the participants. It also uses the NASSP mentor and coaching model. Early in the process, all participants are assigned mentors from their schools or districts or from outside their districts. Candidates spend the duration of the program (two years) with the same mentors. Each candidate must spend 70 percent of the day in a leadership capacity.

For the classroom portion of the program, trainers use case studies that draw from the Quality School Leaders Strand and use workbooks with in-basket items. They also use role playing and simulations. They do some skill building, such as learning to run effective meetings. They have to apply their training at their sites and return with evidence of how the meeting went. Skill building is taught in each area except law and ethics, which is taught in a more traditional style. Participants also work on media skills by training in front of a camera to react to different scenarios — speeches, news conferences, interviews with aggressive reporters, and so on.

Students are encouraged to subscribe to at least one professional journal to keep up with some of the literature and to follow education news items, which are often incorporated into classes.

Candidates are taught to use the Web for research; they also use the Center for Creative Leadership, as well as on-line training sponsored by the Colorado Education Department on conflict resolution. Candidates are encouraged to research the Web to familiarize themselves with the views of controversial critics of education.

Curriculum. The curriculum is currently under revision. Candidates are required to participate in four hundred hours of noninternship training aligned to the state's seven standards for school leaders, Texas's version of the ISLLC standards. Students have to pass a state exit exam that is aligned with the standards, which focuses on ethics and morality, communication, management, instructional leadership, curriculum, school improvement, and resource development. The program administrator indicated that of these, ethics and communication seem to be the critical knowledge and skill areas. The program has a three-day module on ethical aspects of practice but tries to weave ethics throughout the curriculum.

The primary focus of the program is the internship and its related administrative duties. Districts choose mentors, but the program has final approval of them.

Core and Supplementary Faculty. The Educational Service Center conducts a variety of professional development activities for area districts. This program has five staff members who conduct training. In addition, national speakers are hired to make presentations, and the program gets agreement from them to allow use of their materials for other sessions. Around one hundred people in the area do some guest lecturing. Among the core faculty are district mentors who are trained using the NASSP mentoring and coaching model. They are trained on how to gather data, give feedback, conduct observations, and coach others.

Recruitment and Selection. The program invites applications from people with master's degrees in "just about anything" who are interested in school leadership. Participants must have 130 hours of "pretraining" up front, but they can substitute relevant experience for some of the requirements. A rigorous application process includes an IQ-like test and a personality profile to ensure that candidates have at least some of the attributes of successful principals. Applicants must also have excellent references. Applicants are interviewed, with follow-up questions based on the application materials and assessments. Consistent with state requirements, applicants must have at least a 3.0 GPA, a valid teaching certification, at least two years' teaching experience, and some form of leadership responsibility.

The program markets itself to superintendents and principals. It also runs advertisements on its Web site and in newspapers statewide. It has a good relationship with university programs and gets referrals from them of candidates who are not interested in the traditional university approach.

Among the three cohorts to complete the program to date, the first was highly experienced and all white; the second has two African American females and two Hispanic males; the third is all white. All participants except one have had ten to fifteen years of experience. Students choose this program over traditional ones because of the significant quality of the training they get. Graduates are typically hired as principals by their placement district.

Relation to State Policies. State policy allows for alternative certification programs approved by local districts. It also requires participants to pass an ISLLC-based assessment for licensure. Continued state approval for the program requires that 90 percent of participants pass the assessment.

Program Effects. Only one cohort has completed the program to date; 100 percent of its participants passed the state licensure assessment. Program officials frequently survey participants and districts regarding program features; these are formative rather than summary evaluations and are used to modify the program.

Program Costs and Other Challenges. The program charges $400 per course, comparable in cost to university-based programs in the area. Participating districts hire interns at a relatively low wage; they also agree to allow participants off campus for five days during the year for training in addition to the evening sessions. The mentors receive a $500 stipend from the district; some districts provide compensatory time off. Districts also have the incentive of having an intern on the job who is paid at a lower rate than the assistant principal.

Conclusions

Our analysis of the role of the principal, the knowledge and skill it demands, and this set of promising principal training programs together suggest a number of characteristics that may be useful in developing and improving administrator preparation programs. These characteristics differ from the norm of typical preparation programs. In many cases, evaluation data or anecdotal evidence from program administrators suggest that these characteristics have contributed to program quality. It is worth reiterating that these programs tend to be more demanding of participants than traditional ones, yet the programs are all in demand because of their reputation for producing highly qualified, competent administrators and for placing their graduates in administrative positions.

The programs differ from traditional programs in *selection and screening* as well as in *structure and content*. Administrators who had data on placement rates prior to the development and implementation of their model programs report that placement rates for participants are much higher in the model program than in traditional ones. They attribute these higher rates to enhanced preparation of candidates, which leads graduates to be more open to and interested in taking on challenging principalships. It also makes these candidates more attractive, so that those that seek placement actually land the job. The higher placement rates are important because model programs are typically smaller than their traditional predecessors. Although the number of graduates is lower, their rate of placement into actual administrative positions is high.

Important features of these programs include coherence, curriculum focus, sequencing of courses, structured scheduling, collaboration with districts, screening and selection, and membership. Each of these will be discussed in turn.

Unlike the prototypical administrator preparation program, each of these programs was characterized by significant *coherence in curriculum, pedagogy, structure, and staffing*. Significant collaboration was involved in development of the program vision, and each element of the program was carefully designed to reflect program goals rather than happenstance or convenience. In several of the programs, the experiential component was viewed as the core, with classroom-delivered curriculum content designed to support and make meaning of the experiential component. The internships themselves tended to be much longer than in a typical program (usually six hundred hours or more over at least one year), and they were structured to take advantage of cyclical variations in the principal's role. Thus school-based budgeting would be taught to coincide with the budget cycle at the school site.

Program structures were designed to support the core vision and operational goals of the program. The programs were virtually all cohort-based, with typical cohorts of about twenty to twenty-five students. Evaluation, feedback, and purposive program design provided cohorts with an opportunity to engage in more meaningful conversations about administrative practice. The programs provided a forum for making explicit the values and decision-making processes underlying principal leadership and the management decisions observed or experienced in the internship. The cohort structure also provided a significant support system and professional network for graduates in the early stages of their administrative careers.

Schedules were designed around students' working lives, but several programs required that students obtain significant release time from their districts to participate. Others designed program structures to minimize the inconvenience to students while remaining true to the overall objectives of the program.

Program staffing was purposive. Many programs were team-taught, and all had significant faculty discussions about the curriculum, with careful assignment of academic faculty and practitioners as demanded by the subject under study. The programs also typically found ways to work around traditional semester-length course structures, which were viewed as inappropriate for classroom content designed to meet student learning needs and the ebb and flow of administrative cycles. Since primary learning occurred in the field and classroom work was designed to support that, traditional semester-length classes did not fit well with the pedagogical approach.

Each of these programs had a *clear, well-defined curriculum focus*. Each program had a hallmark, a big idea that drove the curriculum design of the program—for example, moral leadership and organizational change at the University of Washington, research-based practice at Wichita State, ethics and communication at San Antonio, instructional leadership and transformational leadership at CSU-Fresno, and standards-based reform in Kentucky and Louisville.

In many of these programs, the *curriculum was sequenced and mapped* against the annual cycle of regular work responsibilities and the random, nonroutine responsibilities of the principal or else against a vision of the knowledge, skills, and abilities needed to be an effective school leader. The curriculum sequence varied among the programs; perhaps the most sophisticated sequencing strategy occurred at CSU-Fresno, where students were expected to become instructional leaders first and then transformational leaders. Coursework and state licensing requirements were aligned to serve those sequential purposes.

As with traditional programs, class meetings were arranged around work schedules, although in some cases students were required to obtain leave or to quit their jobs in order to participate. As mentioned earlier, program structure was typically driven by content rather than by university bureaucracy or tradition.

All of these programs were characterized by *significant collaboration* among the faculty and between the university and the practitioner community in the region. Some programs described overcoming the university culture of autonomy as one of the primary challenges of implementing the program effectively.

Another key feature of these programs was the degree to which applicants were *screened and selected*. In some cases, district leaders had to identify participants in order for them to apply. The University of Washington is an interesting example, using both academic and leadership potential as criteria for admission. Applicants must submit recommendations from their principals, another teacher, and a teacher that the principal selects. They are also interviewed and screened for their potential as moral leaders.

Together, these features affect the quality of the candidate, the quality of the experience, the focus of the program, the reputation and links to current practitioner communities and problems, and ultimately the quality of program graduates. Many of the program structures require more effort than a traditional program, potentially reduced revenues, and more time in planning and collaboration. Most of the model programs receive significant support from universities more interested in enhancing the quality of their offerings than in generating additional revenue.

Another important characteristic of the programs we have studied here relates to the challenges of development, planning, and implementation. Unlike traditional programs, each of these was developed through strong collaboration with local districts. In Louisville, Washington, and San Antonio, districts applied pressure on program administrators to develop the program to better meet their needs. The Jefferson County school district plays such an active role in the program that its officials actually screen and select applicants from their district from among those who apply to the program. They also provide considerable in-kind support for maintenance and program operations. Other catalysts for program development include external support, such as the Danforth Foundation grants (in Washington, CSU-Fresno, and ETSU), and program champions who encourage and lead the change effort. Among the examples here are East Tennessee, which has on its faculty the former director of the Danforth program, and CSU-Fresno, whose program director was formerly affiliated with the NAESP. In addition, extensive preplanning and discussion went into the design of these new programs. Finally, it appears that further discussions and continued planning and redesign occurred during implementation.

This examination of several model programs suggests important directions that could be followed to enhance the quality of administrative preparation across the country. One feature that may be difficult to replicate is the time and effort expended by the faculties and practitioner communities to discuss, plan, and agree on a direction for the programs. It was also necessary to make meaningful changes in program structure and content that required significant increases in faculty workload. Finally, it took the collaborative involvement of local districts with university faculties to make the programs successful. Nonetheless, these programs demonstrate that changes can occur that significantly redefine what preparation programs can accomplish.

References

American Federation of Teachers. *Survey and Analysis of Teacher Salary Trends, 1998.* Washington, D.C.: American Federation of Teachers, 2000. [http://www.aft.org/research/survey].

Andrews, R. L., and Basom, M. R. "Instructional Leadership: Are Women Principals Better?" *Principal,* 1990, 70(2), 38–40.

Block, J. H. "Reflections on Solving the Problem of Training Educational Leaders." *Peabody Journal of Education,* 1997, 72, 167–178.

Bossert, S. T., Dwyer, D. C., Rowan, B., and Lee, G. V. "The Instructional Management Role of the Principal." *Educational Administration Quarterly,* 1982, 18(3), 34–64.

Bredeson, P. V. "New Directions in the Preparation of Educational Leaders." In K. Leithwood, J. Chapman, and D. Corson (eds.), *International Handbook of Educational Leadership and Administration.* New York: Kluwer, 1996.

Bridges, E., and Hallinger, P. "Problem-Based Learning in Medical and Managerial Education." In P. Hallinger, K. Leithwood, and J. Murphy (eds.), *Cognitive Perspectives on Educational Leadership.* New York: Teachers College Press, 1993.

Coleman, D. G., and Adams, R. C. "Establishing Construct Validity and Reliability for the NAESP Professional Development Inventory: Simplifying
Assessment Center Techniques." *Journal of Personnel Evaluation in Education*, 1999, *13*(1), 27–45.

Coleman, D. G., Copeland, D., and Adams, R. C. "A Report on the Reliability
and Validity of the ISLLC Performance Standards." Paper presented at
the National Council of Professors of Educational Administration
NCPEA/ASSA Conference Within a Conference, San Francisco, Mar.
2000.

Council of Chief State School Officers. *Interstate School Leaders Licensure Consortium Standards for School Leaders*. Washington, D.C.: Council of
Chief State School Officers, 1996. [http://www.ccsso.org/isllc.html].

Crawford, J. "Trends in Administrator Preparation Programs." *UCEA Review*,
Fall 1998.

Deal, T. E., and Peterson, K. D. *The Leadership Paradox: Balancing Logic and Art-
istry in Schools*. San Francisco: Jossey-Bass, 1994.

Educational Research Service. *Is There a Shortage of Qualified Candidates for Openings in the Principalship? An Exploratory Study*. Arlington, Va.: Educational Research Service, 1998.

Elmore, R. F., and Burney, D. *Investing in Teacher Learning: Staff Development and
Instructional Improvement in Community School District #2, New York
City*. New York: National Commission on Teaching and America's
Future, 1997.

Fleigel, S. "Lured Away and Forced Out, Principals Leave New York City Schools
at Record Pace." *New York Times*, Sept. 20, 1999, pp. 18, 20.

Ford, D., and Bennett, A. L. "The Changing Principalship in Chicago." *Education and Urban Society*, 1994, *26*, 238–247.

Fullan, M. G. *What's Worth Fighting for in the Principalship*. New York: Teachers
College Press, 1997.

Furtwengler, W., and Furtwengler, C. "Performance Assessment in the Preparation of Educational Administrators: A Journey." *Journal of School Leadership*, 1998, *8*, 65–85.

Hallinger, P., and Heck, R. H. "Reassessing the Principal's Role in School Effectiveness: A Review of Empirical Research, 1980–1995." *Educational
Administration Quarterly*, 1996, *32*(1), 5–44.

Hallinger, P., Leithwood, K., and Murphy, J. (eds.). *Cognitive Perspectives on Educational Leadership*. New York: Teachers College Press, 1993.

Hallinger, P., and Murphy, J. "Instructional Leadership in the School Context."
In W. Greenfield (ed.), *Instructional Leadership: Concepts, Issues, and
Controversies*. Boston: Allyn & Bacon, 1987.

Hart, A. W. "A Design Studio for Reflective Practice." In P. Hallinger, K. Leithwood, and J. Murphy (eds.), *Cognitive Perspectives on Educational Leadership*. New York: Teachers College Press, 1993.

Hart, A. W., and Pounder, D. G. "Reinventing Preparation Programs: A Decade of Activity." In J. Murphy and P. B. Forsyth (eds.), *Educational Administration: A Decade of Reform*. Thousand Oaks, Calif.: Corwin Press, 1999.

Keller, B. "Principal Matters." *Education Week on the Web*, Nov. 11, 1998. [http://www.edweek.org/ew/1998/11prin.h18].

Kelley, C. "The Kentucky School-Based Performance Award Program: School-Level Effects." *Educational Policy*, 1998, *12*, 305–324.

Kelley, C. "What Works in Education: Innovative School Management Approaches in the United States." Paper prepared for the Organization for Economic Cooperation and Development, Center for Educational Research and Improvement, Paris, 2000.

Leithwood, K. "Leadership for School Restructuring." *Educational Administration Quarterly*, 1994, *30*, 498–518.

Leithwood, K., and Duke, D. L. *Defining Effective Leadership for Connecticut's Schools*. Hartford: Connecticut Department of Education, 1997.

Leithwood, K., and Duke, D. L. "A Century's Quest to Understand School Leadership." In J. Murphy and K. S. Louis (eds.), *Handbook of Research on Educational Administration*. San Francisco: Jossey-Bass, 1999.

Leithwood, K., Jantzi, D., and Steinbach, R. *Changing Leadership for Changing Times*. Philadelphia: Open University Press, 1999.

Leithwood, K., Steinbach, R., and Raun, T. "Superintendents' Group Problem-Solving Processes." *Educational Administration Quarterly*, 1993, *29*, 364–391.

Levine, D. U., and Lezotte, L. W. "Effective Schools Research." In J. Banks (ed.), *Handbook of Research on Multicultural Education*. Old Tappan, N.J.: Macmillan, 1995.

Louis, K. S., and Marks, H. M. "Does Professional Community Affect the Classroom? Teachers' Work and Student Experiences in Restructuring Schools." *American Journal of Education*, 1998, *106*, 532–575.

McCarthy, M. M. "The Evolution of Educational Leadership Preparation Programs." In J. Murphy and K. S. Louis (eds.), *Handbook of Research on Educational Administration*. San Francisco: Jossey-Bass, 1999.

Meyer, J. W., and Rowan, B. "The Structure of Educational Organizations." In M. W. Meyer and Associates, *Environments and Organizations*. San Francisco: Jossey-Bass, 1978.

Miklos, E. "Administrator Selection, Career Patterns, Succession, and Socialization." In N. J. Boyan (ed.), *Handbook of Research on Educational Administration*. New York: Longman, 1988.

Milstein, M. M., and Associates. *Changing the Way We Prepare Educational Leaders: The Danforth Experience*. Thousand Oaks, Calif.: Corwin Press, 1993.

Mintzberg, H. *The Nature of Managerial Work*. New York: Harper & Row, 1993.

Murphy, J., and Forsyth, P. B. (eds.). *Educational Administration: A Decade of Reform*. Thousand Oaks, Calif.: Corwin Press, 1999.

Murphy, J., and Louis, K. S. (eds.). *Reshaping the Principalship: Insights from Transformational Reform Efforts*. Thousand Oaks, Calif.: Corwin Press, 1994.

Muse, I., and Thomas, G. J. "The Rural Principal: Select the Best." *Journal of Rural and Small Schools*, 1991, 4(3), 32–37.

National Association of Elementary School Principals. *Elementary and Middle Schools: Proficiencies for Principals*. (3rd ed.) Alexandria, Va.: National Association of Elementary School Principals, 1997.

National Association of State Directors of Teacher Education and Certification. *The NASDTEC Manual on the Preparation and Certification of Educational Personnel*. (5th ed.) Dubuque, Iowa: Kendall/Hunt, 2000.

National Center for Education Statistics. *Public and Private School Principals in the United States: A Statistical Profile, 1987–88 to 1993–94*. Washington, D.C.: National Center for Education Statistics, 1997.

National Commission on Excellence in Education. *A Nation at Risk*. Washington, D.C.: U.S. Government Printing Office, 1983.

National Commission on Teaching and America's Future. *What Matters Most: Teaching for America's Future*. New York: National Commission on Teaching and America's Future, 1996.

Newmann, F., and Associates. *Authentic Achievement*. San Francisco: Jossey-Bass, 1996.

Ohde, K. L., and Murphy, J. "The Development of Expertise: Implications for School Administrators." In P. Hallinger, K. Leithwood, and J. Murphy (eds.), *Cognitive Perspectives on Educational Leadership*. New York: Teachers College Press, 1993.

Peters, T. J., and Waterman, R. H., Jr. *In Search of Excellence: Lessons from America's Best-Run Companies*. New York: Warner Books, 1982.

Peterson, K. D. "Making Sense of Principals' Work." *Australian Administrator*, 1982, 3, 1–4.

Peterson, K. D. *Secondary Principals and Instructional Leadership: Complexities in a Diverse Role*. Madison: National Center on Effective Secondary Schools, University of Wisconsin, 1989.

Peterson, K. D. *The Professional Development of Principals: A Portrait of Programs*. Unpublished manuscript, University of Wisconsin, 1995.

Peterson, K. D., and Finn, C. E. "Principals, Superintendents, and the Administrator's Art." *Public Interest*, 1985, 79, 42–62.

Prestine, N. A. "Apprenticeship in Problem-Solving: Extending the Cognitive Apprenticeship Model." In P. Hallinger, K. Leithwood, and J. Murphy (eds.), *Cognitive Perspectives on Educational Leadership*. New York: Teachers College Press, 1993.

Raun, T., and Leithwood, K. "Pragmatism, Participation, and Duty: Value Themes in Superintendents' Problem-Solving." In P. Hallinger, K. Leithwood, and J. Murphy (eds.), *Cognitive Perspectives on Educational Leadership*. New York: Teachers College Press, 1993.

Sirotnik, K. A., and Mueller, K. "Challenging the Wisdom of Conventional Principal Preparation Programs and Getting Away with It (So Far)." In J. Murphy (ed.), *Preparing Tomorrow's School Leaders: Alternative Designs*. University Park: University Council for Educational Administration, University of Pennsylvania, 1993.

Yale Child Study Center. *Professional Development at SDP: The National Events*. New Haven, Conn.: Yale Child Study Center, Yale University, 2000. [http://info.med.yale.edu/comer/profdev.html].

Appendix A
State Principal Licensure Policies, 2000

California

Preliminary Credential: Valid educator credential; three years of experience; fifth year of study (post-baccalaureate); approved professional preparation program in educational administration; recommendation by an approved college; special education (mainstreaming); and CBEST. Nonrenewable. (Candidates prepared outside of California eligible by verifying completion of a master's degree in educational administration, eligibility for the equivalent credential in originating state, three years experience, CBEST, and the valid prerequisite credential).

Professional Clear Credential: Preliminary administrative services credential, two years of successful full-time experience in a position while holding the preliminary credential; and a Commission-approved program of advanced study and field experience. Valid five years, renewable with 150 clock hours of professional growth activities and one-half year of appropriate experience.

Connecticut

Initial Educator: Master's degree from an approved institution; completion of 18 semester hours of graduate credit in addition to master's degree; completion of 50 school months of successful teaching service in public or approved nonpublic schools, in positions requiring a Connecticut public school certification, or in a state education agency as a professional or managerial staff member (portions may be waved for applicants who have completed a one-year internship as part of an administrator preparation program); recommendation by an approved administrator preparation program that indicates applicant is personally and professionally qualified to serve as a public school administrator, and has completed an approved program, with not less than 15 graduate credits taken at the recommending institution. Has completed graduate study in each of the following areas: psychology and pedagogical foundations of learning; curriculum development and program monitoring; school administration, personnel evaluation and supervision, and contemporary educational problems and solutions from a policy-making perspective; and has completed a course of study in special education (comprised of not fewer than 36 clock hours). Valid three years.

Provisional Educator: Successful completion of Initial Educator Requirements, plus successful completion of beginning educator support and training, 10 months of successful service under the initial educator certificate, or 30 school months of successful service as an educational administrator within the 10 years prior to application; served a Board of Education in Connecticut successfully under a provisional certificate for the school year immediately preceding application. Valid eight years.

Professional Educator: Successful completion of 30 school months under the provisional educator certificate; and not less than 30 semester hours of graduate credit at an approved institution or institutions in addition to the master's degree. Valid five years, renewable with 90 contact hours of continuing education activities or six graduate credits.

Illinois

Master's degree from a recognized institution; approved program, or comparable certificate from another state, and 25–27 graduate semester hours in instructional leadership management, program development and operation, and policy; and two years of full-time teaching or school service personnel experience. The Illinois Certification Tests must be passed. Valid five years, renewable.

Kansas

Graduate degree and a state-approved building level administrator program; three years of accredited experience in the school setting at the level of the building administrator endorsement; and recommendation from an accredited teacher education institution. Renewable with six hours of recent credit, or comparable in-service points.

Kentucky

Three years of full-time classroom teaching experience; master's degree; approved Level I curriculum for school administration and instructional leadership; passing scores on the School Leaders Licensure Assessment (SLLA) and the Kentucky Specialty Test of Instructional and Administrative Practices. Upon confirmation of employment, an internship certificate issued for the first year of employment. Upon successful completion of the internship, the certificate is extended for four years.

First renewal requires approved Level II curriculum. Successive renewals: two years of experience as a school principal, or three semester hours additional graduate credit, or 42 hours of approved training.

Tennessee

Master's degree in Educational Administration from an accredited college or university in a member state; PRAXIS (Principles of Learning and Teaching and the Specialty Area Test in Educational Leadership: Administration & Supervision, with a minimum score of 530 points.

Texas

Master's degree, two years of teaching experience; complete required assessments; and complete the required program and induction period.

Washington

Initial Certificate: Current teaching certificate from any state; master's degree through a regionally accredited institution; complete a state-approved program of the principalship; and 540 days of full-time classroom teaching. Valid seven years.

Continuing Certificate: Must have completed all the requirements for the initial certificate; 15 quarters or 10 semester hours through an approved college/university or 150 approved clock hours based on specified performance domains. Verification of 540 days (three contracted years) of full-time experience as a principal, vice principal, or assistant principal; a course or coursework in issues of abuse, including the identification of physical, emotional, sexual, and substance abuse, its effects, legal requirements, and methods of teaching abuse prevention. Valid five years; renewable with completion of 150 hours of continuing education every five years.

Source: National Association of State Directors of Teacher Education and Certification, 2000.

Appendix B
Data Collection, Methodology, and Sources

We collected information from a variety of sources in order to gain a broad picture of issues related to the preparation and professional development of principals. These sources included research and interviews with key individuals and association members and with leaders of the preparation and in-service programs.

Initially, with the assistance of Hanna Alix Gallagher and Steve Kimball, we conducted a selective review of literature on leadership, principals' work, characteristics of preparation programs, and other topics related to preparation and in-service training. We looked for research-based knowledge as well as conceptualizations of the role and examples of best practices.

Next, we conducted structured interviews with a selected group of people who were involved in the training and preparation of principals, who had helped develop new certification standards, or who had been critics of such programs. Additional interviews were conducted with officials of the U.S. principals' associations to learn their concerns and initiatives in this area.

We then collected information on existing credentialing policies, as well as data on a variety of new standards for preparation. These policies and standards were compared to the knowledge base on the nature of principals' work and the needs of first-year principals.

We then developed a formal interview protocol to collect data on preparation programs. This provided the tool for gathering data on preparation programs.

We used a "snowball" sampling technique to find programs that were identified as particularly effective or innovative. We were able to identify several programs that were using a variety of different standards or approaches to preparation and that one or more informants viewed as successful.

The team conducted interviews with a select group of program leaders from every region in the country, spotlighting programs that approached preparation in nontraditional ways. The interviews lasted from one hour to several hours. Interview data were collected and organized around our core rubrics for describing and comparing programs. In addition, written materials, curricula, and schedules were requested from the programs. These materials were reviewed with attention to the core issues under investigation. Case descriptions were prepared and sent to respondents for a member check of accuracy of the information.

Chapter Nine

Principal In-Service Programs

A Portrait of Diversity and Promise

Kent D. Peterson, Carolyn Kelley

Educational leaders, like leaders in business and industry, have opportunities to develop new or enhance and deepen existing leadership skills and knowledge through professional development and training. In addition, numerous programs are available that are intended to extend the capabilities of leaders in a variety of ways, including: reinforcing values and vision, gaining new knowledge in a technical area, building networks of colleagues within an organization or field, or providing opportunities for personal growth and reflection (see Conger and Benjamin, 1999, for some corporate examples).

In education, as in corporate leadership training, organizations and individuals face a wide array of offerings: from one-shot workshops or conferences in beautiful (or warm) locations to multiweek institutes held on university campuses and from intense, curriculum-focused technical programs to broadly conceived personal growth experiences. These offerings also vary considerably in their focus and purpose, curriculum content, coherence, sequencing of skills and knowledge, use of time, and collaboration with the administrator's district. Most often these programs are not described in any detail, nor are they systematically evaluated (Peterson and Wills, 1989).

Professional development for principals, once called "education's disaster area" (Wagstaff and Collough, 1973), has seen considerable improvement recently. New programs, more careful design of training, a more focused set of purposes, and better pedagogy have all ameliorated some of the worst problems. But much still needs to be done to develop coherent, sequential, and pedagogically effective programs for principals at different stages in their careers. In this chapter, we look at a number of examples of in-service programs for principals, seeking programmatic elements that might improve the skills and knowledge of incumbent principals.

In our examination, we provide as in-depth a picture as possible, given the lack of written materials describing purpose, content, and structure. In some cases, the nature of the programs may change from year to year depending on the popularity of particular topics and the availability of speakers. In other cases, such as the California School Leadership Academy (CSLA), curricula and programs are continually refined to reflect new knowledge and needs of principals. In the following descriptions, one sees an incredible range of program quality, coherence, and structure. Within these descriptions, though, programs may be found that possess many useful and well-designed elements and that can help principals improve their leadership. They are promising examples of professional development models.

Sources of Professional Development for Principals

Numerous groups, associations, and organizations provide professional development for principals:

- National and regional professional associations such as the National Association of Secondary School Principals (NASSP), the Association for Supervision and Curriculum Development (ASCD), and the National Staff Development Council (NSDC) hold yearly conferences, with preconference workshops, keynote speakers, short workshops, and time to network. State associations also typically hold yearly conferences and quarterly workshops on specific topics.

- Universities such as Harvard's Principals Center offer two-week intensive programs with a specific focus and time to learn and reflect with colleagues.

- Reform programs such as Accelerated Schools require several days of focused training on leading and implementing their particular reform models.

- Private, not-for-profit organizations develop programs.

- State departments of instruction develop workshops and sometimes longer training efforts focused on particular state needs or more general leadership skills.

- Intermediate districts and county offices of education offer programs for local administrators.

- Districts often offer workshops and in-service programs for principals and will occasionally develop longer, more intensive academies and self-development programs, such as the Principal In-Service Program in Madison, Wisconsin, or the Principals' Academy in Detroit.

- In the past decade, several major programs have been developed in cooperative arrangements with some combination of districts, state education agencies, administrators' associations, and foundations. These include the California School Leadership Academy, the Gheens Academy, and the Mayerson Academy.

- Federal regional laboratories such as the North Central Regional Educational Laboratory (NCREL) frequently design institutes or offer workshops related to their missions.

- For-profit companies and independent consultants design and offer training for school principals, sometimes with open enrollment and offered nationally or specially designed for districts.

Program Variety

These programs vary considerably, in the following ways:

Focus and purpose: Most seem to focus on particular administrative skills or knowledge needed for new initiatives, though others try to provide information and opportunity for reflection on new educational trends, the deeper purposes of education and learning, or personal renewal. Occasionally, programs have not decided what their focus will be and instead offer whatever presenter is available.

Curriculum coherence: Some simply hire popular speakers for a conference-type format; others have integrated sets of topics based on a defined and sequential curriculum with well-defined objectives.

Instructional strategies: Some are mostly lecture courses; others use a wide variety of strategies, depending on the nature of the material taught and learners' needs. These include experiential learning, moderate use of technology, group interaction and discussion, case study, and action research.

Length and time structure: The most common are one-shot workshops or conferences, though others have long and multiple-session programs. A number have a carefully designed set of long and short sessions over several years to build knowledge and skills.

Connection to state educational initiatives and policies: Some professional development offerings are the result of state legislative initiatives (such as the California, Kentucky, and North Carolina programs). Others are linked to state policies in that they provide topical coverage of information and strategies to manage schools effectively in specific state policy contexts.

Links to district values and specific educational initiatives: District-sponsored programs often include the transmission of district values and mission and provide principals with training to support implementation of district policy initiatives.

Such a large, diverse, and fragmented array produces significant problems for the development of coherent, ongoing, integrated, sequential, and cumulatively effective professional development. Many items on this menu are topical, one-shot approaches that are packaged nicely but are unlikely to provide the support needed to develop excellent school leaders. The selection is like a smorgasbord in that it provides a great and attractive variety without much potential for satisfaction or the nutrition necessary for long-term health.

Despite the variety in focus and format, few of these programs use newer information technologies or offer radically different formats, approaches, or materials. Most use short-term seminar approaches. Better models may link a series of seminars together sequentially to weave information exchange with opportunities for principals to build their knowledge or practice skills over time. A few of these programs provide individual support or coaching to help principals implement new skills and strategies at the school site.

Aside from the few good examples, even those that are not "model" offerings may suggest lessons that could enhance professional development opportunities for principals.

Potential Purposes of Professional Development for Principals

Professional development programs serve a variety of potential purposes. When examining particular models, it is useful to consider what purposes these programs could serve (Conger and Benjamin, 1999; Peterson and Wills, 1989). These include the following:

- Developing organization-specific knowledge and skills that would not necessarily be a part of the general knowledge base, such as district culture, norms, and management or instructional strategies
- Maintaining currency for knowledge and skills that are rapidly changing, such as information on new research findings, and upgrading technological skills and competencies

- Providing an opportunity for personal reflection, renewal, and strategic redirection for individuals whose jobs typically allow little time for such reflection

Like many occupations, the principalship requires on-the-job experience to provide the knowledge needed to develop expertise. It also requires significant investment in knowledge and skill development to become proficient, more than could be expected preservice (particularly given compensation levels and job demands). Professional in-service development can fill these needs.

Many in-service programs have consisted of a succession of interesting or popular speakers brought in to attract attendees. A different approach might be more focused on skills and knowledge needed for a particular career stage or context.

Career Stages

Although little systematic research has been done on the career stages of principals (except perhaps on the needs of first-year principals), few observers doubt that changes occur in the knowledge, skills, and values required over the course of the principal's career. As many of our examples in this chapter suggest, the first year is unique. But principals in the middle of their careers, perhaps in years three to five, probably have different needs than principals in later years. For success, senior principals in the last years should also not be ignored; it is important to make that period energized and focused rather than a slide into on-the-job retirement.

In the middle and later stages of the career, it should be important to develop skills as expert leaders, managers, and problem solvers. Refining the skills of the neophyte could both enhance the core skills and abilities of principals as they move through their careers and be a strong anchor for the district, as these administrators would then feel appreciated, supported, and valued. However, as with other professions where new research and ideas are emerging, principals will need to gain understanding around new curricular content, innovative instructional approaches, current thinking about time and class size, and new strategies for assessing students, planning, and school improvement.

Context Considerations

One of the most striking features of the training of leaders in business is the careful and systematic attention given to the context of the company (Conger and Benjamin, 1999). In companies with the most promising training programs for leaders, significant elements of business training focus on developing shared corporate values, deep knowledge of the industry and its technology, understanding what outcomes are valued and assessed, deep ties and relationships among company members and its leaders, and knowledge of the corporate culture (Conger and Benjamin, 1999).

Similarly, professional development for principals should in part attend to the context of the district, state, and region. In large or highly diverse districts, training could focus on the needs of the communities served by the school.

What contextual issues might be important? Training in districts, like training in corporations, should probably attend to the nature of district values, the underlying belief of what learning is (what an educated student is), knowledge of the particular district and its history, knowledge of the approaches to curriculum and instruction considered most useful, the history of district-union relations, specific managerial systems, and a deepened understanding of the district culture. Finally, these programs could cement stronger, more open professional relationships among principals, which could enhance the sharing of craft knowledge, ideas for leading and managing schools, and the social support needed during the regular challenges of leading schools.

A Short History of Principal Academies

Although principal professional development has existed for decades, it became a broader national movement only in the early 1980s. At that time, both principals' academies and principals' centers started to be widely available to administrators. Academies provided long-term professional development programs over several weeks, usually in the summer. Principals' centers became places offering both long-term and short-term opportunities to learn, network, and grow (Peterson, 1995).

Two of the earliest programs, started in 1981, were the Harvard Principals' Center and the Vanderbilt Principals' Institute. These spawned a number of other programs and still serve principals each summer.

A second major movement developed through the leadership of the Harvard Principals' Center, Roland Barth, and hundreds of committed administrators around the country. Meeting yearly in what were called "conversations" (as opposed to the less interactive "conferences"), educators gathered who were interested in developing centers where principals could meet with researchers and practitioners, reflect on practice, and connect with other school leaders. At these meetings, educators talked about how to design, implement, and support centers for school leaders. Many programs resulted nationwide.

Sometimes these were free-standing programs to increase the leadership skills and knowledge of principals. Most notable is the California School Leadership Academy (CSLA). This state-supported program, begun over a decade ago, offers a wide variety of professional development programs for principals, school teams, superintendents, and prospective administrators. Having served thousands of educators, it is one of the most comprehensive and successful of these programs.

Other programs of this sort are found in universities, including Harvard and Vanderbilt. The Bush Program at the University of Minnesota was offered initially to superintendents and then extended to principals. It uses a process approach and teams of principals to develop skills in leadership and management.

Other reform programs and organizations have used added professional development work for principals as part of their implementation (Peterson, 1995). Several of these earlier programs, such as the Coalition for Essential Schools, offer training often focused more on broad principles than on specific skills or strategies for implementing change.

More recently, some of the more systematic and strategic training programs are focusing on implementing standards-based education or specific curricula. These often provide training for the whole school in skills and strategies necessary for a coordinated approach.

The *ATLAS Communities Project* is a collaboration of the Coalition for Essential Schools with the Comer Project (School Development Program), Harvard Project Zero, and the Education Development Center and also offers training for district and community teams. This effort brings together teachers, students, principals, parents, central office administrators, board members, and community members for an annual winter institute to examine critical issues related to more systematic approaches to reform through collaboration. The program training is in the early stages of development, but it demonstrates an approach to broad-based team training.

The *Coalition for Essential Schools* (CES) has for many years supported professional leadership needs for a small select group of principals, identified as "Thomson Fellows," through a multiweek program of reflection, sharing, learning, and networking. It is now starting principal seminars.

The *Comer Project* (School Development Program) also provides training for principals whose schools are involved in the program. The program helps principals understand the structure of the model and develop skills in working with families and staff.

The *Accelerated Schools* model, for principals of settings using that model, not only operates at the site level but also offers an intensive multiday program for technical assistance people who will be working directly with schools.

Success for All provides training to staff and principals on the program and the strategies needed to implement it. While some training is provided for principals, most is focused on implementation strategies rather than on broader leadership skills.

The *Modern Red Schoolhouse* (MRS) uses a leadership assessment instrument that delineates areas of strength and weakness and then offers coaching.

Other programs also provide focused, systematic training to build the skills and knowledge in implementing program structures and reaching learning goals.

The LEAD Academies

The federal government became interested in leadership development in the early 1990s and provided funding for each state to develop a leadership academy or program through LEAD grants (Peterson and Wills, 1989). Every state became involved, designing a wide variety of activities, from traditional drive-in workshops to longer principal academies. A few of these remained after funding ended and continue to provide service to school leaders.

Similarly, the secretary of education's Fund for Innovation in Education provided special competitive grants in the early 1990s to establish a small number of innovative leadership programs in an effort to develop new models. These were held in Maine, Delaware, Alaska, and Illinois, and a few continue in one form or another. These programs tried out new techniques, such as outdoors experiences (ropes courses or Outward Bound), problem-based learning (PBL), technology-enhanced learning, and a variety of time formats. Some states continue to support principal academies, but the number and breadth of the programs have decreased over the past five years.

Foundation-Supported Academies

Another model for professional development has germinated through foundation support: the free-standing professional development academy. The first was the Gheens Academy in Louisville, Kentucky, in the Jefferson County schools. Funded through a combination of foundation and public monies and under the early leadership of Dr. Phillip Schlechty, the school district encouraged and supported the development of the Gheens Academy. It provides a wide variety of services and programs, from individual workshops and seminars to consultation and support for school reform.

This model appears to have been the impetus for a similar Cincinnati venture, the Mayerson Academy. In this case, corporate and civic leaders saw a significant need for quality professional development for the Cincinnati public schools. The Mayerson Academy began with a combination of public and private funds from foundations, businesses, and the school district. The result was enough money to renovate an existing building with the most current training equipment and meeting rooms. The Mayerson Academy offers both public and private school educators a plethora of programs, with a major strand focused on leadership development.

A Portrait of Selected Programs

A number of professional development programs for school leaders have been initiated to support school improvement. A few—like the Harvard Principals' Center, the Vanderbilt Principals' Institute, and the California School Leadership Academy—have been in operation for a decade or more. We shall outline some core features of some of these programs and what has been learned about successful leadership development (Peterson, 1995).

Mayerson Academy, Cincinnati, Ohio

The Mayerson Academy is a professional development academy that provides services to the Cincinnati public schools. The academy was developed as a joint venture between the school district and local business leaders interested in improving the quality of public schools. The district contracts with the academy to provide professional development. Most programs are geared toward professional development of teachers, but the academy also provides leadership training in four areas.

1. *The Aspiring Principals program*. This is strongly encouraged for all aspiring principals in Cincinnati. It targets those who have or are about to get principal licensure, providing twenty contact hours of training, and is focused on instilling the vision and culture of the Cincinnati public schools (CPS), and its expectations for CPS principals. Thus the curriculum focuses on

> The role and responsibilities of the principalship. This begins with a speech by the superintendent on the CPS district vision.
>
> The culture of the CPS school system. CPS employees provide information about the size, type, organization, and diversity of the school district.
>
> The principal's role in communicating with constituents (parents, staff, and students).

2. *A monthly training program for all CPS principals*. The district contracts with the academy to give each principal five hours of training each for eight months, on topics identified by the district. The principals receive training in four groups, with separate instruction for high school principals, middle school principals, and two sections of elementary school principals. Recent topics have included brain research and instructional coaching models. Attendance is not mandatory, and the training is conducted in a traditional workshop format (for example, it has no assigned readings and consists of a self-contained session).

3. *Focus groups for beginning principals*. Once a month, beginning principals are invited to participate in a group discussion on survival for first-year principals. Mayerson staff follow up with site visits to the new principals' schools if needed. New principals are not required to attend, but all of them do.

4. *Distance learning*. The president of Mayerson has developed a distance learning component with Mayerson's blessing, but it is in fact part of a separate entity, the Instructional Leaders Institute. CPS principals often take part in the distance classes on site at Mayerson. The program, *Requisites of a Leader*, is televised nation-

wide via satellite to seven to eight hundred schools in thirty districts, including rural and urban schools. It focuses on five requisites: vision and direction, accountability, selection and development of personnel, instructional leadership, and building trust. It includes interaction with presenters and trained facilitators who help implement content in the school settings. This appears to be an interesting, evolving model for using new technologies for training.

Six Mayerson trainers staff the programs, and national experts are brought in to contribute to specific content areas. Private donors provided the initial development and start-up funds; the Cincinnati school district pays the operating costs.

North Carolina Principals' Executive Program

The North Carolina Principals' Executive Program (PEP) was established in 1984 as an intense residential program to improve the leadership and management of school leaders. It was initially highly academic with a liberal arts bent—a one-size-fits-all approach to making leaders more insightful and worldly. The program has evolved to have a mixture of rigor and relevance, with tailored programs to meet the different needs of leaders at different stages of their careers.

PEP provides twenty programs that vary in length and focus over an eight-month period. The longest are the twenty-day residential programs. Separate programs are offered for administrators at various career stages and with various foci (for example, central office leadership, higher school performance, assistant principals, or principals with five or more years of experience; see http://www.ga.unc.edu/pep/programs for more information). In cohorts of twenty to twenty-five, practicing principals attend Tuesday to Thursday, once a month. Between sessions, participants read assigned books and reflect on their practice.

The residential programs are conducted in a thematic fashion. They may have discussions, readings, and assignments focused on resource reallocation, for example. In one session, twenty-six principals attended from low-performing schools (identified by the state accountability system). They held workshops and discussions intended to improve their schools' performance, and twenty of the twenty-six schools showed improvement afterward.

During the sessions, students are given several leadership-style assessments to gauge their strengths. Instructors also request information from the participants' faculty and supervisors. Participants are graded on work products, such as homework and project tasks. For example, they may be asked to videotape themselves working in a formal setting. Professors of communication review the videotapes and talk with the principals about their communication styles and needs. Other faculty are contracted to assess the writing styles and skills of the administrators.

In addition to the curricular emphases, the programs provide significant opportunities for networking; many programs hold weekend reunions for revitalization and renewal. Some traditional full-time faculty staff the programs along with superintendents and principals. All faculty typically hold doctoral degrees and have a strong North Carolina network and level of success that resonate with their peers. Each group in the residential program has a class president. The programs hold formal graduation ceremonies, presenting participants with awards for high academic averages and framed certificates. Superintendents and family members are invited to the ceremony, which features a keynote address that is typically by a noted politician.

PEP also offers two-day workshops and one-day seminars or symposia. The seminars, symposia, and workshops are contemporary and have a special focus on current issues (for example, technology and the future).

Participants self-select and must submit an application approved by their superintendents. If they are accepted to the residential program, all expenses are paid by the state. State appropriations for 1999–2000 were $1.7 million. Costs are approximately $3,000 to $4,000 per participant.

The program receives excellent evaluations from participants and districts. Administrators expressed concern that the principals most in need of training are often the least likely to attend. These principals don't recognize the need, or else their superintendents are not interested in letting them go for fear of problems at their schools in their absence.

Gheens Academy, Louisville, Kentucky

The Gheens Academy was established in the 1980s as a partnership between the Gheens Foundation and the Jefferson County Public School District to ensure a more qualified workforce for Louisville schools. The Gheens Foundation donated over $4 million to develop the teacher center for adult learning, and the Gheens Academy has since been viewed as a national model for professional development. While most of the Academy's work focuses on professional development for teachers, a small part of its programs also provide training for principals.

A coordinator chosen from among current principals in the Jefferson County public schools (JCPS) coordinates the principals' program. The Gheens Leadership Development Center provides workshops, training to meet district or state requirements (most recently, evaluation training for new principals), mentoring for new principals, and individual assistance for experienced principals. The programs focus on current education issues (such as standards-based reform and its implications for curriculum and leadership of schools); the leadership curriculum is centered in instructional leadership and management (time management, parent involvement, and community and business partnerships). Specific topics are based on needs identified by principals and the district.

Groups of participants stay together for the duration of a "strand" of typically three to six weeks. An aspiring-administrator strand lasts six to eight weeks. Classes meet regularly during that time. Information is presented through book study, case study, and group projects (not lectures). The program is in the process of incorporating more technology into curriculum delivery, including a virtual classroom with electronic links to resources and between administrators in the district.

Gheens's work with principals is also coordinated with state training programs for new principals and the Kentucky Leadership Academy (KLA; see "Kentucky Principal Internship Program" later in this chapter). JCPS has also contracted with the KLA to provide training for thirty-five additional JCPS principals every two years for a two-year program paid for by the district.

Chicago Principals and Administrators Association Professional Development Programs for the Chicago Public Schools

The Chicago Public Schools (CPS) and the Chicago Principals and Administrators Association (CPAA) have jointly designed four leadership development programs. The CPAA offers four primary programs: LAUNCH for aspiring principals, LIFT for first-year principals, the Illinois Administrators' Academy for principals, and the Chicago Academy for School Leaders for principals and other administrators.

LAUNCH. LAUNCH is a 280-hour-plus apprenticeship program for aspiring principals. Candidates are screened in a rigorous application process that includes a written application, an interview, an assessment center experience, and recommendations. The program is in its second year. It is designed to prepare aspiring principals who already hold their preliminary license for the CPS context. The program has three main components:

- A five-week summer academy is conducted on the Northwestern University campus, cosponsored by the schools of business and education. The first and last weeks of the program are intensive residential programs.

- Participants attend a fall-semester paid apprenticeship, after which they return to their normal jobs unless they are hired into administrative positions. Aspiring principals are matched with schools and mentors screened for the program. The group meets throughout the apprenticeship with mentors and the whole group of LAUNCH participants.

- Once selected for an administrative position, the principal participants join an urban network that provides continuing support. So far, sixty-seven principals have gone through this program (thirty-seven the first year and thirty the second year), and forty-eight have been hired (sixteen as principals and thirty-two in other administrative positions).

LIFT. LIFT, currently in its fifth year, is designed for *beginning principals* who have not participated in LAUNCH. It is a voluntary program that supports new principals (currently, 88 percent of first-year principals in Chicago participate). The program includes monthly meetings (a full day or an evening with a following day) held during the school day and a coach assigned to each participant. Coaches are geographically paired with participants, and each coach mentors two participants, coaching two hours per week in addition to the monthly meetings.

The LIFT program is grounded in the school year cycle and provides nuts-and-bolts information on how to run a school.

The Illinois Administrators' Academy. The Illinois Administrators' Academy provides internship experience and training required by the new state law over and above the initial license. The training includes seven two-day workshops organized around the seven CPS standards (school leadership, parent and community involvement, student-centered learning, professional development and human resource management, instructional leadership, school management and operation, and interpersonal effectiveness) and a teacher evaluation course required by the state. The program is mandatory for all new administrators or can be replaced by LAUNCH (which exceeds these basic requirements).

The Administrators' Academy has also provided support to schools on probation in CPS.

Chicago Academy of School Leadership. The Chicago Academy of School Leadership (CASL) provides continuing professional development for principals and other district administrators. The program is modeled after and adapted from the California School Leadership Academy (see next section) and includes long-term seminars with eleven modules of content aligned with the CPS's seven standards. All participants must make a two-year commitment to the program, which begins with a three-day retreat followed by sessions lasting one day a month. The program operates on a cohort model and is marketed to all current principals. At the end of two years, participants share their portfolios.

The seven CPS standards drive the curriculum for LAUNCH, LIFT, and CASL. Two more—management skills and communication skills—were added after feedback from practitioners about the key skills many principals lacked.

Program pedagogy and staffing vary by program. LAUNCH is problem-, case-, and experience-based. It is staffed in collaboration with Northwestern University. The others tend to be more workshop-based, using external experts and former or practicing administrators. CASL has a portfolio component and uses an NCREL-developed five-day technology module.

Participants tend to have high levels of experience. Under Chicago's highly decentralized, parent-controlled school governance system, principals are typically older and highly experienced. One problem is that aspiring principals trained by LAUNCH may not be selected for hiring under this decentralized system. Unlike many school districts, Chicago principals are paid considerably more than the median teacher salary.

California School Leadership Academy. The California School Leadership Academy (CSLA) is a statewide professional development program created in 1985. A central office and twelve regional offices carry out program operations. Although funded by the state, the CSLA has also provided technical assistance support for the development of programs in Chicago, Mississippi, Texas, Louisiana, Colorado, and Washington.

Since 1985, the curricular focus of the program has evolved from a foundation in the effective-schools literature to a stronger business focus on school performance to shared leadership and more recently back to the principal as an instructional leader in a standards-based system. The current programs have a core grounding in curriculum and instruction as well as in moral and ethical leadership qualities.

The CSLA offers three primary programs: Foundation 3.0, School Leadership Team, and Ventures. In Foundation 3.0 (the "3.0" derives from computer software terminology to signify a changing knowledge and skill set), experienced, new, and aspiring administrators and teacher leaders engage in a two- to three-year program that involves participation in a series of ten related seminars and culminates in the development of a portfolio. Participants who complete the program are called CSLA Senior Associates.

The core curriculum includes the following seminars:

Leading Through Vision

Building a Vision of Powerful Learning

Reculturing to Create Powerful Learning

Assessment in Service of Powerful Learning

A Thinking, Meaning-Centered Curriculum in Service of Powerful Learning

Teaching in Service of Powerful Learning

Creating a Diversity-Sensitive Environment for Powerful Student Learning

Systems Thinking in Service of Student Learning

Building Relationships and Communication Structures in Service of Powerful Student Learning

Shared Vision and Shared Leadership in Service of Powerful Learning

Several elective seminars are also available, on such topics as safe and productive environments, professional development for low-performing schools, school community, change efforts, curriculum alignment, learning communities, and service learning. The CSLA is continuously refining and expanding curricula to reflect new needs. A variety of instructional approaches are used in the seminars, with a combination of constructivist and more traditional learning strategies. Students develop a collection of portfolio evidence of their own vision, current organization and leadership, and change activities.

The School Leadership Team Program is designed to build capacity for communities of leaders to lead their schools to restructure in ways that will promote student learning. Together, school leadership teams implement comprehensive restructuring and reform strategies focused on improved student achievement. Typical teams include the principal, teachers, staff, parents, community representatives, district office staff, and students (in grades 7–12). The program provides ten to fifteen days of seminars, each approximately six hours long, over two to three years. Team members participate in an equal number of workdays at the school site. Seminar sessions include topics such as the following:

Creating a vision of powerful teaching and learning

Designing a curriculum and assessment in the service of powerful learning

The change process

Shared decision making

High-performance teamwork

Shaping school culture to support collaboration and continuous improvement

Working through resistance

The program takes a continuous-improvement approach to the implementation of reform models and specifically trains principals in these skills.

The Ventures Program is designed for experienced school leaders and is focused on transformational leadership. Participants use methods drawn from ethnographic research to study their own school settings. Over a three-year period, participants document the process of transformation of school culture and their own ability to act as change agents to effect significant action. The program is designed in three phases. In phase 1, participants define their theory and the "field of action" and focus of their change efforts. In phase 2, participants begin implementing a transformation strategy based on their analysis of multiple sets of data. In phase 3, participants present an exhibition of their achievement along with a narrative analysis and data that document changes over time.

The CSLA also operates an executive leadership center that provides professional development for superintendents. These programs help superintendents learn how to support change in a standards-based reform.

Overall, the CSLA offers one of the most integrated and reform-focused programs in the country. Its set of training modules, regional structure, and attention to developing leaders who can implement change in a standards-based setting provides a coherent and well-developed professional development package. The program's ability to build a strong network and cohesive professional culture across the state is unique among programs.

Kentucky Principal Internship Program. The Kentucky Principal Internship Program (KPIP) was established in the late 1980s to support struggling first-year principals. Mentors chosen from current principals provide first-year principals with advice. Licensure requires certification from an accredited program and then passage of the School Leaders Licensure Assessment (SLLA, ETS's Interstate Leaders Licensure Consortium–related assessment) and a Kentucky assessment. Principals then have five years to secure a license. Each beginning principal is assigned a three-member committee composed of a mentor, a university professor, and the superintendent or superintendent designate. Mentors participate in a state university leadership training program and must pass a test to be certified as mentors. A second-year support network is provided by volunteer mentors and managed by the Kentucky Department of Education.

The state has developed a program handbook that was revised in time for the June 2000 entering class. Principals must meet the ISLLC standards and are evaluated by a three-member committee based on observations and an ISLLC-aligned portfolio. Principals must pass the evaluation to retain their jobs.

A $400,000 annual state appropriation funds the program through payments to the university faculty for training, participation on committees, and travel related to committee work. In addition, mentors receive $1,000 for their work. No official evaluation has been conducted, but several individual research projects have provided satisfactory external evaluations of the program.

Principals' Institutes and Academies

Principals' institutes have been around for a long time. In the 1980s, they were among the first approaches to leadership development to serve a large group of principals. Most follow a common format, but each represents a unique approach to working with school leaders. We shall examine two that are among the most respected institutes in the country (Peterson, 1995).

The Harvard Principals' Center Institutes. Initiated in 1981 under the leadership of Roland Barth, the Harvard Principals' Academy has been in continuous operation every summer since, providing development opportunities for hundreds of school leaders. During the summer of 1995, it offered almost continuous institutes for principals and district teams, as well as many institutes on special topics or with a particular focus.

The basic institutes, called "The Art and Craft of the Principalship" and "Leadership: An Evolving Vision," draw over 120 school leaders from around the world. During "Art and Craft of the

Principalship," participants examine critical issues and topics related to leading successful schools, read extensively, meet in small discussion groups to address topics from the larger sessions, use case studies to generate dialogue, and engage in personal writing about leadership and the challenges of creating effective schools for all students. In addition, participants address issues of race and gender, team building and staff development, managing change, and dealing with the complexities of school leadership. The institute is intensive and demanding, but participants establish powerful professional ties with the colleagues they meet.

The second institute, "Leadership: An Evolving Vision," is an advanced program that addresses current issues related to transformational learning, creating a vision for one's school, inclusive education, and several of the key topics of the prior institute. Again, considerable time is spent in collegial discussion and analysis, writing, and networking.

These institutes have an internal thematic structure that has been well received by participants. The content and large-group sessions are highly dependent on selecting quality presenters who share the ideas and approaches of the institute. The small-group discussions, a key success of the institutes, are led by school principals who have gone through the institute and demonstrated the ability to lead quality "conversations." In addition, institute staff meet several times during the day to debrief one another about the large presentations, the flow of discussion, and the needs of participants, fine-tuning progress and ensuring quality control.

Lasting two weeks in July, the summer "Institute for School Leadership" is designed for leadership teams from districts. These teams usually include principals and are from districts interested in school reform or restructuring. The institute brings in presenters from around the country—school leaders, consultants, and researchers who share current thinking and ideas with district teams. Major topics include leadership for change, systems thinking, diversity and community, strategic planning and resource allocation, and ways to support personal growth and change. This institute uses case studies extensively and focuses on the multiple district changes necessary to support reform. In addition, there are numerous chances to meet in small groups and as district teams to discuss, analyze, and share.

The Principals' Center has expanded its offerings to serve many different school leaders. During the summer and over the school year, institutes are held for superintendents, aspiring principals, urban educators, and other educational leaders. Various lecture series, study groups around topics of interest to principals, and short courses are offered throughout the school year. The center also has a regular newsletter highlighting the writing of practitioners about problems of practice.

The Vanderbilt International Principals' Institute. The Vanderbilt Institute started the same year as Harvard's under the leadership of Kent Peterson. At that time, it offered a four-week course in instructional leadership, school improvement, and effective schools. It too has evolved over the years and now lasts about ten days, with a focus on instructional leadership, managing change and improvement, developing an educational vision for the school, and shaping the school culture. The program uses a mix of activities to engage participants: problem-based learning (PBL), lectures, simulations, writing, and the ITCOT computer simulation of decision making. Serving a small group of leaders each summer, it continues as an intensive, rewarding experience for principals from the United States and abroad.

In summary, these principal academies are two of the best and longest-running in the country. Unfortunately, quantitative evidence of the impact of their programs on student learning is scant. Nonetheless, support from participants and the reported changes in leadership behavior suggest that they are influencing the ways principals think and act.

Other programs also serve school leaders and might provide some useful topics, techniques, and approaches of professional development. These include the Maine Academy for School Leaders, the Alaska Governor's Academy for School Leadership, the Delaware Principals' Academy, and various programs provided by the Texas administrators' associations.

Professional Development in Restructuring Projects

A number of training programs for school leaders are designed as part of larger school reform and restructuring efforts. Several of the major reform models have at times included leadership training in addition to immersion in the specific program principles and values (Peterson, 1995).

The Accelerated Schools Project

The Accelerated Schools Project includes training for principals in addition to training trainers who will work with schools wanting to implement the Accelerated Schools model. For principals whose schools want to join, the project offers an initial two- to three-day cohort program, which involves an introduction to the philosophy and values of the program, a close examination of the challenges of implementing the Accelerated Schools model, and work with principals in the program who are at various stages of implementing the model. Careful attention is paid not only to examining the changes needed in governance and decision making about school features but also to investigating "powerful learning" based on constructivist concepts.

Implementation of the Accelerated Schools model occurs through the support of a local site coach and trainer. These trainers receive an intensive eight-day program that covers such topics as group dynamics and meeting management, the core principles and values of Accelerated Schools, the nature of powerful learning and constructivist classrooms, the inquiry process and ways to "take stock" of the school, coaching and training techniques, and the problems faced by schools while implementing these processes. The approaches are themselves constructivist and designed to provide skills and experience in the inquiry method and in teamwork. This training is provided for technical assistance people who will be working on-site with schools and is directly linked to skills and knowledge for principals.

School Development Program (The Comer Project)

The School Development Program (SDP) offers four different training programs, one specifically designed for principals. Called "The Principals' Academy," this five-day program focuses on instructional leadership and the decisions principals make that can support SDP. The academy has an organized curriculum that prepares principals to implement SDP, work with staff, and develop plans. The academy's popularity necessitated the development of a returning principals' track for those who had already been through the first program. Principals seem to value the opportunities to get feedback on their work and to network.

Success for All

Success for All (SFA) does not put much emphasis on leadership development. The program provides extensive training for the school both on-site and during conferences. At the conferences, principals can attend meetings that are of interest but not specifically focused on their roles, such as those designed for superintendents and facilitators. No extensive training focuses on the role of principals.

Modern Red Schoolhouse

The Modern Red Schoolhouse (MRS) program has comprehensive training for its school principals. Once a school has become an MRS site, the coach for the site starts to work with the principal. MRS also has the principal, teachers, and direct supervisor fill out the Skills Scope instrument to gauge leadership qualities. The assessments are used to analyze the skills and knowledge of principals and to develop coaching and learning opportunities to address weaknesses. Extensive opportunities arise over the year for direct and telephone meetings with the coach.

The ATLAS Communities Project

The ATLAS Communities Project is a combined effort of several major reform programs, including the Coalition, the Comer Project, Harvard Project Zero, and the Educational Development Center. ATLAS is now developing training for district and community teams. This effort brings together teachers, students, principals, parents, superintendents, board members, and community members from three sites for several days to examine critical issues related to systematic approaches to reform. This broad-based effort exposes this diverse set of people to reform issues such as new union roles, the need for high expectations for students, the challenges of collaborative leadership, conflict management, and ways to forge new agreements in districts (called "goals of engagement"). The project holds an annual winter institute for principals and assistant principals. The three-day leadership institute gives time for the pathway groups to meet and interact as well as to share knowledge about how to work together for urban school reform. Although the majority of the institute focuses on the project, current issues and topics are also added each year.

The Center for Leadership in School Reform

Dr. Phillip Schlechty founded the Center for Leadership in School Reform (CLSR) when he left the Gheens Academy. Created to provide leadership in the school reform movement through training, support, and information, the center has worked with a wide array of districts across the country.

CLSR views itself as a resource for reformers and assists districts in four areas: capacity building, the nature of student work, leadership development for teachers and administrators, and marketing the need for change. Principal development occurs in districts with customized training by in-house trainers. Principal in-service training is focused on the four areas.

The Coalition for Essential Schools

The Coalition for Essential Schools (CES), a reform program started by Dr. Ted Sizer following a major study of secondary education, developed a set of professional growth activities to support principals in implementing the coalition's principles. Through seminars, meetings, and CES's conference, called "The Fall Forum," the program brought together reform-oriented school leaders to meet, talk, learn about the challenges of implementing change, and share ideas and craft knowledge. For a number of years, it selected "Thomson Fellows," a small group of principals leading coalition schools who met for a week two or three times a year for reflection, sharing, learning, and networking. More recently, it has been developing a program to train principals in change, leadership, and coalition principles.

In sum, these major reform programs vary in the degree to which they focus on leadership development. Some make the professional development of school leaders an important component of their program, while others see it as secondary. Each takes a unique approach to working with principals, some providing long programs, others relatively short periods of training. For all of them, a major focus is development of a thorough understanding of the precepts, principles, and components at the core of their reform efforts. Thus these models are developed to facilitate implementation of their reform ideas and models.

Conclusions

The landscape of professional development programs is diverse and fragmented, at times offering high-quality, coherent, in-depth programs and at other times offering marginal, piecemeal, and short-term workshops. The programs discussed here provide some sense of direction and promise for the future.

We have chosen to focus primarily on programs linked to state, district, university, or reform network efforts because these appear to have more of the characteristics that we believe are likely to produce more effective school leaders.

Some of the most successful programs seem to *have a clear vision or purpose, are systematic, and are organized around a thoughtful sequencing of the career development of knowledge, skills, and abilities* needed for professional excellence in the principalship. Some of these programs focus more narrowly on a particular slice of principal career development, while others, such as the Chicago programs, provide developmental support, acculturation, and survival skills for principals aspiring to replace those retiring. A number of these programs also provide an opportunity to develop the habits of mind and professional network connections that should foster continued growth and development throughout the principal's career.

The curriculum content of the programs varies, but several have *a coherent and coordinated set of skills and information organized in a sequential pattern*. Some have content that depends in part on the specific audience or stage of career development targeted by the program, but others offer a broad set of leadership skills. Although few programs have a formalized, written curriculum, those that do help the participants organize and learn material and skills.

Most in-service programs remain short and topical, but some of the better programs offer *a long-term set of experiences blending multiweek institutes with continuing on-site training, practice, and coaching*. For example, twenty-day programs are divided across one or two academic years, with principals attending in two- or three-day increments. The North Carolina and California programs provide good examples of this approach. These longer programs appeared to build skills and knowledge as well as a strong professional culture among participants.

With these caveats, here is a partial list of curricula from the programs highlighted here:

Early Career Curricula

District, state, or reform network vision and values

Managerial tasks of the principalship

District or state requirements and context

Basic leadership and management skills (communication, evaluation, diversity, people skills, and so on)

Instructional leadership

Culture building

Midcareer Curricula

Instructional leadership

Culture building

Transformational leadership

School improvement

Data analysis

Action research

Problem solving

Personal renewal

Pedagogy is varied, interactive, and selected to enhance learning. In general, programs typically use at least some workshop structures designed to address and take advantage of the day-to-day realities of principals.

Seminars are sequenced to build principal knowledge around a focused curriculum and to enable participants to put what they learn into practice. Extensive follow-up seminars and coaching increase the likelihood that skills can be used on the job.

Although the programs are limited in their use of *new technologies*, they feature more variety than many preservice programs. The North Carolina programs use videotaping to examine principal practices and communication skills. Perhaps the most advanced use of technology is the distance education program for school leaders being developed as a spin-off of the work of the Mayerson Academy. The program director provides interactive distance education to districts and schools across the country. Significant plans are under way to link this work to advanced education and professional certification of school leaders.

The best programs are also *closely linked to participants' work and to the needs of current practitioners, schools, and districts.* While typically much less academic in focus than preservice programs, these in-service programs appear to be much more closely aligned with the needs and realities of practicing principals.

Many of the programs have paid close attention to developing *a program culture and sense of membership.* Using graduation ceremonies, reunions, special roles for participants and graduates, awards, unique language, values, history, and rituals, the programs build networks of participants, provide intrinsic rewards for participation, and provide incentives for new members to participate, despite the fact that these programs are voluntary and can be quite demanding.

Programs are governed by many different groups, including states, districts, reform networks, professional associations, and private interests. Of the programs we examined, state, district, association, and privately sponsored programs tended to be designed specifically for principals. The reform network models and some district models were focused on teachers as well as principals. State-level programs were typically linked to state goals and reforms, had significant investment in program development, and were funded to a greater or lesser extent by the state. District programs often focused on induction of new principals or the development of leadership skills unique to the specific district context.

Our investigation of in-service programs suggests that many probably provide significant opportunities for self-renewal, but only a small portion are likely to have a significant impact on the knowledge base, the leadership abilities, and the efficacy of practicing principals. What is clearly needed is a model of professional practice that is not generic but identifies a clear direction for the principalship, one that would potentially change the structure of schools to enable principals to carry out this work effectively.

Also needed is a clearer model of the professional growth, development, and career stages of the principalship and, similarly, a model of sequenced knowledge and skill development for principals. Such a program might provide a well-designed sequence of knowledge and skill development, with early stages focused on organizational acculturation, context, and management and communication skills; middle stages focused on instructional leadership, human resource development, and culture building; and expert stages focused on transformational leadership for organizational regeneration, growth, and improvement. Alternatively, knowledge and skill progression may be viewed as enhancing the level of skill in a broad set of critical knowledge and skill areas (for example, moving from level 1 to level 4 in instructional leadership as defined by the profession). This work would provide a significant foundation for the enhancement of principal professional growth and development, both preservice and in-service, and would strengthen the profession. It would also give policymakers and district administrators clearer direction in the refinement of the role of the principalship and in recruitment, selection, evaluation, and professional development efforts.

It is clear that professional development for principals can and should be improved. Existing models and approaches provide a panoply of possibilities and opportunities for the design of quality programs.

References

Conger, J. A., and Benjamin, B. *Building Leaders: How Successful Companies Develop the Next Generation*. San Francisco: Jossey-Bass, 1999.

Peterson, K. D. "The Professional Development of Principals: A Portrait of Programs." Unpublished manuscript, University of Wisconsin-Madison, 1995.

Peterson, K. D., and Wills, F. "Historical and Conceptual Underpinnings of Leadership Development Programs: A Quest for Roots." *Educational Considerations*, 1989, *16*(2).

Wagstaff, L., and Collough, T. "Inservice: Education's Disaster Area." *Administrator's Notebook*, 1973, *21*, 1–4.

Chapter Ten

Associations and the Principalship

A History of Advocacy,
a Horizon of Opportunity

Gerald N. Tirozzi

> The key factor to the individual school's success
> is the building principal, who sets the tone as
> the school's educational leader, enforces the
> positive, and convinces the students, parents,
> and teachers that all children can learn and
> improve academically. Our overall assessment is
> that the school principal has the greatest single
> impact on student performance. As a result, we
> believe that increased attention and funding needs
> to be directed toward programs that attract,
> evaluate, train, and retain the best principals.
> —*Arthur Andersen report on the Jersey City*
> *and Paterson Public Schools for the New Jersey*
> *Legislature's Joint Committee on Public Schools*

As the turnstile of history adds another millennium to its count, many eyes are focused on educational leadership. Opportunity abounds in this arena because of attention that has been building for more than a decade. Parents, school boards, state departments of education, standards organizations, and others have come to the realization that school site leaders—principals and assistant principals—are essential to systemic school reform.

347

Educational administration preparation programs and school leadership organizations and associations are being called on to ensure that the highest-quality principals and assistant principals are serving in the nation's schools.

Associations have been actively involved in promoting higher standards for their members and are eager to take assessment and development of school leaders to a new level. In fact, school leadership associations have been involved in developing leadership excellence criteria for nearly twenty-five years. Now, however, disparate efforts, including those of the associations, have begun to coalesce so that now we have an excellent opportunity to achieve systemwide results. Associations represent the voice of those who know best about the demands of educational leadership—educational leaders in the field. Thus associations have a unique responsibility to speak up for high standards in the development and assessment of professionals in school leadership.

This surge in support for the reform of school leadership results not only from the efforts of associations and other organizations but also from the urgency of the need. The political environment, the shortage of highly qualified candidates desiring to become principals, and the call for increased accountability have provided a window of opportunity for advocates of school leadership. Principals stand ready to seize the opportunity and help set the highest standards of leadership for their profession. Through their state and national associations, school leaders are becoming increasingly vocal in their call for better leadership preparation programs and for elevation of the standards required of the profession. The American Association of School Administrators (AASA), the National Association of Elementary School Principals (NAESP), and the National Association of Secondary School Principals (NASSP) have been particularly active. In light of the increased attention to the importance of school leadership in academic achievement, school leadership organizations are optimistic that they will play a major role in the meaningful change on the horizon.

For many years, most funding and policy initiatives have focused on teaching excellence. These initiatives led to such enhancements as the National Board for Professional Teaching Standards and various improvements in certification and standards. Although these reforms were much needed, no similar systemic approach to school leadership was undertaken. Because teachers are seen as having the most direct day-to-day impact on student achievement, the attention to teacher reform seemed natural and hence received tremendous attention. Unfortunately, these initiatives bypassed a key player in systemic reform in a given school: the principal. After all, who frequently has the responsibility of hiring those excellent certified teachers? Who can ensure that the entire staff—not just a handful of staff members—has the skills necessary to improve achievement for all students?

A 1999 report by the National Association of State Boards of Education (NASBE) Study Group on School Leadership, *Principals of Change: What Principals Need to Lead Schools to Excellence,* emphasized this notion when it asserted that "without well-qualified motivated leaders in every school, reform will succeed sporadically, and the goal of having all students in every school and district able to meet high standards will be threatened."

In times of extraordinary reform or need, people call on great leaders to guide them. In the corporate world, leadership is *never* an afterthought. Boards seek the most capable leaders—leaders with significant foresight and vision. They may seek among loyal employees who have been groomed for success and risen through the ranks, or they may look for a leader "from the outside."

In education, these are indeed times of extraordinary opportunity and extraordinary need—extraordinary because nothing is ordinary about handling a shooting in your school. There is nothing ordinary about improving academic achievement for six hundred students, implementing block scheduling, or restructuring your academic program. There is nothing ordinary about meeting with parents of a student to inform them their child has a learning disability. There is nothing ordinary about finding and hiring the perfect teaching team. We could argue about whether these duties should rightly fall to the principal, but the fact remains that they do. The handling of each such situation cannot be left to chance.

The life of each student in the school is, or should be, affected by the principal, either directly or indirectly. It is essential to provide these leaders with the knowledge and skills they need to handle their day-to-day activities as well as the crises.

However, training for many school leaders has been inadequate or ends abruptly after certification. Many university administrator preparation programs are not closely aligned with the instructional and real-world demands placed on principals, and the use of postcertification development programs is the exception rather than the rule. According to *Recognizing and Encouraging Exemplary Leadership in America's Schools*, written by David Mandel (2000) and commissioned by the National Policy Board for Educational Administration (NPBEA), the difference between leadership recruitment in education and leadership recruitment in other organizations is like night and day. "Unlike the common practice of the corporate world and the military, where there are systematic and continuous initiatives to grow and develop a management cadre that can take on greater and greater responsibilities and succeed at each step along the way, education makes no such careful investment of resources in its future leaders. Rather it sends a signal to its freshly minted novice managers that once they have been assigned their first administrative position, serious attention to their professional development has concluded" (p. 4).

An analogous situation in the business world would occur if we sent people to get an M.B.A. and told them upon receipt of their diploma, "OK, you can now become a CEO." The M.B.A. is about the acquisition of knowledge. *Real skills come from applying that knowledge in real business situations, often aided by mentoring and coaching.* This is not to say that the M.B.A. recipient may not be outstanding in his or her field but rather that it is highly unlikely that this person is prepared to step immediately into a CEO position. And once the grad becomes a CEO, it is highly unlikely that he or she will forgo opportunities for additional learning and development.

Much is at stake in a corporation—millions of dollars, the livelihood of the personnel, and the investments of shareholders.

And what's at stake in schools? Significant budgets are commonplace, but it is the hopes and dreams of kids that are really at stake, as well as the future contributions they will make to our nation's culture, economy, and competitiveness as productive citizens.

Snapshot of Principal Statistics

To paint a complete picture of the importance of school leadership, one should have a clear understanding of the large number of schools dependent on principals and the makeup of the profession itself. In *Secondary Schools in a New Millennium: Demographic Certainties, Social Realities*, Harold Hodgkinson (2000) reviews some demographics about school principals and the schools they serve. Of the nation's 79,618 principals:

- 19,027 serve in center-city schools, 21,700 in suburbia, and 38,891 in rural areas or small towns
- 53,684 are in elementary schools and 18,263 in secondary schools
- 60 percent are male; the 40 percent who are female are mostly in elementary schools
- 14 percent are ethnic minorities
- The average principal is 47.5 years old
- 60 percent have master's degrees
- 30 percent have more than a master's degree
- The typical principal taught for eleven years before becoming a principal

With an average of six hundred students per school, the reach of school leadership and its potential impact are unquestionable. Equally unquestionable, if not alarming, is the proposition that if one principal is not properly trained and up to the task of leadership, it will have a damaging effect on six hundred students — a statistic that should be sobering to everyone. Multiply those six hundred students several hundreds or thousands of times, and one can readily see the grave problem society would soon face if a shortage of qualified school leaders were ever to occur.

Shortage of School Leaders?

A 1998 survey by the Educational Research Service (ERS), titled *Is There a Shortage of Qualified Candidates for Openings in the Principalship?* and commissioned by the National Association of Elementary School Principals (NAESP) and the National Association of Secondary School Principals (NASSP), reports that we may in fact be facing a shortage of qualified school leaders. According to the report:

- About half of the surveyed districts reported a shortage of qualified candidates for the principal positions they had attempted to fill. This shortage occurred among all types of schools (rural, urban, suburban) and at all levels of vacancies (elementary, junior high or middle school, high school). However, the interviewees did not indicate that they were dissatisfied with the people they hired.
- In the opinions of the administrators responsible for hiring principals, many factors discouraged potential principal applicants. The most frequently mentioned barrier was salary: compared to the job responsibilities, compensation for the principal position was not sufficient to encourage applications. The stress of the job and the time demands that come with a principalship were additional discouraging factors.
- Increasing the number of women in management positions has not been a focus or a problem in most districts. This finding held for all types of schools. Increasing the number of minorities in management positions has been a larger issue. This is especially true among urban districts. Also, districts were more likely to report qualified female than qualified minority applicants.
- Few districts have an aspiring-principals program, but most do have a formal training program for new principals. It was more likely that an urban district would have an aspiring-principals program than a rural or suburban district.

The ERS report also points to the National Center for Education Statistics' "1993–94 Schools and Staffing Survey" (1997), which found that "new principals were more likely to have participated in a local aspiring-principals program than more experienced principals" (p. 4), suggesting a new emphasis on such programs in the career development ladder. According to the ERS report, however, only one-fourth of the districts reported the existence of an aspiring-principals program to recruit and prepare candidates. Just under half of the districts have a formal induction or mentoring program for new principals.

Why is there such a shortage of qualified school leaders? The NASBE report provides some insights (National Association of State Boards of Education, 1999):

- The job of the principal has changed to become more complex and demanding.
- Good principals are scarce — growing student populations, retirements, and decreasing numbers of applicants are creating significant shortages in some districts and regions.
- Principal training, support, and professional development are largely inadequate and not up to the task of producing the good principals we need.
- States have lacked a coherent vision and system for developing and retaining high-quality principals.

The 1998 ERS study reinforced and added to these perceptions and findings when it asked those responsible for hiring what prevented applicants from applying for these positions. Here is what the study found:

- The job is generally too stressful.
- Social problems (poverty, lack of family support, and so on) make it difficult for students to focus on instruction.
- Too much time is required.
- Testing and accountability pressures are too great.

- It is difficult to satisfy demands of parents or the community (or both).
- The nature of the job is viewed as less satisfying than previously.
- Funding for schools is inadequate.
- Compensation is not sufficient compared to responsibilities.
- Fewer experienced teachers are interested in becoming assistant principals or principals.
- Continuing bad press or public relations problems for the district place additional pressure on principals.
- No tenure is associated with the position, and teachers lose tenure if they move to a principal or assistant principal position.
- The state retirement system permits experienced teachers to retire at a fairly young age.
- Openings are not well publicized.

"Perhaps the most interesting, and certainly the most significant, finding from this section of the survey," the ERS report notes, "was the high level of consistency of responses from school administrators across community type and grade level subgroups" (p. 11). The top-ranked barrier among all groups was "compensation not sufficient compared to responsibilities," followed in either second or third place by "too much time required" and "job too stressful."

Are we in the midst of a crisis? Consider these statistics from the ERS report (Educational Research Service, 1998, p. 2):

- The number of assistant principals is expected to grow between now and 2005 as districts hire additional assistant principals rather than open new schools to cope with an increasing workload and expanding student enrollment.
- Most principal and assistant principal job openings between now and 2005 are likely to result from the need to replace administra-

tors who retire. The average age of principals rose slightly from 46.8 in 1987–88 to 47.7 in 1994–95, with over 37.0 percent of principals over age 50.

While these statistics are unnerving, there are also positive signs, including this statistic from the ERS report (p. 7):

- Superintendents are satisfied with the educational preparation of the candidates that they do get. Nearly all reported that recent candidates for principal positions had at least adequate educational preparation, with one-third characterizing the preparation as excellent.

One-third of candidates having excellent preparation is not close to an acceptable level. But perhaps some progress is being made in university programs revisiting a legacy that many have recently questioned. Muse and Thomas (1991) argue that administration preparation programs do not adequately address the needs of the principalship and that to ensure a selection of qualified candidates for principal positions, such preparation programs must be reorganized.

School leadership organizations can be an excellent resource for universities as they focus on this reorganization. Representing tens of thousands of professionals who are uniquely qualified to judge what it takes to be a principal or other administrator, school leadership associations must play an increasingly active role in helping to restructure administrator preparation programs.

While significant challenges reside in administration preparation programs, increasing the number of highly qualified candidates will require work at many levels of the school leadership education continuum. School leadership associations offer a vision that includes "raising the bar" of what is expected of school leaders. As described in greater detail later in this chapter, their vision includes the launch of the American Board for Leadership in Education (ABLE) to oversee advanced professional certification for exemplary practitioners, the formulation of advanced standards, and recognition of excellence in education leadership.

The member associations of NPBEA envision ABLE as an opportunity to make significant progress in cultivating an elite cadre of exemplary school leaders to lead the charge for higher standards throughout the profession. Building on the historical, current, and proposed initiatives of school leadership associations, as well as on delivery opportunities offered by technology, the members of the NPBEA predict that the coming year will usher in the *foundation* for substantial leadership reform.

Historical Involvement of Associations in Preparation and Training

Associations have had extensive involvement in promoting assessment and development in administration. *Educational Administration: A Decade of Reform* (Murphy and Forsyth, 1999) details the history of some of that involvement. For example, it notes that the American Association of School Administrators (AASA) has been actively involved in proposing the study and increased professionalization of administration preparation programs since the end of World War II. Along with higher education organizations, AASA's early involvement and advocacy for improved training, especially for superintendents, set the stage for many structures that have evolved since. Unfortunately, this early emphasis on professionalism ran into many hurdles. However, as noted previously, a critical mass seems to be building to finally make a difference in the preparation of principals.

Other milestones in assessment and development include NASSP's launch of its Assessment Centers in 1975 and the launch of NAESP's Professional Development Inventory (the earliest version was developed in the mid-1980s). One of the most important collective initiatives of several school leadership associations was the creation of NPBEA, nicely detailed by Scott Thomson (1999) in *Educational Administration: A Decade of Reform*. As Thomson notes, formation of NPBEA was a key recommendation of *Leaders for America's Schools* (Griffiths, Stout, and Forsyth, 1988), a report by the National Commission on Excellence in Educational Administration (NCEEA). NCEEA was composed of prominent educators and laypeople, and was sponsored by the University Council for Educational Administration (UCEA).

According to Thomson, AASA, NAESP, NASSP, the National School Boards Association (NSBA), and UCEA, with support from the Danforth Foundation and the University of Virginia, seized on this recommendation and formed a planning board to bring it to fruition. These organizations endorsed founding NPBEA on July 14, 1987. Soon thereafter, several other associations joined NPBEA: the American Association of Colleges for Teacher Education (AACTE), the Association for Supervision and Curriculum Development (ASCD), the Council of Chief State School Officers (CCSSO), the National Council of Professors of Educational Administration (NCPEA), and the Association of School Business Officials (ASBO). (ASBO resigned from NPBEA in 1995.)

The total of ten national associations thus included three from higher education, six from elementary and secondary education, and one governance body. NASSP's executive director at the time, Scott Thomson, was elected chair of the NPBEA board of directors for 1988. The Danforth Foundation, in addition to providing a representative to serve as an ad hoc member of the board, funded NPBEA with a three-year grant. This support was in addition to member organization dues and support from the University of Virginia.

According to Thomson (1999, p. 95):

NPBEA's [initial] core purposes were to:

- Develop, disseminate, and implement professional models for the preparation and inservice training of educational leaders;
- Increase the recruitment and placement of women and minorities in positions of educational leadership
- Establish a national certifying board for educational administrators.

In addition, three program areas were agreed upon for the executive staff to address:

- Improving the preparation of school leaders;
- Redefining roles for school leaders; and
- Raising certification and accreditation standards for school leaders.

As Thomson also notes, the NPBEA's report *Improving the Preparation of School Administration: An Agenda for Reform* (1989) outlined several initiatives designed to improve educational leadership at the state and local levels:

- Launch vigorous recruitment strategies to attract bright and capable candidates
- Raise entrance standards for administrator preparation programs
- Improve the quality of faculty and maintain a minimum of five full-time faculty in university departments
- Make an Ed.D. the only path to certification and licensure in educational leadership, declaring a master's degree insufficient and abolishing six-year programs
- Require one year of full-time academic residency and one year of full-time field residency in precertification programs
- Revise the common core of knowledge of skills to ground them in practice and to focus on school improvement, the teaching and learning process, organizational studies, management processes, inquiry, the ethical and moral dimensions of schooling, and cultural factors
- Organize permanent cooperative relationships between universities and school districts
- Establish a national professional standards board to manage a program of advanced professional standing
- Withhold national accreditation for programs failing to meet the standards outlined

As seen here and echoed by Thomson (1999, pp. 98–102), associations have been among the leading advocates for professional certification at "the entry and advanced levels of practice, including the formation of an independent certification body to determine professional standards." NPBEA's recommendations also included calls for a connection between "the knowledge base and professional skills necessary for success," especially in the areas of communication, interpersonal relations, and decision-making procedures. It is also noteworthy that NPBEA attempted, without success, to secure funding for a proposal "to establish a national certification board with the instruments and processes for voluntary professional certification." In addition, "two national test development firms indicated separately a strong interest in forming a partnership with NPBEA to develop assessments for national certification. The [NPBEA] board of directors voted to pursue this possibility should funding be found to establish a national certification board."

NPBEA was also active in proposing guidelines for "states considering nontraditional routes to the principalship or superintendency." In 1990, NPBEA published a policy document, *Alternative Certification for School Leaders*. "The publication argues, in sum," notes Thomson (1999, p. 99), "that although alternative routes to certification are acceptable for exceptional candidates, this alternative route must meet the same criteria for demonstrated professional knowledge and skills as does the regular route."

NPBEA went on to use work done by the National Commission for the Principalship, which was organized in 1988 by NAESP and NASSP. NPBEA used the commission's report, *Principals for Our Changing Schools: Preparation and Certification* (1990), "as the framework for developing a description of the core knowledge and skills, and the performance standards, to certify principals" (Thomson, 1999, p. 99). The National Commission for the Principalship addressed the question, "What must principals know and be able to do for successful school leadership today?" The commission identified twenty-one domains or areas of knowledge and skill considered essential to the principalship. The twenty-one domains, organized in four broad fields, blended the traditional, content-driven curriculum with leadership and process skills to create a new architecture for preparing principals. This framework recognized the leadership skills and interpersonal competencies required of principals to succeed in today's school environment as well as the central responsibility of principals for the instructional program.

NPBEA went a step further by describing performance standards for each of the domains and identified the specific knowledge areas and skills central to these domains in its *Principals for Our Changing Schools: The Knowledge and Skill Base* (Thomson, 1993).

Licensure

Thomson (1999) notes that NPBEA organizations also agreed to work with NCATE to cooperate on a single set of NCATE curriculum guidelines for programs in educational leadership. Involved in this working group were AASA, ASCD, NAESP, NASSP, and the following higher education groups: AACTE, NCPEA, and UCEA. The working group looked at a matrix that took into account the work done by several associations and organizations:

NPBEA's *Principals for Our Changing Schools* (1993)

NAESP's *Proficiencies for Principals* (1991) and *Administrator Diagnostics Inventory* (1994)

AASA's *Professional Standards for the Superintendency* (1993)

ASCD's *Proposed NCATE Curriculum Guidelines for the Specialty Area of Educational Leadership* (1993)

Northeast States/Region I DOE document *Framework for the Continual Professional Development of Administrators* (1993)

NASSP's Principals' Assessment Centers (1975)

The curriculum guidelines were adopted by NCATE for 1996 and are administered by the Educational Leadership Constituent Council, which is composed of four national associations that hold membership in the NCATE—AASA, ASCD, NAESP, and NASSP.

The new guidelines encompass eleven knowledge and skill domains in four broad areas and one process domain (internship). The four broad areas are strategic leadership, instructional leadership, organizational leadership, and political and community leadership.

According to Thomson (1999), only two-thirds of all preparation programs for educational leaders currently meet NCATE standards.

This brief history provides perspective on the considerable involvement of school leadership associations in training and preparation and lays a foundation for current efforts. Unfortunately, some of the current trends sacrifice thorough assessment and development for cheaper and faster "paper-and-pencil technology" forms of assessment and training. Significant advances have been made in assessment and development, yet until all superintendents can boast a full complement of highly qualified principals, there is more work to be done. We maintain that the work must not sacrifice quality for expediency. There is no silver bullet. Just as the talents of each child must be cultivated, so too *individual* attention is required to raise the knowledge and skill level of school leaders.

Standards

No discussion of school leader preparation and training would be complete without focusing on the current state of standards, which is visible in an acronym: ISLLC. The Interstate School Leaders Licensure Consortium was an outgrowth of years of work by many different organizations.

In 1993, according to Thomson (1999), NPBEA member organizations "decided to convene all states interested in discussing the question of common standards as a basis for licensing school leaders" (p. 106). The meeting was held in January 1994 and attended by representatives from thirty-seven states and ten national associations. Participants agreed that common standards would be of benefit and voted to develop and implement them.

Also in that month, according to Thomson (1999), the Council of Chief State School Officers (CCSSO) board of directors voted "to establish an Interstate Principals Licensure Consortium as a parallel to their national program to develop common standards for entry-level teachers. . . . After discussion of several issues and the CCSSO plans, the NPBEA Board of Directors agreed that competing initiatives would be counterproductive to achieving the professional goal of common and higher licensing standards for school leaders" (p. 106). Consequently, NPBEA decided to become a "working partner with CCSSO" to develop the standards.

The ISLLC standards (Council of Chief State School Officers, 1996) were the result of this effort. "The standards were drafted by representatives of 24 state education agencies and several professional associations, which had extensive experience in assessment and development issues for school leaders" (Thompson, 1999, p. 107). Currently, thirty states use the following ISLLC standards in some way:

Standard 1: A school administrator is an educational leader who promotes the success of all students by *facilitating the development, articulation, implementation, and stewardship of a vision of learning that is shared and supported by the school community.*

Standard 2: A school administrator is an educational leader who promotes the success of all students by *advocating, nurturing, and sustaining a school culture and instructional program conducive to student learning and staff professional growth.*

Standard 3: A school administrator is an educational leader who promotes the success of all students by *ensuring management of the organization, operations, and resources for a safe, efficient, and effective learning environment.*

Standard 4: A school administrator is an educational leader who promotes the success of all students *by collaborating with families and community members, responding to diverse community interests and needs, and mobilizing community resources.*

Standard 5: A school administrator is an educational leader who promotes the success of all students *by acting with integrity, fairness, and in an ethical manner.*

Standard 6: A school administrator is an educational leader who promotes the success of all students *by understanding, responding to, and influencing the larger political, social, economic, legal, and cultural context.*

Each of the standards is supported by characteristics that emphasize situational learning. Several programs that encapsulate the ISLLC standards are offered by school leadership organizations and others. The details of these programs will be covered shortly.

Testing: A Silver Bullet?

One additional outgrowth of the ISLLC standards is the School Leaders Licensure Assessment, offered by the Educational Testing Service (ETS). This $400 paper-and-pencil test is used by several states as part of their licensure process for principals. Each state may set its own pass rate. According to ETS (http://www.ets.org), the test "is based on both a national job analysis study and a set of standards for school leaders identified by ISLLC."

The test "consists of 25 constructed-response questions, ranging from short vignettes requiring a brief response to much longer case study exercises," according to ETS. There are three modules within the test: "Evaluation of Actions," "Synthesis of Information and Problem Solving," and "Analysis of Information and Decision-making."

The "Evaluation of Actions" module has two sections. The first "includes vignettes that deal with situations drawn from and distributed among such content areas as due process and other legal issues, exceptional-needs students, safety, facilities, budget, discipline, technology, and scheduling." The test-taker must develop a response describing the way that he or she would handle the situation.

The second section presents dilemmas "based on learning and teaching issues. . . . The response requires the test-taker to balance competing claims for resources, prioritize actions, articulate the instructional issues raised by the situation, explain instructional and curricular strategies appropriate in responding to the situation, and discuss the situation's instructional implications."

The "Synthesis of Information and Problem Solving" module focuses on a case analysis that includes several documents and a short scenario describing a school and its community. Test-takers are asked to address different problems under relevant information provided in the documents.

The "Analysis of Information and Decisionmaking" module requires the test-taker to respond to questions on several documents. Informational materials offered by ETS indicate that the documents "may include: assessment data, portions of school improvement plans, budget information, schedules, resource allocation documents, staff evaluations, or curriculum information."

According to ETS, the exercises "are scored by school leaders who have been carefully trained in the *ISLLC Standards* and the content specifications for the assessment."

While the test is intended to measure knowledge and the minimum proficiencies a school leader would need to undertake the job effectively—in essence to ensure that a candidate "does no harm" to the profession—the fear is that states may see it as an easy way to assess principals. In reality, true assessment requires a more rigorous approach that includes not only knowledge of the necessary skill sets *but also an ability to implement those skills in real life or simulations.* Unfortunately, a paper-and-pencil test cannot assess skill in collaboration, interpersonal relations, and communication, nor does it predict the way a person will act in a given situation.

Although no assessment can perfectly determine the quality of a principal, the paper-and-pencil method can be viewed as a first step among many. If viewed as the minimum needed to be considered for future leadership, it sets the bar at a certain level. Other programs must step in to raise the bar to new heights. As advocates for professionalism, school leadership organizations cannot allow the bar to remain at the level set by the ETS test alone.

An additional fear is that the test may allow states to say they support the ISLLC standards while they ignore the long-term assessment and development needs of school leaders, which the test is not designed to address. *Recognizing and Encouraging Exemplary Leadership in America's Schools* (Mandel, 2000) warns about the dangers of stopping at any first step:

> This is all well and good, but once in possession of a license, administrators typically find themselves at the end of any organized effort to build their capacity to serve as an education leader. . . . Yes, state licensing requirements encourage them to take an occasional graduate course or to accumulate some fixed number of continuing education units, but the notion that there are higher standards to which they might aspire, that there are greater levels of competence and professionalism that they might work toward, or that they are just at the beginning, not the end, of their development as leaders are concepts foreign to school administration [p. 4].

School leadership organizations have been active in encouraging participation in ongoing development, yet efforts have been stymied by a lack of funding at the district and school levels, as well as by an inability to reach effectively those responsible for deciding on and funding the development needs of principals. With the proposed advanced standards, improved preparation programs, and ever-increasing access to technology, associations are actively pursuing remedies to these hurdles and are confident that the audience for these programs will be receptive. Current programs are detailed in the next section. Other programs are on the drawing board and will be detailed in subsequent sections.

Association Assessment and Development Models

School leadership organizations have an extensive complement of programs intended to support assessment and development for principals. The following are examples. Many of these programs incorporate, conform to, or reflect the ISLLC standards. In addition, several offer continuing education units as an added benefit.

NASSP

The National Association of Secondary School Principals works closely with its state affiliates in the area of assessment and development to offer a variety of publications, programs, and services. NASSP has been working with school districts, state departments of education, universities, and others for more than two decades to develop and refine programs for selection and development of school leaders. Through the generosity of the Danforth, Kellogg, W. Alton Jones, and Spencer Foundations, high-quality programs have been developed that focus on the skills that school administrators need to be effective and successful.

Assessment. NASSP's Assessment Center project began in 1975 with technical assistance from a special committee of industrial psychologists and the American Psychological Association. The committee formulated a plan to assist school districts in identifying and developing highly skilled school leaders at the elementary and secondary levels. Currently, comprehensive assessment centers are functioning in twenty-five states, Canada, England, and Bermuda to help identify school district personnel with the requisite skills to succeed as assistant principals and principals. To date, more than ten thousand assessors have been trained and twenty thousand practitioners (half from the elementary level) have been evaluated with the original Assessment Center model, including at various times all candidates in Kentucky, Maryland, Missouri, New Jersey, and South Carolina.

The Assessment Center was originally designed to improve the selection processes for entry-level elementary, middle-level, and high school building administrators. In addition to objectively assessing specific skills, the process offers opportunities for meaningful staff development. As the project matured, a long-term comprehensive professional development link was added.

An Assessment Center offers a psychometric procedure emphasizing multiple activities, including individual and group exercises used to develop behavior profiles of candidates seeking employment as assistant principals or principals. Candidates for administrative selection, promotion, or development participate in an assessment process involving a daylong series of simulations. These provide opportunities for collecting data on actual behavior in the typical administrative and instructional situations that principals encounter on a daily basis. Analysis also reveals skills in key dimensional areas. Assessment Center methodology is based on the identification of generic skills that can be observed during performance of certain job-related activities. A combination of exercises is typical: simulations, paper-and-pencil "in-baskets," personal interviews, and fact-finding exercises. Often simulations include leaderless group discussions and case studies involving school problems in scheduling, grading, curriculum modifications, staff meetings, negotiations, enrollment reduction, and finances.

Each Assessment Center is headed by a director approved and trained by the national staff. Directors are responsible for maintaining quality control for efficient and effective center operation as well as recruiting candidates for assessor training. The makeup of the assessor team varies but typically includes former principals, practitioners, university professors, superintendents, or state department of education personnel.

There are two Assessment Center models. One assesses twelve participants with a ratio of participants to assessors of 2:1. This was the original NASSP model, but in an effort to reduce assessor workloads and time commitments, a six-participant model with a ratio of 1:1 was adopted. This new ratio of participants to assessors is rigorously maintained throughout all the projects.

Assessors are assigned to observe, record, and report on participants' behaviors during the exercises. Participants are observed by a different assessor during each exercise. Written reports covering behavior in all exercises are required for each participant. These reports contain observations relating to each skill dimension and result in a diagnostic tool on behavior dimensions for use by each participant. The written reports serve as the basis for a discussion among the assessors about each participant's performance. The assessors, working as a team, produce a final report that identifies strengths, improvement needs, and suggestions for each participant's development. The final report is the product of a consensus discussion among the assessors about each participant's performance on all the behavior dimensions.

Skills assessed with the original model were problem analysis, judgment, organizational ability, decisiveness, leadership, sensitivity, stress tolerance, oral communication, written communication, range of interest, personal motivation, and educational values.

As the concept of school leadership has evolved from a more managerial setting to one of instructional leadership, these areas of assessment have also evolved. NASSP assessment and development programs now use NASSP's Skills for Principals, delineated as follows:

Educational Leadership

- *Setting Instructional Direction:* Implementing strategies for improving teaching and learning, including putting programs and improvement efforts into action; developing a vision and establishing clear goals; providing direction in achieving stated goals; encouraging others to contribute to goal achievement; and securing commitment to a course of action from individuals and groups.

- *Teamwork:* Seeking and encouraging involvement of team members; modeling and encouraging the behaviors that move the group to task completion; and supporting group accomplishment.

- *Sensitivity:* Perceiving the needs and concerns of others; dealing tactfully with others in emotionally stressful situations or in conflict; knowing what information to communicate and to whom; and relating to people of varying ethnic, cultural, and religious backgrounds.

Resolving Complex Problems

- *Judgment:* Reaching logical conclusions and making high-quality decisions based on available information; giving priority and caution to significant issues; seeking out relevant data, facts, and impressions; and analyzing and interpreting complex information.
- *Results Orientation:* Assuming responsibility; recognizing when a decision is required; taking prompt action as issues emerge; and resolving short-term issues while balancing them against long-term objectives.
- *Organizational Ability:* Planning and scheduling one's own and the work of others so that resources are used appropriately; scheduling the flow of activities; establishing procedures to monitor projects; practicing time and task management; and knowing what to delegate and to whom.

Communication

- *Oral Communication:* Clearly communicating and making oral presentations that are clear and easy to understand.
- *Written Communication:* Expressing ideas clearly in writing; demonstrating technical language proficiency; and writing appropriately for different audiences.

Developing Self and Others

- *Development of Others:* Teaching, coaching, and helping others; and providing specific feedback based on observations and data.

- *Understanding Own Strengths and Weaknesses:* Understanding personal strengths and weaknesses; taking responsibility by actively pursuing developmental activities; and striving for continuous learning.

Although the original Assessment Center is still used in a few locations, the program has evolved two new assessment models, the Developmental Assessment Center (DAC) and Selecting and Developing the 21st Century Principal.

NASSP assessment and development programs are delivered in the following ways:

- Through a network of Assessment and Development Centers
- As single offerings by NASSP trainers
- Through an agreement in which NASSP trains local facilitators to deliver NASSP programs according to local needs

Other NASSP Assessment programs include the following:

- *Selecting and Developing the 21st Century Principal* is a contemporary assessment tool that can help identify and develop effective school leaders. It is designed to measure leadership potential by diagnosing behavioral strengths and development needs of prospective principals. It is a simulation-based one-day assessment center that is an outgrowth of the original Assessment Center. Participants receive a detailed report on their strengths and improvement needs.
- *Developmental Assessment Center* (DAC) is an assessment program designed specifically for development, with an emphasis on establishing (or revising) a personal plan for career advancement. DAC provides potential leaders and current administrators with specific information about their strengths, potential derailers, and development possibilities they can use to build the skills they need to be effective school leaders. Activities simulate administrative situations, and both assessors and participants engage in a reflection session following each activity. This one-day process provides ver-

bal and written feedback to each participant, including developmental suggestions tailored to individual needs. Assessors spend one day observing activities and one day producing final reports for participants.

- *Superintendent Leadership Development Program* (SLDP) is a partnership between NASSP and AASA that gives current and future school superintendents the information they need to construct a development plan. SLDP does *not* provide information for candidate selection; rather, it provides participants with information for career development planning. The program was initiated in 1991 by NASSP in partnership with the Kentucky State Department of Education, Applied Research Corporation, and AASA to develop a process to assist current and prospective superintendents with in-depth career planning and development. Working with a technical advisory task force of nationally recognized superintendents and educational leaders, NASSP and AASA identified the key skills, knowledge, and abilities of successful contemporary superintendents. SLDP is a day-and-a-half experience for participants and an additional day-and-a-half for assessors. Originally developed for Kentucky, this assessment program is now being used in several other states.

Development Programs. NASSP offers a variety of development programs that address the specific skills administrators need to be successful. All are based on the applied learning model and incorporate adult learning principles. Each program focuses on skills built on a foundation of key behaviors. Focused simulations, integral to these programs, provide participants with a safe environment in which to practice and receive feedback about key behaviors. All programs conclude with a tie back to the school that includes planning for further skill development at the work site.

- *The 21st Century School Administrator Skills (SAS) Program* is designed to provide an opportunity to develop the skills assessed in *Selecting and Developing the 21st Century Principal* and the standards endorsed by the ISLLC. This three-day program provides a safe environment for new and potential school administrators to practice skills and receive feedback.

• *Breaking Ranks Leadership* is designed to develop and enhance the knowledge and skills of high school leadership teams as they seek to create whole-school change using the recommendations cited in *Breaking Ranks: Changing an American Institution*, a report from NASSP and the Carnegie Corporation (National Association of Secondary School Principals, 1996).

• *From the Desk of . . .* is designed to develop and refine the written communication skills of the site administrator. The three- to five-day seminar is based on the unique communication needs of school principals. Activities include more than thirty simulations and role-plays.

• *LEADER 123* is a three-day program designed to help principals build instructional leadership skills. This unique experience focuses on planning, developing, implementing, and measuring skills required to support quality learning in the school and includes practice in team leadership and shared decision making. It is designed for principals, assistant principals, potential school administrators, and college personnel who are counseling and teaching principals and assistant principals.

• *Leading from the Middle* is designed specifically for aspiring and practicing middle school administrators; it combines the research on effective practices with the instructional leadership skills needed to make middle-level schools more effective. This three-day training includes simulations, feedback, and the planning of an instructional project to improve the school.

• *Let's Talk* helps administrators use oral communication skills. The content involves conversation, dialogue, and presentation of information. This three-day program gives school leaders the opportunity to integrate communication theory with effective on-the-job behavior and develop the ability to make a clear and effective presentation of facts or ideas; communicate with various audiences; be a receptive listener and observer; and use voice effectively.

- *Mentoring and Coaching* assists school districts, educational service units, state departments of education, and universities in preparing experienced school leaders to serve as mentors to prospective and new school leaders. *Mentoring and Coaching* is a two-day seminar designed to help experienced school leaders reflect on their own leadership skills and learn how to share their expertise effectively with less experienced educators.

- *Succession Planning for School Leaders* is a customized program for school districts or other agencies that allows them to choose from NASSP's assessment and development programs for a locally designed program to build a cadre of leaders.

NAESP

In addition to development opportunities offered through its various workshops and publications, the National Association of Elementary School Principals offers an assessment tool for school leaders. NAESP's assessment program was developed in the mid-1980s by Washington State principals and faculty at the University of Washington (it was then called the Center for Assessment of Administrative Performance, or CAAP). NAESP purchased the program in 1991 and renamed it the Administrator Diagnostic Inventory (ADI) to emphasize NAESP's intention that it be used solely for professional development planning.

In 1995, NAESP received funding from the Mott Foundation for a two-year project to revise the process and develop a computerized reporting capability. The project was able to reduce the simulation from two days to one day and reduce scoring time from several days to one day (for a maximum of twelve participants). The name was changed once again, to the Professional Development Inventory (PDI). Approximately four hundred K–12 practicing and aspiring principals, mostly those entering graduate programs at universities, have participated in the program since it was re-named PDI.

NAESP relies primarily on licensed assessment centers to administer the program. The centers are typically state affiliate associations, universities, a partnership of the two, or (in Texas) regional education service centers. NAESP also has the ability to conduct PDI sessions for districts or other groups not located in states with a licensed center. In these instances, the simulation is conducted and scored by NAESP's PDI consultants.

Licensed centers have their own teams of assessors, and NAESP has a group of assessors to accommodate centers that prefer not to score locally. The numbers vary; however, fourteen assessors are recommended to complete scoring for twelve participants in one day. The assessors are not present when the participants go through the simulation. All responses are either written or videotaped and are then read or viewed by assessors at a later date.

NAESP's PDI construct and validity research is conducted by Dr. Donald Coleman of the University of California-Fresno. Coleman recently presented two papers at the AASA conference in San Francisco, one on validity studies he did on the ISLLC standards and one on studies he did comparing PDI dimensions to the ISLLC standards. His study indicated a high degree of correlation between PDI and ISLLC. (In the second comparison, he points out that the ISLLC standards reflect performance outcomes, while the PDI dimensions reflect administrative application of management and leadership procedural skills used to produce those outcomes.)

NAESP also offers a Certificate of Advanced Proficiency series. This series of five three-day workshops was designed to provide development in the leadership and management proficiencies (or standards) identified in this section. During the course of each workshop, participants are asked to plan related improvement projects they will complete back at their schools. Follow-up reports on projects are required for program completion.

NAESP has devised *Proficiencies for Principals* that provide guidance and direction for the preparation and professional development of K–8 school principals. The *Proficiencies* are based on both research concerning effective principals and the experience of practicing administrators. What results is a set of proficiencies that describe leadership and management skills and behaviors that effective principals need.

Leadership Proficiencies

Effective principals are leaders of leaders who place as their highest priority the teaching and learning of students. They sustain a quality environment and act morally and ethically at every turn.

Leadership Behavior: Proficient principals possess values, beliefs, and personal attributes that inspire others to achieve school goals, build a school environment marked by collegiality and common purpose, work collaboratively and innovatively, encourage shared decision making, and recognize achievement among students and staff.

Communication Skills: Proficient principals know how to project ideas and images—verbally, nonverbally, through technology, and in written communication. They also keep the school community informed about the school and interact with diverse groups of people with sensitivity and understanding.

Group Processes: Proficient principals mobilize others to collaborate in solving problems and accomplishing school goals and capitalize on the talents and expertise of others. They also understand the dynamics of change and effectively apply group process skills.

Curriculum and Instruction: Proficient principals ensure that their school's curriculum is aligned with school goals, that it has been developed cooperatively, and that it is appropriately specific about knowledge, skills, values, habits, and attitudes that students should develop. They also seek support for the instructional program, ensure that instruction is appropriate and purposeful, and use staff expertise to promote a common core of learning.

Assessment: Proficient principals monitor the school daily to ensure that program and service goals are being met. They also know the importance of evaluating student and staff performance, reinforce success and remedy failure, understand the sensitive nature of evaluation, and seek evaluation of their own performance.

Administrative and Management Proficiencies

Effective principals possess strong organizational skills, manage fiscal resources well, and are effective at dealing with political pressures.

Organizational Management: Proficient principals work with members of the school community to set the school's organizational goals and priorities, manage a wide variety of tasks and responsibilities, participate in professional development and in reflective thinking, and are open to change.

Fiscal Management: Proficient principals understand the relationship between school goals and the budgeting process, creatively find resources to support school programs, and project future needs.

Political Management: Proficient principals deal effectively with forces outside of school, generate public support for the school, are involved in a variety of civic activities, and have a practical knowledge of local, state, and national political processes and their impact on the school.

NAESP is also in the process of developing six two-and-one-half-day workshops addressing each of the six ISLLC standards. Two have been completed so far:

Changing Systems, Changing Schools features the key concepts of systems thinking, personal mastery and models, shared visioning, and team learning. This interactive workshop will support participants as they complete the ISLLC Standard 1 self-assessment, learn storyboarding as a strategy to help the school community revision itself in the twenty-first century, and conduct an internal audit of the school's learning community. Participants will learn how to build their own professional development portfolio.

Reflective Practice in Teaching and Learning features the key concepts of focusing the school's vision in the day-to-day practices of teaching and learning, continuous improvement of all school personnel, and portfolio-based assessment for teachers and administrators. The workshop will support participants as they complete the ISLLC Standard 2 self-assessment, learn the roles of school administrators supporting positive school climate centered in teaching and learning, and develop a learning-organization culture that is enhanced by changing curriculum conversations, curriculum on the wall, and reflective journaling.

The consultant primarily responsible for developing the workshops is one of six principals who serves on ISLLC and conducted one of their pilot portfolio projects at Illinois State University. The workshops will provide research-based theory and best-practice applications and will focus on principal professional development as well as school improvement. At the conclusion of each workshop, participants will have completed their own portfolio and reflections for the particular ISLLC standard addressed in that workshop.

NAESP also offers a wide complement of workshops at its convention and throughout the year. It works closely with state affiliates to offer programs of relevance to the development needs of its membership.

ASCD

The Association for Supervision and Curriculum Development has launched aggressive new efforts to promote the professional nature of school leadership. These include publications as well as institutes (meetings of one, two, or three days), academies, and workshops. Several of the programs have the added benefit of qualifying for graduate credit. Rather than assessment, many of the programs involve professional development and raising the level of understanding or experience on a given issue. Recent examples, as described in ASCD's marketing materials, include these:

- *The Leadership Academy*, designed to allow school teams to align the vision, values, and purpose of the school; manage change and maximize the return on scarce resources; use technology to leverage educational outcomes; measure organizational performance; and link strategic goals to classroom performance. Participants are able to continue the work of the academy for sixty days through ASCD's Web-based virtual learning community.
- *Supporting Teachers of Diverse Learners*, a review of various instructional strategies that enhance student learning, including differentiated instruction, brain-compatible strategies, and performance assessment; and an opportunity to gain a greater understanding of how the many ways honoring, celebrating, and incorporating diversity can enhance achievement.
- *The Principal as Staff Developer*, focusing on providing more support to the teaching staff, how to be a better facilitator of staff development, characteristics of a school culture conducive to learning and achievement, and ways to transform faculty meetings into invitations to learn.
- *Site-Based Decisionmaking* introduces school leaders to the skills, tools, and ideas needed to align education with economic interests of business, political interests of constituents, social interests of parents, and the instructional needs of students; the dimensions of effective stewardship; and ways to enhance results, relationships, and risk taking.
- *Using Brain Research in Working with Adults*, designed to enable participants to be more successful when working with school councils, curriculum committees, and parent groups, by applying new scientific discoveries on how people think and learn. This institute investigates ways to think more creatively and motivate colleagues and parents to stretch their imaginations.

Block scheduling institutes are offered for different levels of elementary and secondary schools:

- *Curriculum Mapping* discusses tools for schoolwide and districtwide curriculum development and how mapping helps align, improve, and integrate curriculum and assessment.
- *Designing Standards-Based Schools, Districts, and Classrooms* guides participants through the process of designing a standards-based system for the participant's situation. Included is advice for dealing with the most important issues of standards-based education, such as the relationship between content standards and performance standards; using performance tasks and portfolios in a standards-based program; how to write your own standards; and report cards and other strategies for reporting student progress in standards-based schools.
- *Building Local Support for Your School* focuses on effective communication and provides school leaders with a comprehensive communications approach that includes discussion of the types of information that need to be communicated; why and how to address the needs of varied audiences; ways to reassure all participants in decision making; and skills that can be used to help promote positive relationships in the community.
- *The Principal's Role in Building a Professional Learning Community* helps principals develop the capacity of their staffs to function as professional learning communities and learn specific strategies for school improvement. Participants learn to identify and overcome barriers to school improvement initiatives and to create procedures and practices that ensure collaboration and continuous improvement.
- *Increasing Parental Involvement* imparts skills to involve parents from diverse linguistic, social, and cultural backgrounds in schools and districts in meaningful and effective ways. This institute introduces ideas and strategies that lead to successful home and school partnerships, with topics such as how to recognize and build on the strengths of the families and using community resources and agencies.
- *Building Capacity for Change* explores school improvement processes that raise achievement for all students and helps participants understand how to engage all key stakeholders in the

improvement processes. Participants also learn to use data on student performance and improvement process indicators in their decision making and to focus school and district staff on issues that have the greatest potential.

In addition to these examples, ASCD's extensive offerings include interactive multimedia courses specifically designed for Web-based training. Each course includes interactive lessons and is supplemented with reading material and access to discussion groups. Topics include the brain, differentiating instruction, effective leadership, global education, multiple intelligences, parents as partners in schooling, planning for technology, and systems thinking.

Models of Success

In addition to the offerings from AASA, ASCD, NAESP, and NASSP, many excellent district and state programs to recruit and retain high-quality principals are available. An entire section of the ERS report *The Principal, Keystone of a High-Achieving School: Attracting and Keeping the Leaders We Need* (Educational Research Service, 2000) focuses on dozens of excellent model programs that have proved effective. Districts and states, often in conjunction with the national or state principals' associations, have been quite innovative when it comes to "grow your own" principal programs and in encouraging individuals who already hold principal certification to serve as principals for the first time. Examples include the following:

• *Aspiring Principals Program Workshops* developed by the National Association of Elementary School Principals. Offered through NAESP's state affiliates, "these one-day workshops are designed to offer insights into the day-to-day roles and responsibilities of the principalship." In *Previewing the Principalship*, participants learn about a principal's daily routine, prioritize tasks, review the latest materials about principals' current roles, and begin to map personal career plans. To add greater depth, participants interact with a panel of principals willing to share their professional experiences.

• Two programs by the Jefferson County (Kentucky) Public School District and the University of Louisville Department of Administration and Higher Education—*Identifying and Developing Educational Administrators for Schools (IDEAS)* and *Principals for Tomorrow*. *IDEAS* was "developed to provide an opportunity for current district personnel who have been identified as well-qualified but who do not have a principal certificate" to learn more about leadership in the school environment. Participants spend eight to ten hours per week with a principal and participate in "observations and interviews of school and community leaders, completion of leadership modules, presentations, portfolio development, case study development, opportunities for teamwork"; they also "attend panel presentations made by people such as principals, counselors, and supervisors, and internship activities." Participants in the *Principals for Tomorrow* program must be certified for the principalship but not currently working as a principal. The goal of the program is to "improve the readiness of the candidates for the principalship by enrolling them in a comprehensive year-long program designed to enhance instructional and administrative skills. Planned instructional activities, simulations, field experiences, internship experiences, mentoring, and constructive feedback characterize the program," which includes more than four hundred intern hours and training under the guidance of an NASSP-trained mentor. How successful is the program? ERS reports that "of the 19 principalship vacancies for 1998–99, 14 were filled by past participants" in this program (Educational Research Service, 2000).

• Pennsylvania's *Governor's Institute for School Leadership*. Participants in this weeklong program can include teachers and administrators. They engage in "critical self-analysis, peer observation and feedback, cognitive coaching, and collaborative research." The institute encourages superintendents, educational associations, and private schools to nominate potential participants. Developed by the state department of education, Shippensburg University, and the Pennsylvania Association of Elementary and Secondary School Principals, the institute demonstrates the potential for collaboration among different stakeholders with the same goal: effective school leadership.

• The Association of Washington School Principals is developing "performance indicators" for a principal's job responsibilities and a list of "authentic assessment options for each responsibility."

• The two-year *New Principal Assistance Program* developed by the Cooperative Council of Oklahoma School Administrators and Oklahoma State University is designed to build skills that first- and second-year principals may not have received in a university-based administrator training program. The curriculum of the program focuses on dilemmas faced by new principals and relies on the expertise of "veteran principals as well as university and association staff."

• The Elementary and Middle School Principals of Connecticut and the Connecticut Association of Schools provide mentoring-skills training to veteran principals and then partner them with new principals. Participants use e-mail as well as face-to-face and other communication to share best practices. Also offered is "Surviving and Thriving in the First Years of the Principalship," which gives practical advice and encourages participants to analyze their schools "in relationship to those school characteristics that ensure greater academic achievement for all students" and to "assess areas for change and identify the processes and timelines necessary to ensure success."

• *Principals Make the Difference in Standards-Based Reform*, a professional development program for middle school principals in the Corpus Christi, Texas, and Jefferson County, Kentucky, school districts. Funded by the Edna McConnell Clark Foundation and coordinated by NASSP, participating principals in this program have worked to identify "ways in which principals might work with teachers to improve instructional planning," "how principals can ensure that teacher evaluation is meaningful and productive," and ways in which the principal can work with the faculty to promote quality work among students. Results of the project will be shared with educators across the country.

Association Initiatives on the Horizon

As detailed in the preceding section, school leadership associations have been active in providing assessment and development programs that are often quite effective. Why haven't these programs led to more systemic elevation of the profession? Why haven't leadership preparation programs received more attention? Often it is because these initiatives are highly specialized and attack one issue — they are not part of a more systemic effort. A systemic effort requires that many organizations combine resources. In offering a rationale for the dearth of attention paid to the profession, David Mandel, author of NPBEA's *Recognizing and Encouraging Exemplary Leadership in America's Schools* (2000), writes, "The institutional leadership functions in schools and school districts are one step removed from the core functions of the institution, teaching and learning. Consequently, the policy community has correctly placed substantial emphasis on what is to be taught, how we teach, and who teaches. This is all to the good, but by itself insufficient. It is insufficient because the way in which schools are organized, structured, financed, and governed requires that a major dose of leadership be applied if we are to achieve real improvement in who teaches, how they teach, and what they teach" (p. 2).

Now, however, significant attention is being paid to this issue of leadership. As previously mentioned, all the school leadership organizations support eliminating institutional weaknesses through elevation of the profession and high professional standards. The ISLLC standards have made some progress in redefining what school leaders need to know and be able to do. This has in turn spotlighted improving preparation programs and viewing school leaders as instructional leaders. But that job is far from complete. In fact, there is no substantial consensus among university preparation programs on how this will be accomplished. School leadership associations must be ardent advocates for the reforms required in preparation programs.

American Board for Leadership in Education

These efforts at the "entry level" will reap dividends in the future. As important, however, is the cultivation of the school leader who has made it past the first hurdle of licensure. We seek to promote among principals themselves the "notion that there are higher standards to which they might aspire, that there are greater levels of competence and professionalism that they might work toward, [and] that they are just at the beginning, not the end, of their development as leaders," concepts that Mandel (2000, p. 4) describes as foreign to school administration today.

One promising initiative that school leadership organizations have proposed, most recently through *Recognizing and Encouraging Exemplary Leadership in America's Schools*, is the advanced certification of school leaders. It describes a system that closely mimics National Board Certification for teachers, which focuses not on minimum standards for beginning teachers but on growing novice and existing teachers "into highly accomplished practitioners" (Mandel, p. 5).

The NPBEA report foresees the following benefits of the American Board for Leadership in Education (Mandel, 2000, pp. 5–7):

- *Standards.* For the first time, members of the profession would come together not to formulate what beginning practitioners need to know and be able to do but to establish a set of professional norms for exemplary practitioners. Codifying such a professional consensus around best practices is the mark of a genuine profession, for only when a profession can articulate what expertise characterizes a full-fledged member of its field can it claim to be a profession.
- *Professional education.* The existence of advanced standards means that for the first time, there will be a set of high standards to guide all phases of the education and training of administrators,

from initial preparation through licensure and initial practices and then on to advanced practices.

- *Recognition of excellence in education leadership.* Administrators who have developed over time into first-rate practitioners deserve, like teachers, to be recognized by their peers for their accomplishments. This affirmation of the quality of their work would create an incentive for excellence and professional growth where few such incentives currently exist. It would also establish a vehicle for school systems to encourage such growth by tying both improved compensation and greater responsibilities to board certification.

- *Quality assurance.* As school systems seek to develop and put in place highly effective administrators who can lead the transformation of schools and school districts, the existence of a valid, reliable, and fair system to identify such administrators would be of substantial assistance in selecting new leaders and placing highly competent administrators in settings most in need of renewal and improvement.

- *Mobility and the administrator labor market.* Although advanced certification of administrators will not by itself solve the problem of state retirement systems that tend to pin down able administrators, it could contribute to a general opening of the labor market for such professionals by introducing an objective qualitative dimension to evaluations and hiring decisions.

Though licensure is ultimately the domain of the individual state, association involvement in advanced certification is essential and appropriate in the quest to raise the standards of the profession. As NPBEA echoes, school leadership professionals and the associations that represent them "have the responsibility to establish high standards of excellence that are inappropriate for beginning practitioners, but set a goal to which members of the profession can aspire over time as they gain experience, build their knowledge, hone their skills, and develop the ability to make tough professional judgments" (Mandel, 2000, p. 7).

A Blueprint

NPBEA (Mandel, 2000) provides the following blueprint for this voluntary advanced certification:

1. Standards Development. The first step must be to create an open and public process for the profession to reach consensus positions on the essential ingredients of exemplary practice. Mandel recommends a close examination of NPBEA, the Educational Leadership Constituent Council, and ISLLC work, among others, as well as a review of the broader management and organizational literature. To achieve this, Mandel recommends creation of one or more standards committees representing a variety of professions and that the committee work be subject to professional and public critique prior to submission to the governing body.

2. Architecture of the Certificates. The NPBEA report lays out several options for the structure of the certificate:

- One certificate for both principals and superintendents
- Two certificates: one for principals and one for superintendents
- Four certificates: one for elementary principals, one for middle school principals, one for high school principals, one for superintendents
- Differentiation through endorsements (for example, offering a single principal certificate along with the option of allowing candidates to earn an endorsement as an elementary, middle, or high school specialist)

3. Prerequisites. Regardless of personal style or knowledge on the first day as principal, to become an exemplary leader requires experience and the gaining of additional knowledge and skills. Mandel recommends an experience requirement of three to five years as a prerequisite for consideration for advanced certification.

"The number of years should be low enough to allow for the exceptional individual to apply, but not so low as to blur the distinction between licensing and certification. Conversely, it should be high enough to avoid the [board's] having to compromise its principles and set a standard below par (to ensure a plausible pass rate), but not so high that it discourages promising candidates by making them wait an inordinate number of years to apply" (p. 10).

4. Assessment Development. Mandel cites the possibility of on-site administrator observations, computer administered examinations, and video portfolios to aid in the assessment process.

5. Renewal. If the certificates "are not to be certificates for life, as there is broad agreement that a mark of a professional is keeping abreast of developments in one's field and continually striving to strengthen one's practice" (p. 12), then the renewal cycle of the certificate as well as the renewal process must be addressed.

To implement this blueprint, Mandel recommends the creation of a new institution. Although the governing board of this new institution would include individuals from a wide variety of professions, the institution would be independent to guard against the "appearance, if not the reality, of potential conflicts of interest that inevitably can arise in such professional enterprises" (p. 13). Regarding the board, Mandel also recommends (pp. 14–15):

- That a majority of the governing board members should be practicing principals and superintendents
- That up to one-third of the board membership should be drawn from outside the profession
- That a possible mix of the twenty-plus board members might be fifteen administrators (five each from the ranks of elementary, secondary school, and superintendents) and seven or eight educators and others (teachers, parents, local school

board members, college faculty, state policymakers, and business and community leaders)

- That the advantages and disadvantages of allotting seats (one or two) for each of the administrator organizations (AASA, NAESP, NASSP) should be carefully considered prior to implementation

Mandel further recommends the sending of an unmistakable message that the board represents the profession's taking responsibility for its own high standards for exemplary practices—standards it is prepared to defend and will encourage its members to meet.

NPBEA and its member organizations are carefully reviewing the recommendations and have begun to develop strategies to further the process. By seizing this opportunity, associations are playing a critical advocacy role, representing the voice of the profession. School leaders are calling for higher standards, and their associations must encourage them to play a key role in standards development.

Other Initiatives

In addition to the excitement building around this concept, associations are undertaking several initiatives to improve the number of high-quality school leaders. They confront an ever-present dilemma: their members do not make decisions about their own assessment and development. It is difficult to provide superintendents, principals, and assistant principals the necessary assessment and development training when scarcity of resources prohibits marketing to the professional development decision makers: the state departments of education, the local school board, individual school staff development directors, and so on. This challenge, along with modes of assessment and development delivery, may have entered a new era with the advent of sophisticated and more affordable technological tools.

For many years, associations have served as clearinghouses for research on leadership and best practices. This role will grow and become significantly more specialized and focused on individuals as fast as the technology allows. Peer-tested, individualized clearinghouse resources will be available at the touch of a button. The quality of the content supplied by associations will improve dramatically with the proposed new initiatives in leadership development and the sharing of success stories.

An example of the vision associations have for the profession and new ways to train principals is NASSP's creation of the National Academy for School Leadership Development (NASLD). The academy will serve several purposes:

• It will develop training for new, aspiring, and experienced principals and assistant principals. The content will be based on best practices for training and development and on the guidelines and principles in the major school reform documents, *Turning Points 2000: Educating Adolescents in the 21st Century* (Jackson and Davis, 2000) and *Breaking Ranks: Changing an American Institution* (National Association of Secondary School Principals, 1996).

• It will deliver training that uses a variety of methods and content approaches to meet the needs of all principals, regardless of geographical location or economic means. Efforts will focus on the creation of cooperative arrangements with NASSP's state affiliates and other partners to offer regional and state summer and weekend institutes, computer-based distance learning, on-line developmental activities, and national conferences.

• It will create "tool kits" for new principals and assistant principals that include conferences and on-line services (such as help hotlines, assessment, mentoring advice, networks of colleagues, and "career opportunity centers"). These activities will connect the realities of school leadership to the needs associated with professional growth and certification while helping increase the retention rate of new principals, especially in urban schools.

- It will create an advanced certification program for principals (as detailed earlier). Beyond creating and offering such certification, it is necessary to work with states to create a level of acceptance for the process that results in recognition of "master principals" who receive appropriate monetary compensation for achieving an exemplary level of competence and site-based leadership.

- It will create a national think tank and national policy center that will formulate and present the best thinking and writing on the most important and most timely issues affecting the secondary school principalship. A center that brings together the best thinkers in education and the humanities can have major impact on the principal's role, professional development, and quality of preparation. It can generate ideas, research, influence, and action on major issues, including the principal's image, the principal as instructional leader, secondary school reform, and school safety.

In addition to these proposed efforts, several associations currently offer continuing education unit credits for relicensure. This trend will continue to grow and become a significant benefit to states, principals, and superintendents as the need for ongoing development becomes the norm. Some existing assessment and development programs allow for franchising of the programs (that is, the programs are developed nationally but conducted locally or regionally with quality control exercised by the national or state associations). The creation of new certification criteria will open up new possibilities for programs of excellence to be replicated nationally.

On another front, both national and state associations are working with state departments of education to investigate other possible remedies to the principal shortage, including alternative certification, incentives to encourage qualified individuals to apply for principal positions, changing provisions of state retirement systems to make it financially more attractive for retired principals to return to the public education system, and establishing "grow your own" principal programs. Preliminary results from a new ERS survey show that the number of states allowing or proposing alternative certification programs is significant. As the number of "grow your own" principal and alternative certification programs increases, associations must be vigilant to ensure that they provide the profession with the appropriate resources to encourage candidate and program excellence.

National associations and their state affiliates must be prepared to take the lead in debates about the effectiveness of these efforts as we continue to "police the profession" for the benefit of students, not for the sake of expediency. Even though steps being taken to form a new professional board for certification are exciting and necessary, it is essential that we pay attention to standards at all levels of the profession. If we leave the back door open to less than qualified candidates for the profession while we focus on national board certification, we will have done a disservice to the profession and to the students who rely on us. If we are to truly make a difference, we must be the voice for excellence at all levels *and* at all entry points to the profession.

References

American Association of School Administrators. *Professional Standards for the Superintendency.* Arlington, Va.: American Association of School Administrators, 1993.

Council of Chief State School Officers. *Interstate School Leaders Licensure Consortium Standards for School Leaders.* Washington, D.C.: Council of Chief State School Officers, 1996. [http://www.ccsso.org/isllc.html].

Educational Research Service. *Is There a Shortage of Qualified Candidates for Openings in the Principalship?* Arlington, Va.: Educational Research Service, 1998.

Educational Research Service. *The Principal, Keystone of a High-Achieving School: Attracting and Keeping the Leaders We Need.* Arlington, Va.: Educational Research Service, 2000.

Griffiths, D. E., Stout, R. T., and Forsyth, P. B. (eds.). *Leaders for America's Schools: The Report and Papers of the National Commission on Excellence in Educational Administration.* Berkeley, Calif.: McCutchan, 1988.

Hodgkinson, H. *Secondary Schools in a New Millennium: Demographic Certainties, Social Realities.* Reston, Va.: National Association of Secondary School Principals, 2000.

Jackson, A. W., and Davis, G. A. *Turning Points 2000: Educating Adolescents in the 21st Century*. New York: Teachers College Press, 2000.

Mandel, D. R. *Recognizing and Encouraging Exemplary Leadership in America's Schools: A Proposal to Establish a System of Advanced Certification for Administrators*. Arlington, Va.: National Policy Board for Educational Administration, 2000.

Murphy, J., and Forsyth, P. B. (eds.). *Educational Administration: A Decade of Reform*. Thousand Oaks, Calif.: Corwin Press, 1999.

Muse, I., and Thomas, G. J. "The Rural Principal: Select the Best." *Journal of Rural and Small Schools*, 1991, 4(3), 32–37.

National Association of Secondary School Principals. *Breaking Ranks: Changing an American Institution*. Reston, Va.: National Association of Secondary School Principals, 1996.

National Association of State Boards of Education. *Principals of Change: What Principals Need to Lead Schools to Excellence*. Alexandria, Va.: National Association of State Boards of Education, 1999.

National Center for Education Statistics. "1993–94 Schools and Staffing Survey." In U.S. Department of Education, *The Digest of Education Statistics, 1996*. Washington, D.C.: Government Printing Office, 1997.

National Policy Board for Educational Administration. *Improving the Preparation of School Administration: An Agenda for Reform*. Arlington, Va.: National Policy Board for Educational Administration, 1989.

National Policy Board for Educational Administration. *Alternative Certification for School Leaders*. Arlington, Va.: National Policy Board for Educational Administration, 1990.

Thomson, S. D. *Principals for Our Changing Schools: The Knowledge and Skill Base*. Arlington, Va.: National Policy Board for Educational Administration, 1993.

Thomson, S. D. "Causing Change: The National Policy Board for Educational Administration." In J. Murphy and P. B. Forsyth (eds.), *Educational Administration: A Decade of Reform*. Thousand Oaks, Calif.: Corwin Press, 1999.

Appendix A
The National Institute for School Leadership: Design for a New Institution to Train School Leaders

The chapters in this volume were commissioned as part of a larger effort, described in the Preface, to respond to the request of several national foundations to design a new institution to prepare school principals. In Chapter One, we, the editors, presented our own analysis of the issues, which is the basis for the design we were requested to produce. In this appendix, we describe the design for that institution, the National Institute for School Leadership, and how it will operate.

Broad Shape of the Design

The National Institute for School Leadership (NISL) is headquartered in Washington, D.C., and managed by the National Center on Education and the Economy.

The NISL Charter

The mission of NISL is to enable principals to acquire the skills and knowledge they need to produce substantial gains in student achievement in their schools. Our aim is to deliver a very high quality program for this purpose, designed to extend its reach quickly to the largest possible number of school leaders with no loss of quality.

Partnership with Districts and Local Universities

Figure A.1 shows the outline of the design for accomplishing this goal. NISL will not train or educate individual principals but will rather join in close partnerships with school districts, intermediate districts, states, school management companies, and schools of education for this purpose (in the remainder of this description, when we refer to "districts," we usually mean all of these types of jurisdictions).

Figure A.1. Schematic of NISL Operations.

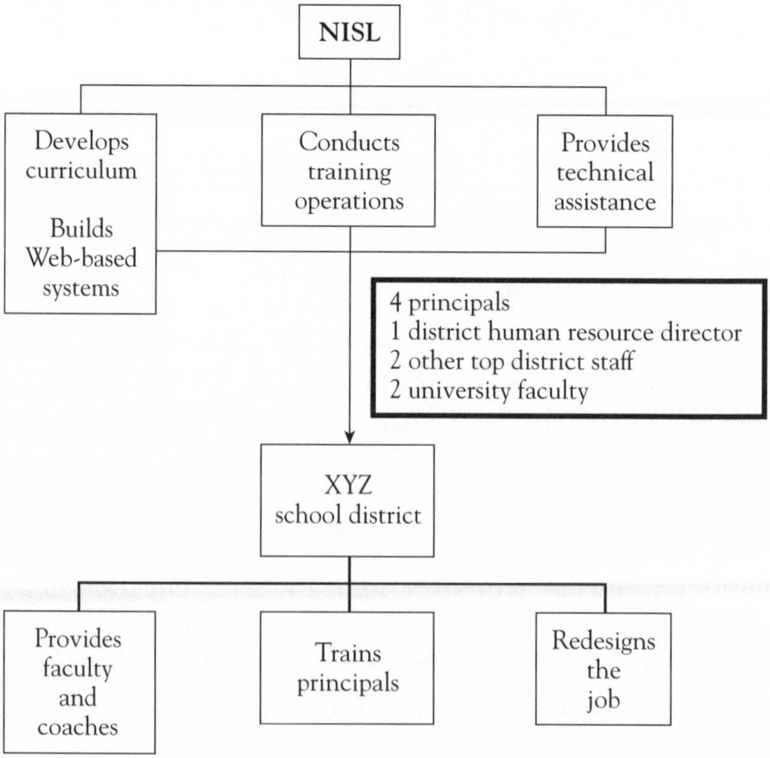

NISL Executive Development Program

The initial program of NISL is an executive development program targeted at experienced school principals.

Local Partners

The districts the NISL partners with must be committed to standards-based, results-oriented policies and strategies for raising student achievement, because that is the kind of system we propose to educate and train school leaders to serve in.

Each partner district is asked to appoint a set of district executives and, when possible, local university faculty to serve on a team whose task it will be to design the local school leadership system and to train the local principals. For a medium-sized district, the team will typically consist of four principals (two for the elementary schools and one each for the middle school and high school level), the district human resource director, two other top district staff, and two university faculty members.

This local team will be trained by NISL to deliver the NISL curriculum (to be described shortly) to the principals in the system and to serve as their coaches. The local team will also have the task of redesigning the job of the principal to make it practicable. In all these roles, the team will have strong support from NISL, as you will see.

NISL's Role

At the core of NISL's role is the creation of a powerful curriculum for the development of school leaders and managers. This curriculum is specifically designed to support the development of principals who see their task not as keeping school but as creating a new kind of high-performance school dedicated to bringing all of its students up to an internationally benchmarked standard of performance as quickly as possible. This curriculum has been designed for delivery in a face-to-face setting and also via the World Wide Web.

NISL trains the district teams to deliver this curriculum to principals in their jurisdiction at a high level of quality. In addition to its own staff, NISL has a national cadre of coaches and consultants that the local teams can engage to assist them as they develop the skills and knowledge of their own school leaders.

At the same time, NISL provides continuing technical assistance to the local team to assist with the design and implementation of both the local professional development system for school leaders and the redesign of the principals' job and the way it fits into the whole local accountability system. NISL assigns one of its staff members to each district to serve as the coach for the whole program and to engage specialized help from others on particular aspects of the development program as needed.

In sum, NISL has three related but distinct operations to support the local program: (1) curriculum development, including elaboration of Web-based systems; (2) training operations, for delivery of the curriculum to the local teams; and (3) technical assistance, to provide assistance for all the purposes just described.

Funding

In the main, aspiring principals pay for their own graduate education, in the expectation that the district will reimburse them for it by moving them up on the salary schedule. The district, by doing that, forfeits any say about the program these people take or its fit with the needs of the district. Later the district may pay for training for school principals, but it is unlikely to fit into any overall design. In the system we have in mind, most of the customers of NISL will be districts and other jurisdictions, not individuals. They will make this investment for the same reason corporations and the military do—as a means of achieving their goals and improving their effectiveness. By our analysis, this will require spending little, if any, monies beyond what they now spend, but it will require spending them differently.

Advantages of This Design

This design presents numerous advantages over existing programs.

- *It focuses on the most important goal.* This goal is not main-taining the current system but rather finding and training the lead-ership needed to put a more effective system in place.
- *It ties training to district goals.* The design overcomes the cur-rent isolation between the university-based training programs and school districts and builds one coherent system for integrating the district strategy for raising student performance, professional devel-opment for leaders, and school practices. Everywhere we went, we were told that effective professional development for leaders and managers requires integration with the goals, strategies, and systems of the employers of the people being trained. This design accom-plishes that.
- *It deals with the problem of the undoable job.* As a practical mat-ter, this problem is most likely to be solved by districts and states moving toward standards-based, results-oriented policy systems by raising principals' pay, restructuring the job, and strengthening principals' authority. By building strong partnerships with the juris-dictions already most highly motivated to make such changes, NISL finds the most fertile ground for its style of training and makes it more likely that the training will pay off in better student performance.
- *It brings universities into the fold.* This design builds in the uni-versities and is designed to change both their programs and their relations with local districts. Local universities have seats on the local teams that will put this design into operation, and their faculty members will be members of the faculty for the local training of school leaders. They will be teaching the national curriculum, but they may add to it and offer their own credits, certificates, and degrees to the people who successfully complete it or parts of it. Just as important, they will be equal partners in a common enterprise

with the district staff. This should put them in a better position to find out what the districts need and to respond to those needs.

Having laid out the broad design of NISL, we will turn now to a more detailed description of some of its key elements.

The Starting Point: An Executive Development Program for New School Principals

The program is designed for principals who have been on the job for one to five years. We think of this as a program very like the executive development programs currently popular in the business world. If the aim is to make the biggest possible difference as fast as possible, then the place to start is with people already in the job.

But there is another reason for focusing on practicing principals early in their career. Research shows that most aspiring principals are interested in learning only what they need to know to survive their first day on the job. Thinking about it in military terms, they are focused on tactics and are not yet ready for operations, much less strategy. After they have been in the job long enough to have confidence in their survival, they begin the process of perfecting their craft, function by function. Only after they have done this for a while, if ever, are they ready to develop their ability to draw on all the functions to create comprehensive strategies for achieving overarching goals. Each stage is important, and our curriculum materials support each stage. But we think that the highest payoff in the near term will come from concentrating on the later stages among people who already have some seasoning.

Curriculum for the NISL Executive Development Program

The NISL curriculum consists of two years of coursework taught locally. There are four courses, each consisting of three or four units each, as follows:

Course 1: World-Class Schooling: Vision and Goals

Unit 1: The Educational Challenge. This unit explains why fundamental changes in the international economy have resulted in greatly raised educational requirements for all citizens in the advanced economies and why social development and ethical behavior are no less important than high academic achievement. It helps the participant make a realistic assessment of the challenges that schools must meet if the new standards are to be achieved, including the corrosive effect of pervasive low expectations for many poor and minority students. And it is designed to help the participants accept and embrace the goal of getting every student ready for college without remediation by the time that student leaves high school.

Unit 2: Standards-Based Instructional Systems. The purpose of this unit is to help the participant develop a sophisticated understanding of the components of standards-based instructional systems and the ways those components can be combined to produce very powerful effects on student performance. Participants learn about different kinds of standards and assessments available and the appropriate uses of each. They learn how to distinguish assessments that are genuinely aligned to standards from those that are not. They learn how to build curriculum frameworks designed to array topics in a logical way to enable students to reach standards over a period of years and how to analyze and select instructional materials that are aligned with the standards and the frameworks. Most important, they learn what the role of the principal is in ensuring that his or her school has a fully aligned instructional system that is focused on the standards and is internally coherent and consistent.

Unit 3: The Principal as Strategic Thinker. The purpose of this unit is to enable the participant to think strategically about the challenges he or she faces and to put together a clear and powerful strategy for addressing these challenges. Much of this unit draws on literature and experience from business and the military, but participants are asked throughout the unit to apply what is learned to the world of the school. Participants are introduced to the distinctions among tactical, operational, and strategic thinking. They are shown how to take all aspects of the problem to be solved into account, how to systematically assess the challenges to be overcome and the assets to be mobilized. And they are introduced to the elements of planning required both to construct a viable strategy and to execute it successfully.

Unit 4: The Principal as School Designer. The purpose of this unit is to enable the participant to take on the role of leading the faculty in the development of a powerful, coherent school design. This incorporates a design for the school's instructional system, the elements of which we have already described, as well as all the other elements of the school operation, which must be aligned with and supportive of the instructional system if it is to succeed. This includes everything from the master schedule to the budget allocation process to the way parents are involved in the education of their children. Participants also learn how to assess designs offered by third parties, how to select such designs in light of the needs of their own schools, and how to adapt and extend those designs to fit those needs.

Course 2: Focusing on Teaching and Learning

The purpose of this course is to give the participant access to the best research the world has to offer on the issues that relate to standards-based education and the role of the principal in leading his or her school to high performance. The research is distilled into a series of principles related to learning, teaching, and curriculum. The principal is asked to consider the implications of those principles for the redesign of the school in the context of the new accountability systems and standards.

Unit 5: The Foundations of Effective Learning. This unit focuses on the particular role of the school leader in making sure that the way the school operates reflects each principle of learning, teaching, and curriculum.

Unit 6: Leadership for Excellence in Literacy. The purpose of this unit is to enable the participant to be an effective instructional leader in this crucial area of the curriculum. The aim is not to turn the principal into a literacy expert but rather to enable the principal to recognize the key elements of best practices in the field of literacy and provide the principal with sound criteria for judging whether the school has an effective literacy program and some practice in using those criteria. Also included in this unit is instruction designed to enable the participant to recognize the key features of effective safety net programs in literacy so that he or she can exercise leadership, if necessary, in the development of such programs to ensure that all students are literate, regardless of their level of literacy when they entered the school.

Unit 7: Leadership for Excellence in Mathematics. The purpose of this unit is to enable the participant to be an effective instructional leader in this crucial area of the curriculum. The aim is not to turn the principal into a mathematics expert but rather to enable the principal to recognize the key elements of best practices in the field of mathematics and provide the principal with sound criteria for judging whether the school has an effective mathematics program and some practice in using those criteria. Also included in this unit is instruction designed to enable the participant to recognize the key features of effective safety net programs in mathematics so that he or she can exercise leadership, if necessary, in the development of such programs to ensure that all students have the necessary mathematical skills and knowledge regardless of their level when they entered the school.

Unit 8: Promoting Professional Knowledge. The purpose of this unit is to enable the participant to lead a schoolwide effort to continuously develop the professional knowledge and skills of the faculty. This means establishing a culture in which every professional on the staff is expected to be learning all the time and in which professional development is seen by the whole faculty as the most important tool by which it acquires the skills and knowledge it needs to implement successfully the strategies and designs the school has adopted for improving student achievement. Participants learn how to promote organizational learning through analysis of its successes and failures, through benchmarking best practices beyond the school, and through disciplined searches for proven knowledge that bears on the challenges the school faces. Finally, the participant learns what to look for as he or she walks around the school and observes classrooms and how to use those observations as the basis for mentoring the faculty over time.

Course 3: Developing Capacity and Commitment

Unit 9: The Principal as Instructional Leader. The purpose of this unit is to enable the participant to reflect on his or her role as an instructional leader and to learn how to play that role effectively, alone or in combination with other members of the leadership team. The participant looks back in time to understand how the role of the school principal came to be disassociated from instruction in the United States, as opposed to most other industrialized nations, and reflects on the forces now at work to restore the principal's role as instructional leader. The participant is introduced to a variety of ways in which the role of instructional leaders can be allocated among two or more people who together assume the function of the principalship and considers how best to allocate responsibility in his or her own school for this function.

Unit 10: The Principal as Team Builder. The purpose of this unit is to enable the participant to understand the power of teams to get the work of the school done and to develop the knowledge and skills needed to build effective teams in his or her school. Participants learn how to define the goals for teams, recruit and select their members, and motivate and coach them to success.

Unit 11: Creating a Culture That Is Ethical, Results-Oriented, and Professional. The purpose of this unit is to enable the principal to understand the role that organizational culture plays in determining the capacity of the school to raise student achievement, to give the participant the skills and knowledge to build an effective culture, and in particular to enable the participant to be an effective moral leader of the school. The participant learns how to analyze the culture of the school from a variety of perspectives and how to build a healthy, positive culture that is focused on results and values, supports professional behavior, and upholds ethical and moral principles.

Course 4: Driving for Results

Unit 12: The Principal as Driver of Change. The purpose of this unit is to enable the participant to design, lead, and drive a change process calculated to produce steady improvement in student achievement. The participant learns to analyze the motivations of the various participants in the process, to identify friends and foes, and to maximize the former at the expense of the latter over time, moving steadily from small wins to substantial gains. The principal should also learn how to identify root problems and causes, gather intelligence and formulate a plan on the basis of appropriate data, set performance targets, select strategies, and develop sound implementation plans.

Unit 13: Managing for Results. In this unit, the participant focuses on the crucial role of data in the drive for results, including setting targets and collecting, displaying, and analyzing data on program implementation and student progress in relation to standards. The participant also learns how to use data in the process of setting goals, monitoring progress, allocating and reallocating resources, and managing the school program. Finally, the participant integrates materials from earlier units that relate to the crucial role of the principal in providing a vision of the results worth achieving, keeping that vision constantly in front of the school community and allocating responsibilities to everyone involved for realizing that vision.

Unit 14: Standards-Based Reform Project. In this last unit, the participant focuses on a project defined by the school district that provides an opportunity for the participant to use much of what has been learned in the executive development program. The project must meet certain criteria defined in the course materials, one of which is that it is a project with real value and importance to the district, apart from its educational value for the participant.

Program Pedagogy

Part of the curriculum is delivered in face-to-face format and part using Web-based technology. The Web-based part of the program is highly interactive. Heavy use is made of case studies in both video and print form. Games, simulations, scenarios, and action projects are employed. Access is provided to a wide variety of on-line information sources. Dozens of national and international experts from the fields of education, cognitive psychology, organizational studies, sociology, policy studies, economics, business, the military, and other fields were interviewed for this program and appear in video throughout the curriculum.

The pedagogy grows out of the kinds of problems these principals can be expected to encounter on the way to achieving a high-performing school. Participants work together in cohorts and study groups. At times they work on the tasks set by the curriculum. At times they are pursuing issues that grow out of the challenges they currently face in their schools and districts. The projects they work on result in products of real value to them as they learn how to think strategically about how to achieve their goals and implement their plans.

As the participants proceed through the curriculum, they are supported by their coaches. All the courses will be on the Web, sometimes as the primary learning mechanism and sometimes for review after completion of the face-to-face version.

Program Delivery and Technical Assistance

The training program for jurisdiction teams, conducted by the NISL national staff, lasts three years and takes place at national training locations for four weeks in the first summer institute and two weeks in each of the following summers. NISL also provides follow-up training for the jurisdiction teams at two sessions each year, for three days each session, one in the fall and the other in the spring.

Following the first summer training session, the district team returns to the home district to plan the local training program, develop a design for the career development system, and initiate work on the redesign of the principalship. Each district has a senior NISL staff person serving as a coach to the team, who provides six days of on-site assistance a year. This coach has access to a team of specialized experts on the NISL staff and on call from other organizations.

The next summer, the district team continues with its members' own training and begins to deliver the curriculum to their own principals. The training of their own principals will take place locally.

The program for school principals, conducted by the district, lasts two years—in residence for three weeks the first summer and two weeks the second summer. These summer programs are supplemented by fall and spring institutes of three days each in which the jurisdiction teams reinforce the summer materials, discuss challenges that arise when principals apply what they have learned, and identify action projects in the context of the jurisdiction's school reform program.

In addition to the program just described, the principals in the program are expected to participate in continuing local study groups during the school year, for a minimum of three hours a month for eight months a year. These study group sessions focus on action learning projects that address the issues of greatest priority for that district, given its strategic agenda and the particular problems it faces.

NISL provides the training for the jurisdiction teams, as well as the curriculum materials to support both the face-to-face and Web-based components of the program for both the jurisdiction teams and the principals. NISL also provides on-site, phone, and Web-based technical assistance to the teams.

For additional information on the NISL program, please contact Bob Hughes, acting director, National Institute for School Leadership, One Thomas Circle NW, Suite 700, Washington, D.C. 20005; phone: (202) 783-3668, ext. 152.

Appendix B
People Consulted in the Design of the National Institute for School Leadership

Patricia C. Barron, Clinical Associate Professor of Information Systems, Entrepreneurship and Innovation, Leonard N. Stern School of Business, New York University

Roland Barth, Professor Emeritus, Harvard Graduate School of Education, Harvard University

Alison Bernstein, Vice President, Ford Foundation

Gale H. Bitter, Executive Director, Executive Education, Graduate School of Business, Stanford University

Kathleen Burke, Executive Director, Stupski Family Foundation

Deanna Burney, Senior Fellow, University of Pennsylvania

Michele Cahill, Senior Program Officer, Carnegie Corporation of New York

Brian Caldwell, Dean of Education, University of Melbourne

Ingrid Carney, LAUNCH Leadership Training Program, Northwestern University

Michael Cohen, former Assistant Secretary for Elementary and Secondary Education, Senior Fellow, Aspen Institute

Mike Copeland, Professor, Stanford University (program founded by Ed Bridges)

Tom Corcoran, Associate Director, Consortium for Policy Research in Education and Professor, University of Pennsylvania

Rudy Crew, Director, District Reform, Stupski Family Foundation; formerly Chancellor, New York City Board of Education

Gloria Crum, Director, Texas Administrators Academy

Terrence Deal, Professor of Education, University of Southern California

Greg Dees, Professor, Stanford Business School, Stanford University

Delaine Eastin, Superintendent of Public Instruction, California Department of Education

Bobbi Eddins, Executive Director, Texas Principal Leadership Institute

Russ Edgerton, former Director of Education, Pew Charitable Trusts

Karin Egan, Program Officer, Carnegie Corporation of New York

Marie Eiter, Director of Executive Development, Sloan School of Management, Massachusetts Institute of Technology

Dan Fallon, Chair, Education Division, Carnegie Corporation of New York

Vincent Ferrandino, President, National Association of Elementary School Principals

Mary Lee Fitzgerald, Program Director for Education, DeWitt Wallace–Reader's Digest Fund

Patrick Forsyth, Director, University Council for Education Administration, Oklahoma State University

Leslie Fosset, Deputy Superintendent, California State Department of Education

John Fryer, Superintendent, Duvall County (Florida) Public Schools

Susan Furhman, Dean, Graduate School of Education, University of Pennsylvania

Marcy Singer Gabella, Office for Initiatives in Education and PROJECT GRAD, Vanderbilt University

Tom Genesse, President, University Access

Leslie Graitcer, Executive Director, Bell South Foundation

Vartan Gregorian, President, Carnegie Corporation of New York

Patricia Harvey, Superintendent of Schools, Saint Paul (Minnesota) Public Schools

Guilbert Hentschke, Professor and former Dean, Rossier School of Education, University of Southern California

Peter Hill, Director, Research and Development, National Center on Education and the Economy

Harold Howe, Hanover, New Hampshire

Bob Hughes, former Provost, National War College; Acting Director, National Institute for School Leadership

Robert Joss, Dean, Graduate School of Business, Stanford University

Tom Kabora, On-Line Learning.Net

Dan Katzir, Director of Program Development, Broad Foundation

Robert Kegan, Professor, Graduate School of Education, Harvard University

Carolyn Kelley, Graduate School of Education, University of Wisconsin-Madison

Carl Kester, Chairman, M.B.A. Program, Harvard Business School, Harvard University

Sherry King, Superintendent, Mamaroneck (New York) Public Schools

Susan King, Vice President, Public Affairs, Carnegie Corporation of New York

Peter Kleinbard, Program Officer, DeWitt Wallace–Reader's Digest Fund

Kathy Klock, Program Officer, Education, Bill and Melinda Gates Foundation

Kenneth Leithwood, Professor of Education, Center for Leadership Development, University of Toronto

Arthur Levine, President, Teachers College, Columbia University

Michael Levine, former Deputy Chair and Senior Program Officer, Carnegie Corporation of New York

David Mandel, Director, Management, Planning and Research Center for Curriculum and Professional Development

David Marsh, Robert A. Naslund Professor of Curriculum and Instruction, Director, Center for School Leadership, Graduate School of Education, University of Southern California

Wayne Martin, Assessment Center Director, Council of Chief State School Officers

Amy Mast, Senior Project Associate, Interstate School Leaders Licensure Consortium, Council of Chief State School Officers

Anne Miller, Director, Development and Strategic Alliances, National Association of Secondary School Principals

Susan Mitchell, Vice President, University of Phoenix

Ted Mitchell, President, Occidental College

Jerry Murphy, Professor and former Dean, Graduate School of Education, Harvard University

Joe Murphy, Professor of Education, Peabody College, Vanderbilt University

George Parker, Associate Dean for Academic Affairs, Director of the M.B.A. Program, Graduate School of Business, Stanford University

Kent Peterson, Professor, Department of Educational Administration, Graduate School of Education, University of Wisconsin-Madison

Vicki Phillips, Superintendent of Schools, Lancaster, Pennsylvania

Kathleen Ponder, Director, Design Center Services, Center for Creative Leadership

Roy Romer, Superintendent of Schools, Los Angeles Unified School District

Earl Sasser, Senior Associate Dean, Executive Education, Harvard Business School, Harvard University

Robert Schwartz, President, Achieve

Eileen Shapiro, Management Consultant, Hillcrest Group

Frank Smith, Professor of Education, Teachers College, Columbia University

Kim Smith, President, New Schools Venture Fund

Tom Sobol, Professor, Teachers College, Columbia University

Theresa Stahlman, Principal, Chets Creek Elementary School (Jacksonville, Florida)

Vivien Stewart, Vice President, Asia Society

James Stigler, CEO, LessonLab

Gary Sykes, Professor, Michigan State University

Gerald Tirozzi, Executive Director, National Association of Secondary School Principals

Susan Traiman, Director of Education, Business Roundtable

Tom Vander Ark, Director of Education, Bill and Melinda Gates Foundation

Vera Vignes, Superintendent, Pasadena (California) Unified School District

Anthony Wagner, Professor, Graduate School of Education, Harvard University

Gordon Wohlers, Associate Superintendent, Planning, Assessment and Research, Los Angeles Unified School District

Focus Groups

- Twenty-five *America's Choice* practicing principals and central office administrators from across the United States
- Principals from a wide variety of District of Columbia public schools
- Principals from Westchester County, New York, several of whom had worked in New York City public schools
- Principals from Los Angeles County public schools

Index